Strategic Manageme

What role can strategic thinking play in contemporary sport management? It can be the difference between leading or languishing – it's *that* important! Covering sport at all levels, from community-based sport to elite sport, this is the first textbook to focus on strategic management in a sport context.

The book introduces the fundamentals of strategic planning, environmental analyses, strategic direction and leadership, strategy formulation and selection, implementation, strategic control, and change management. Designed to encourage students to develop a strategic mindset, as well as critical thinking and problem-solving skills, the book unpacks key concepts such as leadership, governance, organizational change, and the multiple layers of strategy in sport.

Full of real-world case studies from diverse, international sport business environments, and useful pedagogical features such as review questions and guides to online resources, this is an essential text for any sport management course and an invaluable resource for sport development, recreation management, or events management courses.

Danny O'Brien is Associate Professor in Sport Management in the Bond Business School, Bond University, Australia. He is Visiting Professor at both the Center for Surf Research at San Diego State University, USA, and the Plymouth Sustainability and Surfing Research Group at Plymouth University, UK. His research is in sustainable surf tourism, event leverage, and organizational change in sport. Each area shares a common strategizing for sport-for-development thread. He is Editorial Board Member for *Sport Management Review* and *Journal of Sport & Tourism*.

Milena M. Parent is Full Professor in Sport (Event) Management in the School of Human Kinetics at the University of Ottawa, Canada. Internationally recognized for her research in the management and governance of major international sports events, she is a North American Society for Sport Management Research Fellow and former holder of a Government of Ontario Young Researcher Award. She also consults with government and industry organizations on their governance, management, and sport event hosting.

Lesley Ferkins is Professor and Director of the Sports Performance Research Institute New Zealand (NZ) at Auckland University of Technology, New Zealand. She has worked closely with boards of national sports in NZ and Australia as part of action research interventions to develop board strategic capability. She has an ongoing program of research in leadership and governance with NZ Rugby and is part of an international team evaluating action research impact in multiple countries. She is Associate Editor of *Sport Management Review* and sits on the Editorial Board of the *Journal of Sport Management*. She also sits on the board as Independent Director for Tennis NZ.

Lisa Gowthorp is Assistant Professor in Sport Management within the Bond Business School at Bond University, Australia. Her research interests include sport governance and sport policy within Australian high-performance sport. She consults with industry and is the Vice President of Sport Management Australia and New Zealand (SMAANZ) and a Director on the Board of Paddle Australia.

Strategic Management in Sport

Danny O'Brien, Milena M. Parent,
Lesley Ferkins and Lisa Gowthorp

Routledge
Taylor & Francis Group

LONDON AND NEW YORK

First published 2019
by Routledge
2 Park Square, Milton Park, Abingdon, Oxon OX14 4RN

and by Routledge
52 Vanderbilt Avenue, New York, NY 10017

Routledge is an imprint of the Taylor & Francis Group, an informa business

British Library Cataloguing-in-Publication Data
A catalogue record for this book is available from the British Library

Library of Congress Cataloging-in-Publication Data
A catalog record for this book has been requested

ISBN: 978-1-138-29002-0 (hbk)
ISBN: 978-1-138-29003-7 (pbk)
ISBN: 978-1-315-26667-1 (ebk)

Typeset in Minion Pro
by Apex CoVantage, LLC

MIX
Paper from
responsible sources
FSC™ C013985   Printed in the United Kingdom
by Henry Ling Limited

Brief contents

Detailed contents

Figures

Tables

The genesis of this book came through the authors' collective frustration at the fact that no available textbooks adequately covered the subject of strategic management in the context of sport. Like most academics teaching in this area, we were forced to use excerpts from mainstream strategic management texts, then go about sourcing additional sport-specific readings and cases from academic journals, textbooks, news media, and the popular press. This was cumbersome and time-consuming for both academic and student! So this book is somewhat unique in that it addresses the foundations of strategic management, but it does so in a manner that utilizes the many faces of the sport industry as the backdrop for explaining and demonstrating the relevant concepts and theories.

This book is targeted more at upper-level undergraduate students, but will also be a useful resource for postgraduate students to develop their understanding of the strategic management process in sport organizations. The book is designed as a tool to help develop students' ability for strategic thought and action as well as their capacities for critical thinking and problem-solving.

Through the book's structure, we work through the various phases of the strategic management process in the context of sport. This entails chapters on environmental analysis; strategic leadership and governance; setting strategic direction; formulating strategy at the business and corporate levels; strategy evaluation and selection; implementation of strategy; strategic control mechanisms and managing organizational change; and, of course, strategic planning. This approach will encourage students, first, to develop their understanding of fundamental strategic concepts; second, to apply strategic thinking to real-world case studies in diverse sport business environments; and third, to recognize and apply this knowledge to their own experience of sport.

We chose to adopt an inclusive approach in terms of the sport contexts utilized throughout this book. We thought carefully about the cases and examples used so as to produce a good cross section of sport and its many industry contexts. What we've produced are cases ranging from the corporate, for-profit, supply side of the industry through to cases representing the non-profit, community-based, demand side. We have also integrated material from a variety of national contexts.

In covering this diversity of sport sectors, we ran the risk of "trying to be all things to all people." But the alternative would have been to focus on just one or a few aspects of the sport spectrum, which could have alienated the majority of the international sport management community. Also, too often we come across students who, upon graduation, have a singular focus on going into ONE aspect of the sport industry (e.g., "I'm going to work in professional football!"). While ambition is good, such a singular focus can mean students sometimes "switch off" when a particular case or example is not in their particular sphere of interest. This means they may miss valuable learning opportunities to appreciate the potential cross-pollination of ideas and concepts across industry contexts. So the message for students here is clear: focus on the concepts and less on the contexts! That said, we've produced a nice mix from across the many nooks and crannies of the international sport management environment.

Key themes running through the book reflect the breadth of reach that strategic management has into the very essence of sport organizations. Themes such as organizational change, leadership, governance, and culture – all are focused around sport and its related industries. In writing the book, we set ourselves the following objectives:

1   To explain the key aspects of the strategic management process in the context of sport and sport-related contexts;
2   To identify the unique attributes of sport management that require specific strategic thought and action;
3   To help students understand each aspect of the strategic management process through meaningful case studies centered on diverse elements of the sport industry from community-based sport through to elite and high-performance sport, while not forgetting other sport-related contexts such as sport media, sport events, sport tourism, and sport apparel and equipment providers; and
4   To contextualize the management of organizational change within sport as an omnipresent aspect of strategic management.

This book is the first to offer a specific focus on explaining the strategic management process in the context of sport. Other books have variously explored management, leadership, policy, organization theory, human resource management, organizational behavior, or marketing in sport. Meanwhile, mainstream management texts have explored strategic management in a generic sense or in contexts such as tourism, for example; but none has specifically focused on strategic management in *sport*. Moreover, many of the texts that have explored management-related themes in sport have been edited texts that present discrete, preordained chapters by invited authors. Indeed, the authors of this text have contributed a number of these! While many of these individual chapters can be extremely useful, this edited book approach does not lend itself to a thorough, cohesive, user-friendly approach that is directly applicable to (1) a subject specifically focused on strategic management in sport and (2) a 10- to 12-week semester classroom environment. By contrast, this book offers a cohesive, ten-chapter approach to explicating the theory and practice of strategic management in the context of sport. We hope you find it useful!

At the 2018 European Association for Sport Management Annual Conference in Malmö, Sweden, Professor Mike Weed made a keynote presentation that decried the lack of evidence underpinning the claims made for sport by managers, politicians, policy makers, and researchers. Professor Weed argued that claims about sport's positive impacts on society, the economy, and individuals' lives in relation to education, culture, health, and well-being are too often completely unsubstantiated – or worse, fabricated. Fixing this problem is certainly *way* beyond the scope of this book, but by imbuing sport management students – our industry's future leaders – with a mindset that highlights the merits of strategic thinking, transparency, accountability, and critical thinking, perhaps we go some way toward alleviating the very real issues highlighted by Professor Weed.

As an authorship team, we would like to thank our colleagues, contributors, and students for their encouragement and feedback on earlier versions of the book's manuscript. We are also indebted to Simon Whitmore and Rebecca Connor from Routledge for their faith and endless patience in us to complete this book – a book that we believe makes an important contribution to the international sport management body of knowledge. Finally, we are also indebted to our respective partners and families for their patience and support for the long hours that went into this arduous though extremely worthwhile project.

Danny O'Brien
Milena M. Parent
Lesley Ferkins
Lisa Gowthorp

Acknowledgments

We would like to thank the following people for the collegial spirit in which they collaborated with us in compiling the case studies for this book. The support and professional insights they generously shared with us have been central in our efforts to illustrate theoretical concepts with real-world scenarios:

- **Brigid Carroll**, Department of Management and International Business, The University of Auckland Business School, New Zealand.
- **Matt and Jenny Cruden**, Owners, Resort Latitude Zero, Telo Islands, North Sumatra, Indonesia.
- **Don Knapp**, ex-CEO (retired), UniSport Australia.
- **Erik L. Lachance**, Ph.D. Student, School of Human Kinetics, University of Ottawa, Canada.
- **Julie Paterson**, CEO, Tennis New Zealand.
- **Celia Patrick**, Chair, Tennis New Zealand Board.
- **Terri-Ann Scorer**, Deputy Chair, Tennis New Zealand Board.
- **Donna Spethman**, General Manager, Education, Training & Risk, UniSport Australia.
- **Ashley Thompson**, Ph.D. Student, School of Human Kinetics, University of Ottawa, Canada.
- **Richard I. Toomer**, Ph.D. Candidate, School of Human Kinetics, University of Ottawa, Canada.

1 The process of strategic management in sport

OPENING CASE: UNDER ARMOUR'S QUEST FOR WORLD DOMINANCE

In the late 1990s, a walk-on player for the University of Maryland Terrapins football team, Kevin Plank, was irritated with the cotton T-shirts he and his teammates were forced to wear under their shoulder pads. The shirts would become soaked with sweat, which made them heavy and uncomfortable. Always a tinkerer, Plank experimented with making his own T-shirt by emulating the figure hugging, moisture wicking garments he had seen athletes wear in sports like cycling. His teammates were so impressed with Plank's microfiber innovation that he ended up outfitting the entire squad. These were, of course, the humble beginnings of the sport apparel success story, Under Armour. At the time, Nike and adidas dominated the sports apparel market, but Plank soon grew his fledgling company and diversified into multiple products in numerous categories, while never deviating from his focus on sport and innovation and his vision to rival and eventually overtake adidas and Nike.

Fast-forward to 2014–2015, and Under Armour had spent close to USD 1 billion on the purchase of three mobile applications that specialize in physical activity and diet tracking. On the surface, these seem completely unrelated to Under Armour's core sporting goods and apparel sector. But Plank spent large amounts of time explaining to his staff the company's goal to use these new capabilities to amass the world's largest digital health and fitness community, which would then fuel a big data engine to help drive Under Armour's future product development, merchandising, and marketing. Although Nike still dominates the US market, Plank's strategy has already seen Under Armour leapfrog adidas to second place in that massive geographic market. Internationally, however, Under Armour still ranks third behind Nike and adidas (Foster, n.d.). An extremely capable general, Plank's ultimate vision for Under Armour is nothing short of global market leadership.

Strategic management in sport

The opening case highlights the uniqueness of sport as a context for studying, understanding, and practicing strategic management. Large sport organizations, like Under Armour, do not achieve their ultimate vision without strategic management – financial lenders require the accountability offered by formalized planning, and senior managers need strategic direction to help guide decision-making around resource acquisition, production, and distribution processes, which helps them position their respective organizations to effectively fulfill their mission and compete against rivals.

Indeed, perhaps the defining feature of sport is the presence of institutionalized competition. Shilbury (2012) observed that "competition . . . is the heart and soul of sport management" (p. 2). This makes perfect sense in the arena of organized sport, where individual athletes and teams compete against each other to win leagues, world titles, and Olympic medals. But even in seemingly non-competitive sport, the sport management environment is still characterized by competition. Take recreational skiing, for example: snowsport-related hardware companies compete with each other to sell skis, snowboards, bindings, and apparel. Meanwhile, ski tourism operators compete with each other to provide transport, accommodation, and instruction services, while ski destinations rival with each other to attract tourists and host events. In and among all of this, different snowsport disciplines such as downhill, slalom, cross-country, biathlon, and snowboard compete with each other and other sports to attract participants, sponsors, media coverage, and government funding.

Therefore, while the sport environment is diverse and involves many seemingly non-competitive aspects, from an organizational perspective the fact remains that sport organizations compete with each other for access to valuable tangible and intangible resources. These resources allow sport organizations to provide certain products and services and to compete for the loyalty of customers, members, and clientele. Competition is indeed at the core of sport management, and how sport organizations identify their core purpose, stake out their domain, and differentiate themselves from rivals ultimately determines their level of competitiveness and ultimate survival – hence the need for strategic management in sport.

Critical thinking Box 1.1

Go to: https://careers.underarmour.com/life-at-ua

After perusing this website, explain how Under Armour's vision, mission, and core values influence the company's strategic direction.

What is strategy and strategic management?

The term *strategy* is used so widely that a discrete and unambiguous definition *should* be simple. We hear the word used in so many different sporting contexts – for example, in relation to Olympic bid strategies, the New York Yankees' recruitment strategy, the Indian Premier League's cricket growth strategy, or Real Madrid's digital strategy, plus myriad other instances. So clearly, defining the term "strategy" in one discrete sentence is not as straightforward as you might think! Strictly speaking, the word *strategy* actually derives from the Greek *strategos*, which translates to "the general's view." This militaristic perspective provides a useful analogy: the army general is like a chief executive officer (CEO), and the officers below the general equate to department heads and middle-level managers. However, even generals are accountable for their performance as they report to the political leadership of their nation. Similarly, a sport organization's CEO is employed by, and is accountable to, the board of that organization. It is the responsibility of the board to monitor and evaluate the performance of the CEO. What is emerging here is a more inclusive conception of sport leadership, one that will be picked up on later in the book that conceives of leadership as a shared responsibility, which contrasts the traditional single person "command and control" conception.

Rather than proposing a strict definition of strategy, de Kluyver and Pearce (2012) suggested it is more useful to identify what strategy actually pertains to. They proposed:

Strategy is about *positioning* an organization for *competitive advantage*. It involves making *choices* about *which industries to participate in, what products and services *to offer*, and *how to allocate corporate resources*. Its primary goal is to *create value for shareholders and other stakeholders* by providing *customer value*.

(de Kluyver & Pearce, 2012, p. 2; emphasis in original)

The statement "*positioning* an organization for *competitive advantage*" is crucial to our understanding of strategy. Simply put, *competitive advantage* refers to an organization's ability to create value that its rivals cannot, which then allows the organization to gain an edge over those rivals. In the opening case, Under Armour seeks to create competitive advantage over key rivals like Nike and adidas by creating a relationship with its customers that competitors may struggle to match. In another example, Evolve MMA is the market leader in Singapore for mixed martial arts (MMA) instruction/coaching and competition. In an industry sector characterized by small operators, Evolve MMA stands out because it operates across four five-star facilities and boasts the largest, most experienced instructor team in Asia with over 1,000 years of collective world championship experience (Evolve MMA, n.d.). This broad scope of operations allows Evolve MMA to offer clients an integrated service throughout their MMA involvement, from introductory experiences and coaching for children through to competing at world championship levels and everything in between (Evolve MMA, n.d.). So we can see how Evolve MMA differentiates itself from its competitors by its sheer size and its unique position as a one-stop shop that allows clients premium access to five-star sport facilities and instruction.

Obviously, sport organizations like Under Armour and Evolve MMA, or Manchester City Football Club, a university athletic department, or your local hockey club, do not operate with one single strategy. Rather, organizations employ numerous strategies at various levels and with respect to any number of stakeholders – hence the need to *manage* strategy. It is true that not all sport organizations practice strategic management, but to maximize the chances of organizational success while minimizing the prospect of organizational failure, the management of strategy – *strategic management* – is imperative. Harrison and St. John (2014) define strategic management in the following way:

> Strategic management is the process through which organizations analyze and learn from their internal and external environments, establish strategic direction, create strategies that are intended to help achieve established goals, and execute those strategies, all in an effort to satisfy key organizational stakeholders.
>
> (p. 4)

The context of strategic management in sport

The international sport environment is multifaceted; it influences and is influenced by any number of other sectors such as media, tourism, fashion, technology, education, and religion, to name a few. It has supply and demand sides, where the former is characterized by for-profit companies, like Under Armour in the opening case, that produce and trade in sporting goods and services; the latter consists of participants seeking involvement in sport activity as individuals or within teams or clubs, either as amateurs or as their primary source of income. Hoye, Smith, Nicholson, and Stewart (2018) helpfully delineate sport into three main sectors:

1   The state or public sector (national, state, regional, and local governments);
2   The non-profit/voluntary sector (community-based clubs, sport governing bodies that regulate and manage participation opportunities); and

3   Professional and commercial sport organizations (professional leagues and teams, sport apparel and equipment producers [think Under Armour in the opening case], media companies, major stadium and event managers, etc.).

While the sport industry may seem incredibly complex, the principles of strategic management can help to cut through this complexity because the concepts explored in this text are designed to offer insight to all layers of the sport environment. For example, board members of a local non-profit football club must consider the club's value proposition in relation to competitors, and while the scale is vastly dissimilar and there will be different influences, so too do board members of Nike need to consider the company's position relative to competitors. It is the *context* that changes, not the *concepts*. With this in mind, as you read this text, it is important for you to constantly make connections across cases and focus on the concepts being explored rather than the contexts within which they are presented. What you learn about managing the organizational culture of a local football club may indeed hold true for managing the organizational culture at Nike!

The strategic management process: an overview of this book

So how do sport organizations like New Zealand Rugby (and its All Blacks rugby team) achieve success and maintain that success over such long periods of time? They do this by differentiating themselves from their competition; that is, by deviating in key ways from the more widely accepted practices of their competitors. This entails major risk because "accepted" ways of conducting business are accepted because they are considered "safe" – or in strategic terms, *legitimate*. This means there are two main ways for an organization to stand out from competitors: either by success, or alternatively, by failure. Obviously, the former is more desirable than the latter, and this is where strategic management plays a key role in enabling sport managers to provide at least a measure of certainty in an uncertain environment.

Figure 1.1 depicts the various steps involved in managing strategy. As in all textbooks, these types of figures simplify what happens in the real world, but nevertheless they provide

FIGURE 1.1 The strategic sport management process

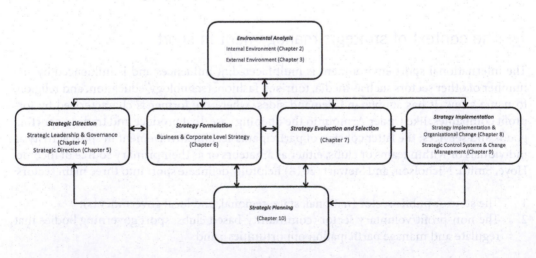

a foundation upon which we build deeper understanding. Strategic management is far more complex than a static snapshot, and it involves more than producing a strategic plan every few years or every Olympic cycle. Rather, strategic management should be perceived as an iterative process that evolves over time, with no "right" place to begin. For the sake of analysis and building understanding, we have chosen to start with environmental analysis.

As an iterative process, strategic management involves making choices. Decisions need to be made about the sector(s) the sport organization is best suited to compete in and what products and/or services it can viably offer to satisfy the needs of key stakeholders. The term *stakeholder* refers to groups or individuals who share some level of interdependency with the focal organization; whose actions affect, or are affected by, the focal organization; and who have the sense of an interest or right in the focal organization (Merrilees, Getz, & O'Brien, 2005). As in any walk of life, sound decision-making is founded upon equally sound information about the available alternatives. In the strategic management process, this information is derived from *environmental analysis*.

Obviously, there are many ways to scan an organizational environment, but essentially, senior management needs hard data and detailed information upon which to base its strategic decision-making. Organizations typically undertake both internal and external environmental analyses. For *internal environmental analysis* (Chapter 2), management needs to examine within the organization's structures, processes, and people for strengths and weaknesses. Meanwhile, *external environmental analysis* (Chapter 3) consists of identifying opportunities and threats in the organization's immediate competitive industry environment as well as its broad environment where pressures emerge in terms of trends and influences that can affect all industries. Based on data generated from this environmental scanning, management can then generate, evaluate, and select appropriate strategies to steer the organization toward achieving its mission.

This function of "steering" the sport organization is the responsibility of senior leadership. Leadership in sport organizations, depending on the context, manifests in many guises from an individual or team unit to a more role-oriented view of leadership, including team captains and coaches, department heads, senior executives, and CEOs. It is the CEO who typically reports to a board of management, sometimes referred to as an executive board. In this text, we are more concerned with *strategic leadership* (Chapter 4). As such, our focus will be on those leaders and leadership teams, such as CEOs, senior executives, and board members who profoundly influence the strategies, performance, and governance of their respective sport organizations. And, as recent corruption scandals at both Fédération Internationale de Football Association (FIFA) and the International Association of Athletics Federations (IAAF) demonstrate, *sport governance* that features both ethical leadership and an effective board structure are crucial for transparency and the maintenance of goodwill toward the focal sport organization. This is why Chapter 4 addresses *sport governance* and how it relates to strategic leadership in sport organizations.

How executive boards are structured is significant here. In sport, the representative democracy model, also known as the delegate or federated structure, has traditionally been the board structure of choice. However, with the trend toward the professionalization and commodification of sport throughout the 1980s and 1990s, the delegate structure proved inefficient in dealing with the unique pressures these trends presented (Hoye & Cuskelly, 2007). In its place, skills-based boards that follow a more corporate style of governance have emerged as more appropriate (Ferkins & Shilbury, 2012). In this model, rather than board members representing parochial stakeholder interests, they are appointed based upon the skills, experience, and leadership capabilities they bring to the role of board membership and sport governance. Regardless of structure, the board determines the parameters around which the CEO is hired and fired and performs an oversight function as the ultimate governance authority in the sport organization.

But perhaps the most profound responsibility of the board and senior leadership is to establish the sport organization's *strategic direction* (Chapter 5). Strategic direction is expressed formally as mission and vision, and these are typically underpinned by enduring values and beliefs as well as goals and objectives designed to guide the organization toward achievement of its mission. The world governing body for football, FIFA, has three core value statements in its mission:

(i)   developing football everywhere and for all;

(ii)   organizing inspiring tournaments; and,

(iii)   caring about society and the environment.

(FIFA, 2016)

For many years, critics of FIFA have made allegations of corrupt practices and a lack of transparency in decision-making and governance that contravened FIFA's espoused values and mission. So when US authorities arrested senior FIFA executives in May and December of 2015 on charges that included racketeering, money laundering, and fraud (Ruiz, Apuzzo, & Borden, 2015), FIFA's critics were vindicated. Football's many stakeholders around the world now look forward to widespread changes in leadership and governance practices and a much firmer commitment to the organization's claimed strategic direction.

Critical thinking Box 1.2

Google the phrase "iterative process." Using what you find, explain the nature of strategic management as an "iterative process."

Clearly, there is rarely only one route to a given destination. In the same way, there is seldom only one viable strategy to achieve organizational success. Therefore, management needs to engage in a robust *strategy formulation* process to work out the most effective route to organizational success. Strategy can be broken down into functional, business, and corporate levels. The functional level, as the name suggests, deals with functional areas or departments within the organization such as marketing, high performance, or human resource management. These functional-level strategies are an important part of strategy implementation, but they are not addressed in any real detail in this book because they are more operational rather than strategic in nature. *Business-level strategy formulation* (Chapter 6) deals with the particular industry sector, sometimes referred to as domain, which the sport organization has staked out for itself. Specifically, business-level strategy pertains to how management seeks to navigate this domain and position the organization relative to competitors. Meanwhile, *corporate-level strategy formulation* (also Chapter 6) relates to the selection of domains in which to compete. Some larger sport organizations, such as Under Armour discussed earlier, are involved in multiple business areas. These diversified organizations, called *conglomerates*, can become incredibly complex due to the breadth and scope of operations they are engaged in. This complexity makes the strategy formulation process particularly important.

Quite often in the strategy formulation process, numerous strategies will emerge that have merit in contributing to the sport organization's strategic direction. At this point, with a suite of strategic choices available, management may evaluate each strategic choice before making a final selection. This means a thorough *strategy evaluation and selection process* (Chapter 7) needs to be undertaken to analyze each strategy for its feasibility (can it be realistically achieved?), suitability (will it help us meet objectives?), acceptability (how will stakeholders react to it?), and ultimately, will it help us achieve competitive advantage? Strategic decisions such as Under Armour's, to diversify into the technology sector, are not made on a whim but are the product of rigorous environmental scanning, detailed strategy formulation, and a robust evaluation and selection processes.

Part of selecting an appropriate strategy is planning for its implementation. *Strategy implementation* (Chapter 8) requires decisions around the organizational structure and design elements that best predispose the chosen strategy to success. At this point, management needs to consider the types and number of specialist skills and capabilities that are required; whether these should be grouped by function, product, project, regional affiliation, or some combination; and then what the reporting relationships among the various subgroups will look like. Further, strategy implementation typically involves various degrees of organizational change. Resistance to change, or *inertia*, can often derail even the best-laid plans (O'Brien & Slack, 2003, 2004). Systems and processes to consult with, train, and compensate staff, and to collect, analyze, and communicate information in a manner consistent with organizational culture and values, can help to minimize resistance to change and increase the chances of implementation success. Communication that is couched in an organizational culture focused on learning and innovation, and which is accepting of trial and error *to a certain degree*, is often considered helpful.

As with most human endeavors, we like to know how successful we have been! *Strategic control systems* help managers gauge the success or otherwise of particular strategies. In Chapter 9, we explain the three main facets that constitute a comprehensive strategic control system: feedback, concurrent, and feedforward mechanisms. Taken together, these mechanisms provide a means of assessing effectiveness, but they also provide a level of accountability by helping us identify the actual sources of strategic success or failure, which then allows us to recognize areas requiring remedial action. When this is the case – that there are aspects of the organization that are not functioning as well as they could be – some level of organizational change is the natural outcome. Therefore, it is important for us to also understand some of the main ways of managing change processes.

When our strategic control systems tell us that strategy is in alignment with environmental trends and organizational objectives are consistently being met, the need for remedial action is minor. In this case, the type of organizational change taking place is evolutionary – small, almost imperceptible adjustments. However, from time to time, unexpected events take place in our external and/or internal environments, or managers simply misread the environment, strategy no longer aligns with environment, and the organization loses competitiveness and perhaps goes into decline. In such periods, revolutionary organizational change may be necessary to restore competitiveness – and sometimes to secure the organization's very survival.

Revolutionary change involves wholesale shifts across strategy, people, and processes. This type of all-encompassing change can be traumatic on stakeholders who may be financially and/or emotionally invested in maintaining the status quo. In the opening case, Kevin Plank devoted serious time to explaining Under Armour's technology diversification strategy to senior managers. By doing so, Plank was attempting to educate these key stakeholders as to the logic behind significant future changes, thus hopefully overcoming potential sources of resistance to change. Organizational change is perhaps the most enduring aspect of organizational life (Bedeian & Zammuto, 1991). Thus, it is helpful for an effective sport manager to develop skills in recognizing when, where, and importantly *why* inertia occurs and how to respond appropriately. These aspects of managing change are also addressed in Chapter 9.

We exist in an era characterized by questionable ethics and a lack of transparency in some of the world's most prominent sport organizations. As never before, it is the moral imperative of organizational leaders in sport to ensure accountability and transparency in their pursuit of organizational success while also conducting sport business in a financially responsible way that minimizes harm to local communities and the ecological environment. Engaging in a robust process of strategic management and utilizing the tools and processes described in this text is one way to maximize the chances of achieving this. The formalized expression of the strategic direction of the organization is a document referred to as a strategic plan, and *strategic planning* is the focus of Chapter 10.

Summary

This chapter opened by explaining what we mean by the terms *strategy* and *strategic management*. We distinguished between the two terms and also differentiated strategic management from strategic planning, the latter being a document that articulates where the sport organization has recently been, where it currently is and hopes to get to, and how it is proposed that it will get there. Meanwhile, strategic management is an ongoing, iterative process that is aimed at achieving competitive advantage and realizing the sport organization's mission – its purpose for being. We also explored the context of strategic management in sport and followed the lead of Hoye et al. (2018), who delineated sport into the state or public sector, the non-profit/voluntary sector, and last, professional and commercial sport organizations. While each context is distinct, it is important to remember that the concepts we explore in this text are equally applicable across all three. Last, we worked through each of the facets that make up the strategic management process, and in so doing, we also provided an overview of the text.

Chapter review questions

1   How can engaging in the process of strategic management help to provide sport organizations with a sense of purpose and direction in an uncertain and sometimes chaotic environment?

2   Go to www.patagonia.com/company-info.html and peruse the site. The values of sustainability are absolutely central to this company that specializes in what they refer to as "silent sports." Explain the link between mission, values, and strategic direction at this company, and the ways in which we see Patagonia's values manifest.

3   Nominate a national sport organization (NSO) that you are familiar with or have an interest in. Identify whether this NSO's governance is more aligned with the delegate or corporate model of sport governance.

4   The purpose of strategic control systems is to provide management with information as to the effectiveness of their organization's strategies. Think about the NSO you identified

in Chapter Review Question 3. What strategic control systems does this sport organization have in place? Are they effective? Why or why not?

5   Google the phrase "IAAF governance scandal." Peruse the top 5–10 articles and discuss what you believe were some of the key problems at IAAF that led to its problems. What type of organizational change – evolutionary or revolutionary – would you recommend is required at IAAF? Explain your answer and also identify where and how potential sources of resistance to change (inertia) may appear.

Additional resources

- Websites
  - McKinsey 7-S tool: www.mckinsey.com/business-functions/strategy-and-corporate-finance/our-insights/enduring-ideas-the-7-s-framework
  - Harvard Business Review: How Coca-Cola, Netflix, and Amazon learn from failure: https://hbr.org/2017/11/how-coca-cola-netflix-and-amazon-learn-from-failure?referral=03758&cm_vc=rr_item_page.top_right
- Videos
  - IAAF Council "could not have been unaware" of doping in athletics – as it happened: www.theguardian.com/sport/live/2016/jan/14/athletics-doping-scandal-wada-releases-part-two-of-report-live
  - Global sport boards – gender balance. www.youtube.com/watch?v=OkPe-dT4uMA
- Books
  - MacCallum, L., & Brew, E. (2019). *Inspired INC: Become a company the world will get behind*. London: Whitefox Publishing Co.
  - Mintzberg, H., Ahlstrand, B., & Lampel, J. (2005). *Strategy bites back: It is far more, and less, than you ever imagined.* . . . Harlow, Scotland: FT Prentice Hall/Pearson Education Ltd.

References

Bedeian, A. G., & Zammuto, R. F. (1991). *Organizations theory and design*. Chicago: Dryden Press.

de Kluyver, C. A., & Pearce II, J. A. (2012). Strategy: A view from the top (4th Ed.). Upper Saddle River: PrenticeHall.

Evolve MMA. (n.d.). *About Evolve MMA*. Retrieved February 4, 2019 from https://evolve-mma.com/about-us/about-evolve/

Fédération Internationale de Football Association. (2016). *About FIFA: What we stand for*. Retrieved October 28, 2016 from www.fifa.com/about-fifa/who-we-are/explore-fifa.html?intcmp=fifacom_hp_module_corporate

Ferkins, L., & Shilbury, D. (2012). Good boards are strategic: What does that mean for sport governance? *Journal of Sport Management*, *26*, 67–80.

Foster, T. (n.d.). Kevin Plank is betting almost $1 billion that Under Armour can beat Nike. *Inc*. Retrieved February 3, 2019 from www.inc.com/magazine/201602/tom-foster/kevin-plank-under-armour-spending-1-billion-to-beat-nike.html

Harrison, J. S., & St. John, C. H. (2014). *Foundations in strategic management* (6th Ed.). Mason, OH: Thomson South-Western.

Hoye, R., & Cuskelly, G. (2007). *Sport governance*. Oxford, UK: Elsevier.

Hoye, R., Smith, A. C., Nicholson, M., & Stewart, B. (2018). *Sport management: Principles and applications* (5th ed.). London: Routledge.

Merrilees, B., Getz, D., & O'Brien, D. (2005). Marketing stakeholder analysis: Branding the Brisbane Goodwill Games. *European Journal of Marketing, 39*, 1060–1077.

O'Brien, D., & Slack, T. (2003). An analysis of change in an organizational field: The professionalization of English rugby union. *Journal of Sport Management, 17*, 417–448.

O'Brien, D., & Slack, T. (2004). The emergence of a professional logic in English rugby union: The role of isomorphic and diffusion processes. *Journal of Sport Management, 18*, 13–39.

Ruiz, R., Apuzzo, M., & Borden, S. (2015, December 3). FIFA corruption: Top officials arrested in pre-dawn raid at Zurich hotel. *New York Times*. Retrieved October 28, 2016 from www.nytimes.com/2015/12/03/sports/fifa-scandal-arrests-in-switzerland.html

Shilbury, D. (2012). Competition: The heart and soul of sport management. *Journal of Sport Management, 26*, 1–10.

2 Internal environmental analysis

OPENING CASE: THE WINNING FORMULA IN FORMULA 1

At the start of the 2017 Formula 1 season, Mercedes AMG Petronas and Scuderia Ferrari appeared to have a competitive edge over the rest of the field – a carbon copy of the year before. In fact, Mercedes had dominated the previous year and hoped for a repeat. However, teams like Red Bull Racing, Williams Martini Racing, and McLaren Honda, which all dominated the sport at various points over the past few decades, had different ideas.

With a great deal of anticipation, the teams arrived in Melbourne, Australia, in March for the start of the season, where Sebastian Vettel took top honors, giving Ferrari its first win of the championship campaign. By mid-season, after 11 races, Mercedes and Ferrari topped the constructors' standings, with Mercedes leading by 39 points. Sebastian Vettel led Mercedes' Lewis Hamilton by 14 points in the drivers' standings. Red Bull had started to score points on a regular basis, as did Force India, rounding out the top four in the constructors' championship.

But two months later, at the 2017 US Grand Prix in Austin, Texas, Mercedes claimed its fourth straight constructors' championship. Two weeks later, Lewis Hamilton clinched the 2017 drivers' championship (his fourth title) after finishing ninth at the Mexican Grand Prix, with two races in hand.

What contributed to Mercedes' domination? Was it the drivers, the team leaders, the pit crew, the research and development teams, the engineers, the marketing department, the finances, or the car itself? These are all different types of resources that a Formula 1 team needs in order to be competitive. All Formula 1 teams arguably have these resources. But what makes Mercedes able to consistently dominate and sustain this competitive advantage over rival teams?

Introduction

To find out the answer to the opening case, you would have to do an internal environmental analysis of Mercedes' resources as compared to those of the other teams (assuming they would let you in their top secret facilities).

As the opening case highlights, different sport organizations may appear to have the same resources, but on closer inspection, slight differences in skills, abilities, and capacities can make a big difference, as can how these resources are assembled or combined. This is why the internal environment is so important for a sport organization to gain and sustain a competitive advantage compared to its competitors.

Sport managers need to have a good understanding of their internal environment for this reason, but also because it happens to be part of the first step in the strategic planning process. More precisely, when embarking on a strategic planning process, a sport manager must first ask herself: where are we now?

The Strengths-Weaknesses-Opportunities-Threats (SWOT) analysis is a means to answer this question (see Figure 2.1). As Hansen and Wernerfelt (1989) demonstrated, both

FIGURE 2.1 The SWOT analysis

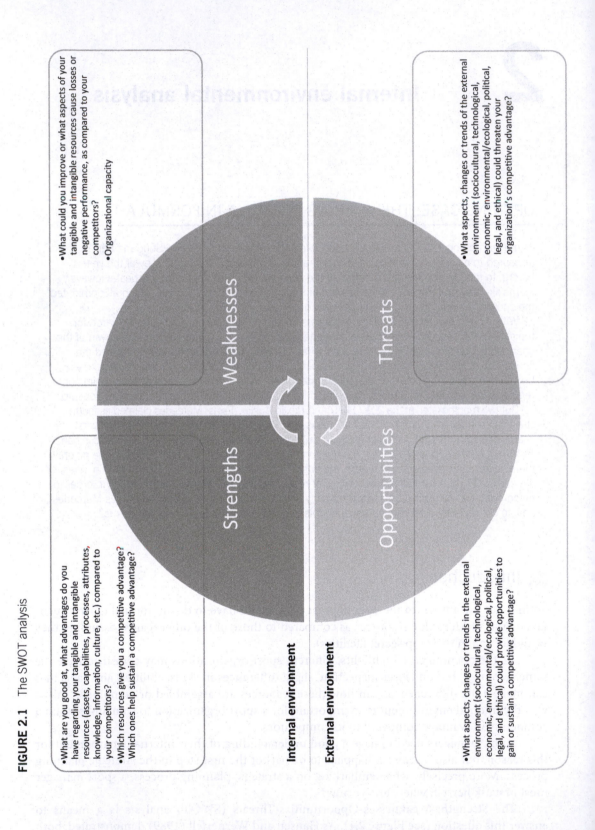

- What could you improve or what aspects of your tangible and intangible resources cause losses or negative performance, as compared to your competitors?
- Organizational capacity

- What aspects, changes or trends of the external environment (sociocultural, technological, economic, environmental/ecological, political, legal, and ethical) could threaten your organization's competitive advantage?

Weaknesses

Threats

Strengths

Opportunities

Internal environment

External environment

- What are you good at, what advantages do you have regarding your tangible and intangible resources (assets, capabilities, processes, attributes, knowledge, information, culture, etc.) compared to your competitors?
- Which resources give you a competitive advantage? Which ones help sustain a competitive advantage?

- What aspects, changes or trends in the external environment (sociocultural, technological, economic, environmental/ecological, political, legal, and ethical) could provide opportunities to gain or sustain a competitive advantage?

the organization's characteristics (climate, management, etc.) and its positioning relative to other organizations in the industry are important for its performance. In this chapter, we focus on the strengths and weaknesses of the organization's internal environment. In Chapter 3, we will examine the opportunities and threats found in the external environment.

Organizational resources

In order to analyze a sport organization's strengths and weaknesses, we must look to its resources. Resources are an organization's assets, capabilities, processes, attributes, knowledge, information, and so forth, which it controls, and which help the organization develop and implement a strategic plan or strategies to increase its effectiveness and efficiency (Barney, 1991). In other words, resources are the identified strengths of the organization, which it can use to build and implement its strategic plan. What is important to note is that when examining strengths and weaknesses, these are relative to your organization's competitors.

There are various ways to classify resources. At a basic level, you have tangible versus intangible resources. But perhaps more appropriately, you have (cf. Barney, 1991; Horton et al., 2003):

- *Physical resources*: those tangible, material resources such as buildings, technologies, equipment, raw materials, and even geographical location;
- *Human resources*: the intangible capital found within individuals – that is, their knowledge, training, experiences, judgement, intelligence, abilities, skills, and network of relationships;
- *Organizational resources*: the more intangible capital found within the organization, its capabilities, capacity (see below), its culture, values, and informal relations between groups, as well as its formal and informal reporting, planning, controlling, and coordinating systems; and
- *Financial resources*: although some would include financial resources (i.e., revenues/expenses, assets/liabilities) in the organizational resources category, given the emphasis on limited financial resources within many (volunteer) sport organizations, we place financial resources as a distinct category.

So, it is important for you to look at the visible, tangible resources and the intangible and less visible resources or capabilities of the organization and its individuals. Figure 2.2 illustrates the four key types of tangible and intangible resources.

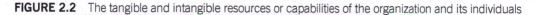

FIGURE 2.2 The tangible and intangible resources or capabilities of the organization and its individuals

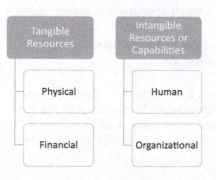

As organizations are social communities, they can actually be seen as repositories of capabilities, where individuals' and groups' experience and expertise are transformed into products and services (Kogut & Zander, 1992). As we will see below, some researchers (cf. Eisenhardt & Santos, 2002; Grant, 1996, 1997; Jasimuddin, 2012; Parent, MacDonald, & Goulet, 2014; Schenk, Parent, MacDonald, & Proulx Therrien, 2015; Zander & Kogut, 1995) argue that the intangible knowledge within the organization's members – both paid staff and volunteers for sport organizations – are the most important types of resources to examine for strategic planning purposes, and to use to gain and sustain a competitive advantage.

How do you identify your strengths and weaknesses? If strengths are the resources you can use to create and implement a strategic plan, what resources – tangible and intangible physical, human, and organizational capital resources – do you have within your organization that you can use? It is also important to identify what you are good at doing, the organization's capabilities, and members' knowledge, abilities, and skills.

In terms of weaknesses, you should look to what you are not good at but also your organization's capacity, or more precisely, the limits of the organization's capacity.

◼ Organizational capacity

Organizational capacity, in effect, translates the organization's resources into performance, or success (competitive advantage). "In simple terms, an organization's capacity is its potential to perform – its ability to successfully apply its skills and resources to accomplish its goals and satisfy its stakeholders' expectations" (Horton et al., 2003, p. 19). Organizational capacity includes tangible and intangible resources (e.g., management). It is a multidimensional concept of interconnected aspects (cf. Hall et al., 2003; Misener & Doherty, 2009). More precisely, organizational capacity includes (Hall et al., 2003):

- *Human resources capacity*: competence within the organization (i.e., core competencies of the organization, individuals' knowledge, skills, and know-how);
- *Financial capacity*: revenue versus expenses, and assets versus liabilities;
- *Relationship and network capacity*: relationships between internal and external stakeholders;
- *Infrastructure and process capacity*: physical infrastructure, organizational culture and processes, technology, and day-to-day operational products, processes, and procedures; and
- *Planning and development capacity*: an organization's planning, research, and development processes (such as strategic planning or program design).

Core competencies were first defined by Prahalad and Hamel (1990) as a key part of competitive advantage. They are defined as:

> the collective learning in the organization, especially how to coordinate diverse production skills and integrate multiple streams of technologies . . . it is also about the organization of work and the delivery of value. . . . Unlike physical assets, which do deteriorate over time, [core] competencies are enhanced as they are applied and

shared. . . . Competencies are the glue that binds existing businesses. They are also the engine for new business development.

(p. 82)

Another way to see it is that the organization's core products/services are the physical embodiment of its core competencies (Prahalad & Hamel, 1990). How do you identify core competencies? Prahalad and Hamel suggest three tests:

1   Does it provide access to potential new markets?
2   Does it provide "a significant contribution to the perceived customer benefits of the end product" (p. 84) or service?
3   Is it difficult for competitors to imitate?

Note that we presented core competencies within the context of human resource capacity, which is a critical place to look for core competencies – people and their knowledge. However, core competencies in themselves could include other areas such as technological processes or how the organization approaches client servicing, conflict resolution, or decision-making.

If you are in a non-profit organization, whether at the local or national level, you may very well say that you have great human resources, just not enough of them to do what you would like to do. This is a limit of the organization and demonstrates the organization's capacity. This may or may not be a weakness for the organization, but it will certainly be a limitation to consider as you progress through your strategic planning process.

This example also points to some experts (e.g., Hall et al., 2003; Misener & Doherty, 2009) arguing human resources are at the center of organizational capital, especially if knowledge is the most important resource to gain a competitive advantage. This also demonstrates the critical importance of effective leadership (i.e., intangible human resource) in organizational capacity building, and thus in strategic planning.

Misener and Doherty (2009) noted that, for non-profit sport organizations, human resources capacity as well as planning and development capacity were of relatively greater importance to achieve organizational goals than the other aspects. This means that these two types of capacities should be of particular interest during a strategic planning process and they should be examined during the internal analysis portion.

Hall et al. (2003) argued that organizations can more easily acquire new human resources than undertake or increase planning and development processes. As such, the organization's planning and development capabilities can be an important source of competitive advantage. Still, in a sport context, quality human resources can be difficult to obtain, thereby demonstrating a potential competitive advantage.

Critical thinking Box 2.1

Examine a variety of advertised sport job descriptions. What are the capabilities required for particular roles? If you cannot find any, a popular Australian sport recruitment site is www.sportspeople.com.au. Examine the desirable traits for various sport positions. Can you find some commonalities? What traits do you have? What will you need to work on?

Resources to gain and sustain a competitive advantage

Although you can create a list of all your organization's resources, not all of them contribute to gaining and/or sustaining a competitive advantage. For a resource to have this potential, it must have the four following attributes (cf. Barney, 1991, 1995):

- *Valuable*: the resource must allow the organization to exploit an opportunity in the external environment or counteract a threat; only then can it be considered valuable and "worth" considering as a resource for the SWOT analysis and the strategic planning process.
- *Rare*: the resource must be uncommon or unusual in the organization's external environment; only when rare can the resource be considered as a potential source of competitive advantage.
- *Imperfectly imitable*: the resource must be difficult or costly to copy by other organizations; only if the resource is considered imperfectly imitable can the valuable and rare resource help sustain a competitive advantage for the organization. Imperfect imitability is derived from:
  - *Unique historical conditions* (e.g., over a long period of time or because of unique/particular historical events) that allowed for the resource to be created;
  - *Causal ambiguity*, meaning the organization has difficulty pinpointing the specific resource that is allowing for a competitive advantage, or understanding why it even has a competitive advantage to begin with; or
  - *Social complexity*, meaning the organization may not be able to truly manage or control the particular resource because it is the result of a complex social phenomenon.
- *Non-substitutable*: there should not be other valuable resources the organization's competitors can use as a substitute for the given resource; only if no other resource can serve as a facsimile can the valuable, rare, and imperfectly imitable resource help sustain a competitive advantage.

However, even if a resource meets all four attributes, the organization must have the capacity and capability to use this resource to gain and sustain a competitive advantage; the organization must be able to capture the resource's value, as resources do not confer value on themselves (Barney, 1995). Combining the *Valuable, Rare*, and *Imperfectly imitable* resource attributes with the organization being *Organized* to capture value, results in what is termed the VRIO analysis of the internal environment (Barney, 1995). Figure 2.3 illustrates the VRIO.

Tangible resources are often easier to imitate or substitute compared to intangible resources. In addition, of all the intangible resources, knowledge is seen as the most valuable, to the point a strategic management theory has even been developed around it: the knowledge-based view of the firm (see Eisenhardt & Santos, 2002; Kogut & Zander, 1992; Winter, 1987).

In turn, knowledge can be broken down into explicit (formalized, written down) and tacit (informal, not written down) forms (Polanyi, 1966). Explicit knowledge can be found on websites, in technical manuals, or in other organizational documents. However, tacit knowledge is found within individuals; it derives from their training, experiences, and even gut feeling. As you can guess, tacit knowledge is the more valuable, rare, imperfectly imitable, and non-substitutable resource.

FIGURE 2.3   The VRIO analysis of the internal environment for competitive advantage

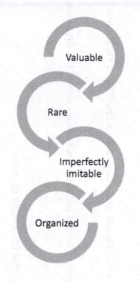

In fact, whole knowledge management and transfer systems are developed to get at and transfer tacit knowledge. Most of these systems include acquisition, creation, application, identification, storage, and transfer activities (Heisig, 2009). For example, the International Olympic Committee developed the Olympic Games Knowledge Management program to capture and transfer knowledge from one edition of the Olympic Games to the next. Within this program we find documents, reports, and technical manuals hosted on an extranet (i.e., storage), but we also find observer programs and city-to-city debriefs in order to transfer tacit knowledge so the next organizing committee can acquire knowledge it identified as necessary. What information it cannot acquire must be created. For more on this, see Parent et al. (2014) and Schenk et al. (2015).

Before we further explore resources to gain and sustain a competitive advantage in sport and the particularities of the sport context, an additional tool can help you analyze an organization's internal environment: the PRIMEFACT checklist (Parrish, 2016), described in Figure 2.4.

Sport-specific internal environmental issues

As an industry, sport employs millions of people globally (Hoye, Nicholson, & Smith, 2008), even more volunteers, and generates billions in revenues. The industry's commercialization has doubled since 2005, growing from USD 46.5 billion in 2005 to an estimated USD 90.9 billion in 2017 (Statista, 2014). Along with this commercialization has been a sometimes difficult professionalization process of volunteers and non-profit organizations (Clausen et al., in press).

Sport is unique due to a number of attributes, as illustrated in Figure 2.5. First, public (government-based), private/for-profit, and non-profit organizations coexist and govern the global sport system together. Sport is governed as a series of interlocking networks of individuals, groups, and organizations. While some organizations may be the titular heads of a

FIGURE 2.4 The PRIMEFACT checklist

P • **People:** your employees and staff, as well as your stakeholders, including advisors and consultants.

R • **Reputation:** what is your organization's reputation?

I • **Intellectual property:** what copyrights, design rights, trademarks, etc., that need to be protected but that can also be turned into a competitive advantage by commercializing them?

M • **Market information:** what intelligence do you have regarding the markets in which you operate and your various clients and customers?

E • **Ethos:** organizational values and culture, the way the organization "does things," and the extent to which individuals within the organization have the same values and culture (strength of your values and culture).

F • **Finances:** financial capacity, financial reserves and assets, financial reputation to be able to borrow or enter.

A • **Agility:** the degree to which the organization is flexible, able to change to address the clients' changing needs.

C • **Collaborators:** the organizations/businesses with which we collaborate, the degree and effectiveness of existing partnerships to meet organizational goals.

T • **Talents:** the existing skills in the organization as well as those that are lacking, and how the organization needs to improve these skills and core competencies.

FIGURE 2.5   Sport's unique attributes

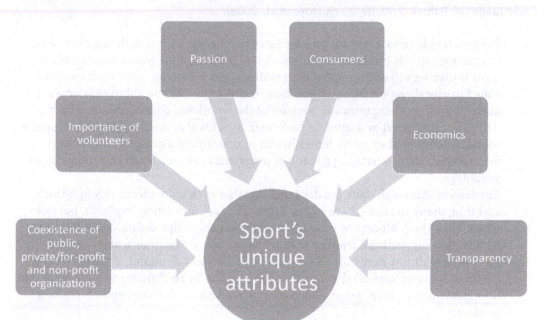

sport (i.e., international sport federations or professional leagues/associations), they cannot deliver their products and services without a number of stakeholders, such as the athletes, officials, coaches, media, governments, community/fans, sponsors, paid employees, and volunteers.

In fact, the significant number and influence of volunteers in the sport industry is a unique feature of sport. At the London 2012 Olympic and Paralympic Games, 70,000 volunteers were involved, and the Tokyo 2020 Olympic and Paralympic Games are projected to need 90,000 volunteers (The Independent, 2012; Tokyo Metropolitan Government & Tokyo Organising Committee of the Olympic and Paralympic Games (Tokyo 2020), 2016).

These volunteers do not come on gradually; the majority essentially start within a month of the opening ceremonies, with the bulk starting the day after the opening ceremonies. Much effort is placed on recruiting the right volunteers, training these volunteers, and preparing them for their roles as well as recognizing their efforts, as they – just like the paid employees – cannot make a mistake with the whole world watching. You cannot redo a sport event; you only have one chance (Parent & Smith-Swan, 2013). On a smaller scale, local sport clubs also need volunteers for a multitude of jobs, such as ticketing or food and beverage. Volunteers are the face of the organization; they are likely the only interaction a sport organization's customers will experience.

But we also find volunteers at higher organizational levels. In non-profit organizations, boards of directors are usually volunteers. These volunteers have a fiduciary duty to the organization; they are the ultimate decision makers. They notably approve budgets and strategic plans, and therefore have a direct effect on the survival of the organization, together with the top (paid) management, such as the chief executive officer (CEO), executive director, or secretary general. As such, choosing volunteers with the right skills, knowledge, and expertise becomes critical for most sport organizations to gain and/or sustain a competitive advantage.

Sport's other unique attributes can also impact upon an organization's competitive advantage (cf. Babiak & Wolfe, 2009; Hoye et al., 2008):

- *Passion*: It is hard to name another industry that brings with it such emotions when interacting with its products and services. Attending a game where your favorite team is playing will elicit much more emotion than when you wash your hair with your favorite shampoo. Many, if not most, individuals become volunteers or want to work for a sport organization because of the emotional connection they have with sport in general or a sport in particular. Sport is also used as a means to garner social benefits, be they active living/health or developing a sense of community, for example. Thus, leveraging passion appropriately can be a source of competitive advantage.
- *Consumers*: Although there are die-hard fans that stick with a team through thick and thin, many consumers are rather fickle. They are fans when "we" win, but not when "they" lose. Moreover, your sport affiliation also helps define your identity, be it by just supporting a team or even by where you are born or where you live. For example, if you were born in or you live in Glasgow, Scotland, you are either a Celtic or Rangers football club fan. Fan rivalries can be so extreme as to develop into hooliganism. As a manager of such a team, your fans can be a strength, but also a weakness.
- *Economics*: Sport also enjoys particular benefits and demonstrates particular characteristics in terms of economics. More precisely, many professional leagues operate as what are essentially cartels, while international sport federations enjoy the monopoly in the overall governance of a sport worldwide. At the same time, municipal and other levels of government offer economic benefits (free stadia, subsidies, no taxation, etc.) to various sport organizations within their jurisdiction that you do not see for other industries. Sport's economic situation, therefore, provides a competitive advantage compared to other industries.
- *Transparency*: Sport is a unique industry where the statistics of key stakeholders are publicly available and analyzed by the media and other interested parties. Data analytics of professional players, developed in part due to the Oakland Athletics' success in Major League Baseball (MLB) at a relatively low cost (see Lewis, 2003), is a career in itself. Likewise, the scandals and corruption related to sport – be it an organization like FIFA (the international federation for football) or an athlete like Lance Armstrong (caught doping) – result in high global media attention that you do not see in many other industries. Finally, at the time of writing this chapter, wearable technologies – and what you can do with them – were being debated in the National Basketball Association (NBA) and the NBA Players' Association (NBAPA) contract negotiations: on the positive side, such data can add richness to a broadcast, but on the negative side, such data could also be used against a player during contract negotiations.

Of course, these characteristics are not mutually exclusive. For example, some individuals have become leaders in sport by virtue of their passion for that sport, but they have been involved in scandals (e.g., bribes) that hit the headlines (such as the former president of the IAAF, Lamine Diack).

The importance of diversity

An increasing number of studies demonstrate the importance of diversity, whether that is gender-based, race-based, or other. For example, in a study of 700 companies listed on the Toronto Stock Exchange (see www.ctvnews.ca/business/representation-of-women-on-boards-varies-by-industry-company-size-report-1.2584872), about 60% of all listed companies with a market capitalization over CAD 2 billion had at least two women board members and at least two women executive officers. In contrast, listed companies with less than CAD 1 billion in market capitalization had no women board members, and 48% reported they had no women in executive positions.

In sport, many governing bodies set gender targets for boards of National Sporting/Governing Organizations (NSOs/NGOs), following evidence to suggest that increased gender diversity on boards leads to better organizational performance. For example, the Australian Sports Commission (ASC), the governing body of sport in Australia, published mandatory sport governance principles that are expected to be implemented by NSOs receiving significant funding from the ASC (see www.ausport.gov.au). One principle was gender balance on boards, whereby NSOs are to achieve a minimum target of 40% representation of females on executive sport boards.

While the targets are encouraging, there are no mechanisms in place to ensure NSOs achieve the desired gender percentages. Currently, the larger ASC-funded NSOs, such as swimming and athletics, are below the representative target with each organization having three women on their nine-person board of directors (33% women representation). Professional sports in Australia, not reliant on ASC funding, are even less inclined to reach the 40% women representative target. For example, the Australian Football League (AFL) Commission is at 25% and the National Rugby League (NRL) Commission is at 16%. Surprisingly, the International Olympic Committee also advocates for gender quality on its executive board, and yet only 4 of the 15 executive board members are women.

Cunningham (2011) also found that sport organizations with a high degree of diversity in terms of sexual orientation that followed a strong proactive diversity strategy outperformed their competitors. So, as the preceding examples demonstrate, having a diverse workforce (employees or volunteers) typically benefits the sport organization. As such, it can be a source of competitive advantage.

Critical thinking Box 2.2

Do you believe diversity (gender, race, sexuality, etc.) within an organization (and within a board of directors) can be a competitive advantage for an organization? Why or why not? Provide examples from the sport industry to support your argument.

Finally, as we have alluded to throughout the chapter, leadership is a potentially important resource to gain and sustain a competitive advantage. And yet, when empirically investigated (e.g., Fligstein & Brantley, 1992; Smart & Wolfe, 2003), leadership explains sometimes barely 1% of variance on performance when comparing organizations (see Smart & Wolfe, 2003). But the leader's (e.g., chief executive officer) background, the industry's growth, and the product strategy developed by the organization are factors that can have an effect on organizational performance (Fligstein & Brantley, 1992).

What is potentially even more impactful is the culture instilled by the leader within the organization. Culture can become an intangible resource, especially if a learning culture pervades the organization. Although individuals tend to resist change (see Chapter 9), if the leader is able to instill a desire to embrace innovation, it can differentiate the organization from its competitors and therefore be a source of competitive advantage, as culture is a complex phenomenon. Culture can be defined as the shared "stories, ceremonies, language, values, beliefs, ways of operating and physical settings of an organization. It brings people back into organizations without paying attention to psychological measures" (Byers, Slack, & Parent, 2012, p. 110).

A multidimensional concept, organizational culture can be examined at three levels: artifacts, values, and underlying assumptions (Schein, 1985). It is an important consideration within the internal environment analysis, as demonstrated by its presence in the PRIME-FACT checklist (Parrish, 2016) under the ethos component.

Organizational culture impacts an organization's strategy. For example, together with leadership, organizational culture has been shown to be a precondition for an organization's sustainability strategy (Baumgartner, 2009).

Within a sport event context, Parent and MacIntosh (2013) demonstrated that an organizing committee's culture actually includes a variety of subcultures, each tailored to meet the needs of the employees, volunteers, and target stakeholder groups of the particular department. MacIntosh and Doherty (2008, 2010) also demonstrated that in the fitness industry, organizational culture, or more precisely the organization's positive atmosphere, was highly linked to employees' job satisfaction.

Thus, organizational culture is important in strategic planning. But the proper learning culture can also be a source of competitive advantage, if the organization is flexible (cf. Parrish, 2016). As Zong, Duserick, and Rummel (2009) noted,

> in order to successfully compete in an increasingly changing business and technological environment, a firm can be successful in managing change by creating a learning culture as a platform, on which a variety of learning initiatives may be launched for enhancing business performance.
>
> (p. 22)

But the learning culture needs to be instilled throughout the organization: in its business strategies (further down in the strategic planning process), in its human resources, in its business processes, and in its customer relations; only then can the learning culture be considered a strength and therefore, a source of competitive advantage (Zong et al., 2009).

Summary

In summary, the internal analysis is the first step in the strategic planning process. It constitutes the first half of an organization's SWOT analysis and is meant to take a critical look at the organization's characteristics, and especially its resources.

Resources include all the organization's tangible and intangible assets, capabilities, processes, attributes, knowledge, information, and so forth that it controls, to help it develop and implement a strategic plan or strategies to increase its effectiveness and efficiency

(Barney, 1991). Whether the resource is a strength or a weakness must be determined in relation to the organization's competitors. But organizational capacity is often an area where weaknesses are identified.

Combining a resource's *Valuable, Rare,* and *Imperfectly imitable* attributes with the organization being *Organized* to capture value is called the VRIO analysis of the internal environment (Barney, 1995), and points to those resources that can help an organization gain and sustain a competitive advantage.

Each organization will have a unique set of critical resources. However, sport organizations also have particularities to consider that are not found in other industries. Nevertheless, leadership, diversity, and culture will form part of the organization's internal analysis and should constitute part of its strengths.

CLOSING CASE: SUCCESSFUL NOT-FOR-PROFIT BOARDS OF DIRECTORS CONDUCT GOOD GOVERNANCE SELF-ASSESSMENTS

In an era marred by global corruption in sport – be it match fixing, bribery or doping, for example – Canada has enacted its new Canada Not-for-Profit Corporations Act (2017). With this Act, all not-for-profit boards, including in sport, must adhere to good governance principles. It has meant that many national sport organizations have had to clarify and/or modify the roles and responsibilities of their boards versus its executive members and staff (e.g., chief executive officer or executive director).

It has also meant that board members can no longer be appointed ex officio, or according to a position they hold, such as being the president of a regional federation. Board members must now be appointed as individuals in their own right. At the same time, these organizations are facing complex governance challenges such as reduced funding, decreasing volunteer numbers, and higher ethical leadership, accountability, transparency, and trust requirements by stakeholders (and by the Act).

Boards have therefore been forced to look at themselves to identify their needs in terms of skills, but also their performance so they can demonstrate transparency and accountability to their stakeholders. Many boards, however, do not feel they have the capacity, knowledge, or expertise to carry out an evaluation of themselves.

Davidson (2014) suggested key areas for evaluation include:

- Board development: recruiting members, orientation and training process, governance structure;
- Board management: meeting process, roles of each board member, board committee, etc.;
- Board strategic plan, mission and goals, effectiveness, and efficiency; and
- Chief executive officer or executive director evaluation.

A number of tools are available to board members now, such as Dalhousie University College of Continuing Education and Governing Good's (2013) "Board Self-Evaluation Questionnaire: A Tool for Improving the Governance Practices of Non-profit Organizations."

As such, just like publicly traded for-profit organizations that require quarterly or annual reports, or like sports events that require an evaluation component post-event (Parent, 2008), not-for-profit and non-profit organizations also need to undertake evaluation activities to understand their strengths and weaknesses, which ultimately will help organizations improve their performance and gain and/or sustain a competitive advantage.

Chapter review questions

1   How do you analyze an organization's internal environment?
2   What are the characteristics of the resources that can help an organization gain and sustain a competitive advantage?
3   What is organizational capacity? Why is it often a weakness for sport organizations?
4   Use the PRIMEFACT checklist to analyze the internal environment of a sport organization you know.
5   Explain the concepts of diversity and organizational culture and why they are important for organizations to gain and sustain a competitive advantage.

Additional resources

- Websites
  - Resource-based view of the firm: www.strategicmanagementinsight.com/topics/resource-based-view.html
  - Valuable-rare-inimitable-organized tool: www.strategicmanagementinsight.com/tools/vrio.html
  - McKinsey 7-S tool: www.mckinsey.com/business-functions/strategy-and-corporate-finance/our-insights/enduring-ideas-the-7-s-framework
  - An interview with Anita DeFrantz from the United States, the fifth female to be elected as an International Olympic Committee member: www.sportcal.com/Insight/Interviews/115414
  - National Council of Nonprofits: Self-assessments for non-profit boards: www.councilofnonprofits.org/tools-resources/self-assessments-nonprofit-boards
- Videos
  - David Parrish on the internal analysis part of strategic planning: www.youtube.com/watch?v=bJVtaFWyr-Y
  - Facebook chief operating officer, Sheryl Sandberg, on why we have too few women leaders: www.ted.com/talks/sheryl_sandberg_why_we_have_too_few_women_leaders?language=en
- Books
  - Chelladurai, P., & Kerwin, S. (2017). *Human resource management in sport and recreation* (3rd Ed.). Champaign, IL: Human Kinetics.
  - Mintzberg, H., Ahlstrand, B., & Lampel, J. (2005). *Strategy bites back: It is far more, and less, than you ever imagined.* . . . Harlow, Scotland: FT Prentice Hall/Pearson Education Ltd.

References

Babiak, K., & Wolfe, R. (2009). Determinants of corporate social responsibility in professional sport: Internal and external factors. *Journal of Sport Management, 23*(6), 717–742. https://doi.org/10.1123/jsm.23.6.717

Barney, J. B. (1991). Firm resources and sustained competitive advantage. *Journal of Management, 17*, 99–120.

Barney, J. B. (1995). Looking inside for competitive advantage. *Academy of Management Executive, 9*(4), 49–61.

Baumgartner, R. J. (2009). Organizational culture and leadership: Preconditions for the development of a sustainable corporation. *Sustainable Development, 17*(2), 102–113. https://doi.org/10.1002/sd.405

Byers, T., Slack, T., & Parent, M. M. (2012). *Key concepts in sport management.* London: Sage.

Canada Not-for-Profit Corporations Act. (2017). Retrieved from https://laws-lois.justice. gc.ca/eng/acts/c-7.75/

Clausen, J., Bayle, E., Giauque, D., Klenk, C., Lang, G., Nagel, S., . . . Schlesinger, T. (in press). Drivers of and barriers to professionalization in international sport federations. *Journal of Global Sport Management.*

Cunningham, G. B. (2011). The LGBT advantage: Examining the relationship among sexual orientation diversity, diversity strategy, and performance. *Sport Management Review, 14*(4), 453–461. https://doi.org/10.1016/j.smr.2010.11.003

Dalhousie University College of Continuing Education, & Governing Good. (2013). *Board self-evaluation questionnaire: A tool for improving the governance practices of non-profit organizations* (3rd ed.). Halifax, Nova Scotia, Canada: Dalhousie University College of Continuing Education.

Davidson, C. (2014). *Community Literacy of Ontario's board governance resource guide* (2nd ed.). Barrie, Ontario, Canada: Community Literacy of Ontario.

Eisenhardt, K. M., & Santos, F. M. (2002). Knowledge-based view: A new theory of strategy? In H. Thomas, A. M. Pettigrew, & R. Whittington (Eds.), *Handbook of strategy and management.* London: Sage.

Fligstein, N., & Brantley, P. (1992). Bank control, owner control, or organizational dynamics: Who controls the large modern corporation? *American Journal of Sociology, 98*, 280–307.

Grant, R. M. (1996). Toward a knowledge-based theory of the firm. *Strategic Management Journal, 17*(Winter Special Issue), 109–122.

Grant, R. M. (1997). The knowledge-based view of the firm: Implications for management practice. *Long Range Planning, 30*(3), 450–454.

Hall, M., Andrukow, A., Barr, C., Brock, K., Wit, M. D., Embuldeniya, D., . . . Vaillancourt, Y. (2003). *The capacity to serve: A qualitative study of the challenges facing Canada's Nonprofit and voluntary organizations.* Toronto, Canada: Canadian Centre for Philanthropy.

Hansen, G. S., & Wernerfelt, B. (1989). Determinants of firm performance: The relative importance of economic and organizational factors. *Strategic Management Journal, 10*(5), 399–411.

Heisig, P. (2009). Harmonisation of knowledge management – Comparing 160 KM frameworks around the globe. *Journal of Knowledge Management, 13*(4), 4–31.

Horton, D., Alexaki, A., Bennett-Lartey, S., Brice, K. N., Campilan, D., Carden, F., . . . Watts, J. (2003). *Evaluating capacity development: Experiences from research and development organizations around the world.* The Hague, the Netherlands; Ottawa, Canada; Wageningen, the Netherlands: International Service for National Agricultural Research (ISNAR), the Netherlands; International Development Research Centre (IDRC), Canada; and ACP-EU Technical Centre for Agricultural and Rural Cooperation (CTA), the Netherlands.

Hoye, R., Nicholson, M., & Smith, A. (2008). *21st century management: A reference handbook.* Thousand Oaks, CA: Sage.

The Independent. (2012, August 10). *London 2012: Olympics success down to 70,000 volunteers*. Retrieved December 13, 2017 from www.independent.co.uk/sport/olympics/news/london-2012-olympics-success-down-to-70000-volunteers-8030867.html

Jasimuddin, S. M. (2012). *Knowledge management: An interdisciplinary perspective*. Hackensack, NJ: World Scientific Publishing Co Pte Ltd.

Kogut, B., & Zander, U. (1992). Knowledge of the firm, combinative capabilities, and the replication of technology. *Organization Science, 3*(3), 383–397.

Lewis, M. (2003). *Moneyball: The art of winning an unfair game*. New York, NY: W. W. Norton & Company.

MacIntosh, E. W., & Doherty, A. (2008). Inside the Canadian fitness industry: Development of a conceptual framework of organizational culture. *Journal of Sport Management, 9*(3), 303–327.

MacIntosh, E. W., & Doherty, A. (2010). The influence of organizational culture on job satisfaction and intention to leave. *Sport Management Review, 13*(2), 106–117.

Misener, K., & Doherty, A. (2009). A case study of organizational capacity in nonprofit community sport. *Journal of Sport Management, 23*(4), 457–482. https://doi.org/10.1123/jsm.23.4.457

Parent, M. M. (2008). Evolution and issue patterns for major-sport-event organizing committees and their stakeholders. *Journal of Sport Management, 22*(2), 135–164.

Parent, M. M., MacDonald, D., & Goulet, G. (2014). The theory and practice of knowledge management and transfer: The case of the Olympic Games. *Sport Management Review, 17*(2), 205–218. https://doi.org/10.1016/j.smr.2013.06.002

Parent, M. M., & MacIntosh, E. W. (2013). Organizational culture evolution in temporary organizations: The case of the 2010 Olympic Winter Games. *Canadian Journal of Administrative Sciences, 30*(4), 223–237. https://doi.org/10.1002/CJAS.1262

Parent, M. M., & Smith-Swan, S. (2013). *Managing major sports events: Theory and practice*. London: Routledge.

Parrish, D. (2016, June 22). *Strategic planning: Internal analysis an online course with David Parrish*. Retrieved December 15, 2017 from www.youtube.com/watch?v=bJVtaFWyr-Y

Polanyi, M. (1966). *The tacit dimension*. New York, NY: Anchor Books.

Prahalad, C. K., & Hamel, G. (1990). The core competence of the corporation. *Harvard Business Review, 68*(3), 79–91.

Schein, E. H. (1985). *Organizational culture and leadership* (1st ed.). San Francisco, CA: Jossey-Bass Publishers.

Schenk, J., Parent, M. M., MacDonald, D., & Proulx Therrien, L. (2015). The evolution of knowledge management and transfer processes from domestic to international multi-sport events. *European Sport Management Quarterly, 15*(5), 535–554. https://doi.org/10.1080/16184742.2015.1091022

Smart, D. L., & Wolfe, R. A. (2003). The contribution of leadership and human resources to organizational success: An empirical assessment of performance in major league baseball. *European Sport Management Quarterly, 3*(3), 165–188.

Statista. (2014, November). *Global sports market – Total revenue from 2005 to 2017 (in billion U.S. dollars)*. Retrieved December 13, 2017 from www.statista.com/statistics/370560/worldwide-sports-market-revenue/

Tokyo Metropolitan Government, & Tokyo Organising Committee of the Olympic and Paralympic Games (Tokyo 2020). (2016). *Volunteering strategy for the Olympic and Paralympic Games Tokyo 2020* (pp. 38). Retrieved from https://tokyo2020.jp/jp/get-involved/volunteer/data/volunteer-summary_EN.pdf

Winter, S. G. (1987). Knowledge and competence as strategic assets. In D. J. Teece (Ed.), *The competitive challenge* (pp. 159–184). Cambridge, MA: Ballinger.

Zander, U., & Kogut, B. (1995). Knowledge and the speed of the transfer of organizational capabilities. *Organization Science, 6*(1), 76–92.

Zong, D., Duserick, F., & Rummel, A. B. (2009). Creating a learning culture for competitive advantage. *Competition Forum, 7*(1), 17–24.

3 External environmental analysis

OPENING CASE: GOLFSMITH FAILS TO ADAPT TO A CHANGING EXTERNAL ENVIRONMENT
(By Ashley Thompson)

In 1967, Golfsmith was founded by Carl and Barbara Paul as a supply company that sold component parts of golf equipment to avid golfers looking to create their own golf clubs. In the mid-1990s, with the increasing popularity of golf, Golfsmith began to aggressively expand its retail model. The company went public in 2006, and in 2009 it generated revenues of over USD 338 million. In 2012, through a merger with Canada's Golf Town retail stores, Golfsmith was considered one of the largest golf retail companies in the world. By the end of that year, employing more than 1,800 people, the company had approximately 89 mega-sized retail stores with each store having approximately 20,000 square feet of floor space. Despite the early success of Golfsmith in the 1990s and early 2000s, the retail chain filed for Chapter 11 bankruptcy in 2016.

So what happened? As changes in the company's external environment occurred, such as the onset of the 2008 recession as well as shifts in consumer attitudes toward physical retail stores, Golfsmith failed to recognize and adapt to these new trends. Instead, the company continued to open new stores, expanding from 89 stores in 2012 to 109 stores in 2016. As a result of its aggressive expansion and vast amount of retail stores, Golfsmith's costs were too high to sustain. Put simply, the company had too many stores that were larger than needed to meet market demands. Consequently, because of these mega-sized stores with an excess of merchandise, Golfsmith also owed approximately USD 200 million in outstanding loans or credit facilities, including more than USD 20 million to its major equipment suppliers such as Callaway, TaylorMade, Nike, Titleist, and Ping.

The case of Golfsmith sheds light on some of the broader problems that have plagued the sporting retail industry over the last decade in which numerous companies (Sport Chek, Dick's Sporting Goods, etc.) have either downsized or filed for bankruptcy as a result of a lack of recognition and adaption to changing trends in the external environment. This case is based on information in Madden (2016), Stachura (2012, 2016a, 2016b), Torsiello (n.d.).

Introduction

As the preceding case demonstrates, even big, successful companies can read their environment wrong, to dire consequence. This chapter will give you the tools to properly analyze the various aspects of your sport organization's external environment. We will start with the general environment, followed by the task environment. Understanding how to manage your organization's stakeholders will conclude the core concepts for this chapter.

General environment

The general environment is the broad environment that every organization, regardless of industry or country, must deal with. Think at the 30,000-foot level. These environmental forces affect, directly or indirectly, how organizations operate and the types of decisions they can and need to make.

There are various acronyms one can commonly find related to the different parts of the external environment, such as PEST, PESTLE, or STEEPLE (Aguilar, 1967; Andrew, 1980; Drucker, 1994; Porter, 1980). At the core, they all deal with four key sectors: political, economic, social, and technological. In this book, we will use the STEEPLE approach, as it is the more encompassing acronym (see Figure 3.1):

- *Sociocultural*: The sociocultural environment looks at the general population. Aspects to consider can include age and income distributions, demographic changes, social class structure, national/regional/local culture, labor and social mobility trends, lifestyle and consumer taste trends, and fashion trends. Market research typically falls within this sector. An example would be differences in sport preferences in one country over another, such as the cultural dominance of ice hockey in Canada, which is not the case in Australia.
- *Technological*: Aspects to consider can include new inventions, materials, technologies, and developments; information technology (IT) changes; the rate of technology transfer as well as the life cycle and speed of technological obsolescence, and mobile technology changes. An example would be the new materials developed to make able-bodied and para-athletes go faster or higher, such as swimmers' so-called shark suits. Using your mobile phone to pay for purchases by tapping it to a payment machine would be another example.
- *Economic*: The economic environment comprises the economic situation not only in your country, but also throughout the world; this is particularly so given the state of globalization and internationalization (see below for more on this issue). As such, aspects to consider include whether there is an economic boom or recession, the state of unemployment, inflation rates, interest rates and other national monetary policies, the system of banking, and consumer confidence in the market. An example of this environmental influence would be that, for a national sport organization seeking new sponsors, there may be more opportunities during an economic boom than during a recession, when money is tight for consumers and companies.
- *Ecological/environmental*: The ecological environment includes aspects such as environmental regulations and protection, as all organizations impact their ecological environment, whether positively or negatively, and whether to a large or small degree. An example of the ecological environment would be the green, ecologically friendly standards put in place by event rights owners, which cities and stadia must adhere to.
- *Political environment*: The political environment refers to the political structure and system in place in the country of operation. Aspects to consider include the political party in power, its ideology, the political leaders' attitudes/beliefs/behaviors, political stability (or instability) of the country, and the concentration of political power. An example of the political environment would be the election of a president with a strong domestic, protectionist agenda. This may pose some problems if your organization operates internationally.

- *Legal environment*: The legal environment refers to the legal system in place in the country (e.g., common law versus civil law), the tax policies, employment/labor laws, health and safety regulations, and competition laws in the jurisdiction(s) in which your organization operates. An example would be the differences between operating in a socialist country versus a capitalist country. This would have a significant impact if you are a for-profit company. Business operations can be significantly facilitated or hindered by the country's political system.
- *Ethical environment*: The ethical environment refers to social norms, values, duties, and behaviors currently shaping businesses – in other words, (corporate) social responsibility (for more information, see Walker & Parent, 2010). Aspects to consider include the expectations of the organization in terms of social, economic, and environmental responsibility, proper marketing techniques (cf. ambush marketing), respecting employees' religious beliefs, and good governance practices. An example is the current wave of corruption scandals hitting sport and the numerous calls for "good" governance principles to be adopted by sport organizations (see Play the Game, 2013; Transparency International, 2016). An example would be the question as to whether McDonald's, as a then sponsor in The Olympic Program (TOP) – the premium level of sponsorship in the Olympic Movement – should have been permitted to advertise during the 2012 Innsbruck Youth Olympic Games, given that the athletes were teenagers.

FIGURE 3.1   The STEEPLE approach to the external environment

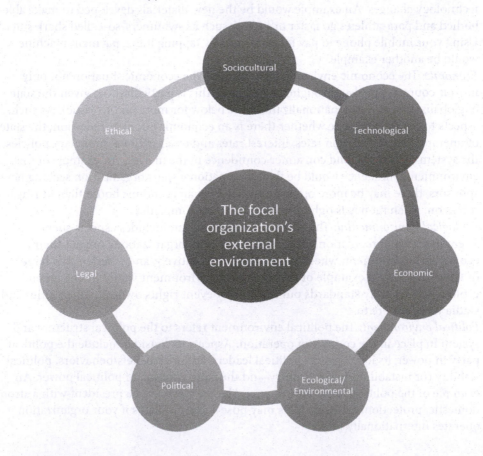

It is not enough to look at the various sectors of the general environment. You have to look at whether these sectors provide *opportunities* for your organization and/or *threats*, for your *SWOT analysis* (see Figure 2.1). Some developing aspects or trends in the external environment could be used to your organization's advantage, such as the advent of online cloud technologies to allow task coordination among managers in different countries. On the flip side, the advent of new technology could become a threat as the market moves away from your organization's "traditional" technology products.

As such, the same trend can be an opportunity for some but a threat to others. With the aging demographic population trend in many Western countries, if your company provides products or services to seniors, then this trend is an opportunity. Conversely, if your company provides products or services to youth, then this trend becomes a potential threat to your survival.

Such perceptions and understanding of the external environment are predicated on your cognitive map, however. In other words, different managers in the organization may have different perceptions, not only because their role or job differs but also because of differing backgrounds, history, experiences, values, beliefs, knowledge, preferences, and biases (cf. Morden, 2007). So, two different managers in the organization may have a different perception of the external environment, as can two different individuals in the same position. As such, it can be useful to conduct external environment analyses in a group.

Next, as a manager, you must also understand the degree of stability or (potential for) change each sector has, as well as the influence of globalization (see below).

Stability and change

Each sector of the external environment noted above "should be analyzed in terms of *the degree of stability* and the *rate of change*" (Morden, 2007, p. 101, emphasis in original). Each sector can be examined to determine whether it is stable, moderately dynamic, turbulent, or turbulent with an increasing rate of change. Figure 3.2 provides an overview of these potential external environment descriptors. What you will notice, though, is that the descriptors are placed on a continuum. The more you find yourself on the right side of the continuum, the more the changes can significantly impact the organization and even affect its overall survival (cf. Morden, 2007).

Globalization

In the 21st century, we are in a knowledge economy, where what you know gives you value and a competitive advantage, but we are also in a digital economy. With the advent of the internet, mobile phones, Web 2.0, social media, new media, satellites, and so forth, our world is more connected than ever. Sport organizations can even operate completely virtually now, with no physical headquarters, as is the case with Waterski Wakeboard Canada, the national sport organization for waterski and wakeboard in Canada.

Globalization can be defined as "the economic, political, socio-cultural and temporal integration of people, values, goods and services enabled through advances in technology, travel, and communication" (Byers, Slack, & Parent, 2012, p. 69). Globalization has also been facilitated with the increase in trade agreements between countries and the decrease in legal and political barriers.

FIGURE 3.2 The stability-change continuum for external environment sectors

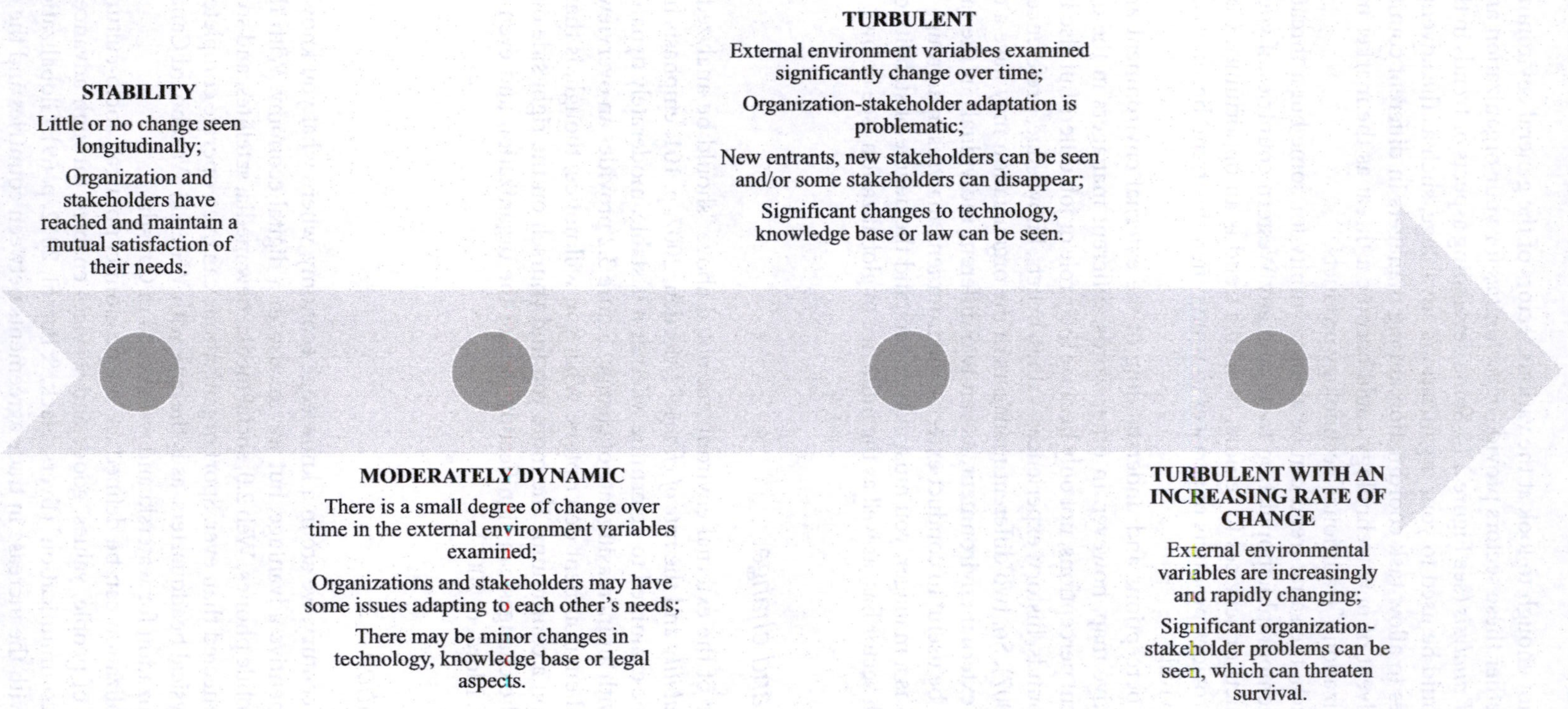

STABILITY

Little or no change seen longitudinally;

Organization and stakeholders have reached and maintain a mutual satisfaction of their needs.

MODERATELY DYNAMIC

There is a small degree of change over time in the external environment variables examined;

Organizations and stakeholders may have some issues adapting to each other's needs;

There may be minor changes in technology, knowledge base or legal aspects.

TURBULENT

External environment variables examined significantly change over time;

Organization-stakeholder adaptation is problematic;

New entrants, new stakeholders can be seen and/or some stakeholders can disappear;

Significant changes to technology, knowledge base or law can be seen.

TURBULENT WITH AN INCREASING RATE OF CHANGE

External environmental variables are increasingly and rapidly changing;

Significant organization-stakeholder problems can be seen, which can threaten survival.

Although some sport organizations see globalization as a threat – for example, cheaper labor and production costs abroad can make your equivalent local product more expensive and less desirable in the eyes of your consumer – other organizations see opportunity. For example, Barcelona Football Club has developed football academies around the world under its international FCBEscola banner. It exported its football school internationally with a wish "to spread the Barça name and transmit the Club's work philosophy and values to the rest of the world" (FCBEscola, n.d.a). Outside Spain, the international FCBEscola schools can be found in 22 countries (FCBEscola, n.d.b):

- Europe: Turkey, Poland, and Russia
- Africa: Egypt, Nigeria, and Zambia
- The Americas: Canada, the United States, Mexico, Dominican Republic, Peru, Brazil, Guatemala, Colombia, and Costa Rica
- Asia: Saudi Arabia, United Arab Emirates, India, Singapore, China, and Japan
- Oceania: Australia.

Critical thinking Box 3.1

Consider globalization and a sport organization you are familiar with. Do you believe globalization is a threat to your organization? Why or why not? Can you list some sport organizations that may be threatened by globalization? Similarly, can you identify sport organizations that will benefit from globalization?

Porter (1990) argues that countries can have a competitive advantage over other nations in a given industry due two four "diamonds," as he called them (see also Morden, 2007):

1 *Factor conditions*: the various resources available, such as the skill and competence of the workforce; the geographical local, physical resources, and sources of energy; the knowledge resources in that particular society; the capital resources to finance or sustain economic development; and the infrastructure (e.g., transportation, financial, health, education, and communication systems).

2 *Demand conditions*: the stronger and more sophisticated the demand in a particular country for a product/service, the more likely that country will dominate international markets in that product/service (e.g., the United States, the United Kingdom, and Japan dominate the entertainment industry worldwide due to this industry dominating at home). The same can be said for sports, with Japan dominating judo; New Zealand with rugby union; the United Kingdom with rowing and sailing; Germany with equestrian sports; India with cricket; Brazil with football and surfing; South Korea with tae kwon do; and the United States with basketball (Shekara, 2015).

3 *Firm strategy, structure, and rivalry*: the greater the sector rivalry and competition in an industry in a country, the more likely those organizations are to be competent and competitive internationally.

4 *Related and supporting industries*: if there are clusters of supporting and related industries in a country, then there can be the potential for greater competitive advantage, as organizations can create supply chains with other organizations that themselves are competent and have a competitive advantage, and thereby have value.

These factors allow organizations to take advantage of particular laws, policies, and resources in a country to create economies of scale; increase quality, effectiveness, and efficiency; and ultimately gain and sustain a competitive advantage (see also the discussion on competitive advantage in Chapter 2).

However, with this globalization and internationalization of processes and activities comes an inundation of data to the manager. At the same time, the advances in technology have provided managers (and researchers) with a new range of tools to address what is termed big data.

Big data

In *Moneyball: The Art of Winning an Unfair Game*, Michael Lewis (2003) exposed how Billy Beane, general manager of the Oakland Athletics of MLB, paid attention to numbers, to data already being collected but not previously used, to his competitive advantage, fielding a team at low cost that no one else would want, but who performed. Thanks to big data analytics, the team with one of the lowest – if not the lowest – payrolls in the league managed to win more regular season games than teams with three times its payroll.

This *Moneyball* revolution in sport is essentially a revolution in the use of large datasets to inform decision-making and strategy. Big data analysis is not only revolutionizing the sport manager's on-the-field activities but also her off-the-field activities.

> A new wave of convergence is emerging that will radically transform marketing methodologies as well as other components of business operations and management. The converging dimensions include social media and networking, mobile devices and platforms, cloud computing, and so-called "Big Data" analytical environments.
> (Bonometti, 2012, p. 209)

Thanks to globalization and the digital age, big data analytics have exploded. One key management activity linked to big data is in marketing: customer relationship management (CRM). CRM systems collect information (data) from customers at every possible interaction with the company or touch point, such as product usage, demographics, and psychographics. The analysis of this big data allows key marketing decisions to be made (Mumcu & Fried, 2017). Making sense of big data therefore helps companies reduce costs; make faster, better decisions; and develop new products and services that meet the current and future needs of their customers (Davenport & Dyché, 2013).

To take advantage of big data, sport managers need to mine (or collect), store, analyze, and present this information in useful ways to make informed decisions. Mining big data can come from social media accounts, consumption patterns, demographics, web logs, documents, images, videos, and so forth (Davenport & Dyché, 2013). Tools such as NCapture or Netlytic can be used for social media account mining. Storing becomes a critical component, as the system must handle huge amounts of information, often done through open source solutions (e.g., Apache Hadoop).

But big data are still not in a useful form until they are analyzed. This can be done with various tools, such as Hadoop's Hive project, MapReduce, or Leximancer, the latter being a big data automated thematic analysis software, and the first two allowing for data restructuring and/or statistical analysis and presentation of data in relational tables or cubes. Once the analysis of big data is in a digestible format, modeling, reporting, and other decision-making activities can be done (Davenport & Dyché, 2013).

Although big data can provide much return on investment for interested organizations (Davenport & Dyché, 2013), there are some issues and caveats. Gerrard (2007), for example, looked at transferring the *Moneyball* approach, performance data, to English Premier League football, while Mason and Foster (2007) examined the transferability in the National Hockey League. Though optimistic, both studies noted issues with transferability due to technological, conceptual, and cultural barriers (Gerrard, 2007) and requiring new statistical measures (Mason & Foster, 2007). More recently, however, Weimar and Wicker (2017) found a potential *Moneyball* effect in German professional football based on an undervalued running distance measure.

At the same time, collecting data from individuals without their knowledge or consent can be legally problematic. Hattery (2017) also raises the question of athletes' right to know in regards to MLB teams' health data mining and modeling; he argues teams have a duty to disclose health risks to their athletes:

> This "Right to Know" should provide individuals, specifically Major League Baseball players, with access to information that indicates significant health risks threatening the quality of life or livelihood of the player. By this inference, the Right to Know requires the possessors of the information to affirmatively give this information to the subjects of data collection and analysis.
>
> (Hattery, 2017, p. 260)

And with increasingly tight personal information protection laws being enacted (e.g., the 2018 reform of the European Union's data protection rules), individuals are getting increased control over their personal data, which means organizations have stricter rules to follow for handling personal data. How this will affect big data analysis, if at all, remains to be seen.

Critical thinking Box 3.2

What data are collected in your sport (or an organization you are familiar with)? Do you know what this data is used for? Can you identify specific "big data" that could be collected that would potentially give you a competitive advantage? How can data literacy among sport managers strategically assist your organization?

■ Task environment

So far we have focused on the general external environment. But the preceding big data discussion has actually brought us to consider those individuals, groups, and organizations that have a more direct effect or can be affected by the actions of a given organization. These are termed *stakeholders* (see Freeman, 1984), and they form the task or immediate environment of an organization.

There are a number of generic stakeholder groups that most organizations will have. Clarkson (1995) suggested organizations have employees as internal stakeholders, and shareholders, customers, suppliers, and public/governmental organizations as external stakeholders. Zeigler (1985) suggested physical education and athletic departments have clients, suppliers, advisers, controllers, adversaries, and publics with opinions as stakeholders. Finally,

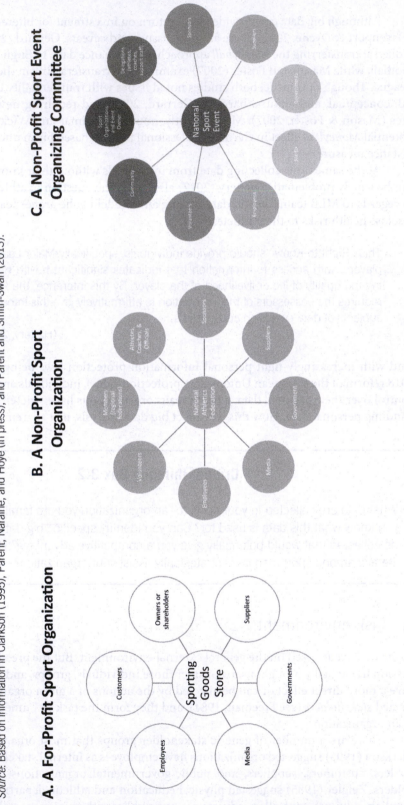

FIGURE 3.3 Generic task environments of different types of sport organizations

Source: Based on information in Clarkson (1995), Parent, Naraine, and Hoye (in press), and Parent and Smith-Swan (2013).

A. A For-Profit Sport Organization

Sporting Goods Store

Owners or shareholders

Suppliers

Governments

Media

Employees

Customers

B. A Non-Profit Sport Organization

National Athlete Federation

Athletes, Coaches, & Officials

Sponsors

Suppliers

Governments

Media

Employees

Volunteers

Members (regional federations)

C. A Non-Profit Sport Event Organizing Committee

National Sport Event

Sponsors

Spectators

Governments

Media

Employees

Volunteers

Community

Sport Organizations and Event Owner

Delegations (athletes, coaches, support staff)

Parent and Smith-Swan (2013) suggested major international multi-sport event organizing committees have paid staff and volunteers as internal stakeholders, and host governments, the community (residents, schools, community groups, activists, local businesses), media (traditional and new media), sport governing bodies (sport federations and event rights owner), sponsors, delegations (athletes, their support staff, and mission staff) as the main external stakeholders.

As you can see, there can be different generic stakeholders depending on the type of organization. Figure 3.3 illustrates this by comparing potential generic stakeholder groups for a for-profit sport organization (e.g., Nike or adidas), a non-profit sport organization (e.g., a national sport federation or governing body), and a non-profit sport event organizing committee.

It is important to point out that, regardless of whether the organization is enduring (e.g., Nike or a national sport federation) or temporary (e.g., a sport event organizing committee) in nature, each organization will have a task environment – and an external environment – to deal with.

Just as the external environment analysis is dependent on a manager's cognition, so too is the task environment. Parent and Deephouse (2007) demonstrated that sport event managers in the same event can have differing perceptions of who their stakeholders are in their task environment as well as how important or salient they are. Thus it is important that you know the boundaries of your market and industry before you can analyze the task environment (Kay, 1993). To do so, we will look at Porter's five forces model and stakeholder analysis.

Porter's five forces model

Porter (1980) argued that competition in a given market is due to forces from five sources: rivals, buyers, suppliers, new entrants, and substitutes. Each source and force is described below (see also Morden, 2007).

1   *The extent of industry rivalry.* The degree of industry competition is impacted by:
    a   The nature of industry rivalry: diversity and number of competitors, degree of equality (or lack thereof) between competitors' relative market strengths, and degree of concentration (or fragmentation) of the industry;
    b   The relative youth (or maturity) of the industry;
    c   The degree to which operational capacity is increased in large (or small) increments;
    d   The presence of high financial burdens linked to fixed costs; and
    e   The presence of high exit barriers preventing organizations from leaving a market.
2   *The bargaining power of suppliers.* The degree to which suppliers have bargaining power is affected by:
    a   The degree of supplier concentration (i.e., small number of suppliers);
    b   The ability of suppliers to differentiate their product/service;
    c   The degree to which the supplier is important to the buyer for the purchase of the product/service;
    d   The degree to which close substitutes are available; and
    e   The degree to which suppliers can threaten forward (vertical) integration to control their distribution channels or market outlets.

3   *The bargaining power of buyers.* The degree to which buyers have bargaining power is affected by:
  a   The degree of buyer concentration (i.e., small number of organizations) compared to suppliers;
  b   The relative size or volume of the buyer's purchases in the market as well as the importance of the purchase for the buyer;
  c   The degree to which close substitutes are available;
  d   The degree to which buyers can threaten backward (vertical) integration to control their supply sources;
  e   The degree to which the product/service is standardized or commodified (meaning less differentiation possible between suppliers);
  f   The potential costs associated with switching between suppliers;
  g   The degree of buyers' price sensitivity; and
  h   The degree to which buyers wish/need to develop a long-term relationship with the supplier.
4   *The threat of new entrants.* The degree to which new entrants have a hard time penetrating a market will be partly determined by:
  a   Building strong customer loyalty to existing competitors;
  b   Having effective product differentiation between existing competitors;
  c   Making it difficult for potential entrants to access the necessary distribution channels;
  d   Making it difficult for potential entrants to access the necessary capabilities, operational experience, or value chain inputs;
  e   Using competition strategies to make it difficult for potential entrants to become competitors (e.g., aggressive pricing or additional discounts/service offers);
  f   Having absolute cost advantage through economies of scale or a premier market position that would be difficult to match by a new entrant;
  g   Having high capital costs associated with entering a market;
  h   Making it difficult for new entrants to build brand loyalty and organizational reputation; and
  i   Having government policies discouraging new entries in a market.
5   *The threat of substitutes.* The degree to which the threat of substitutes can be diminished will be partly determined by:
  a   Buyers' tendency or willingness to substitute a product/service for one from a competitor;
  b   The price attractiveness of existing products/services compared to substitutes;
  c   The perceived value (price/performance) of existing products/services compared to substitutes; and
  d   The perceived costs or risks associated with switching from existing products/services to substitutes.

Porter's five forces model is very popular with management students. Caution is warranted, however. This is one tool among many that can be used by (sport) managers to understand their immediate task environment. It should not be used as a cookie-cutter approach – blindly, for all situations. In fact, research (e.g., Hansen & Wernerfelt, 1989; Rumelt, 1991) on the structure-conduct-paradigm and Porter's five forces has not supported this approach as one that improves performance or competitive advantage; this research actually points to business or organization-specific aspects being more important for performance/competitive advantage than industry characteristics. This therefore demonstrates the criticality of understanding one's organization, as presented in Chapter 2.

Thus, another tool to help managers understand their immediate environment is through stakeholder analysis.

Stakeholder analysis

As sport organizations have many stakeholders, it is important for managers to know which stakeholders are more important, what these key stakeholders want, and how the organization can meet those needs if they are to survive. The stakeholder analysis process allows you to do this, and it includes four main steps (see Figure 3.4 and also Freeman, 1984). As Friedman, Parent, and Mason (2004, p. 171) noted, "Through the use of stakeholder management techniques, sport managers should be better able to achieve their organization's objectives."

Step 1: stakeholder identification – who surrounds the organization?

The first step is to draw a stakeholder map with your organization in the center. You can start with the generic maps and stakeholder groups noted earlier and then expand each stakeholder group to specific stakeholders within each group (see Merrilees, Getz, & O'Brien [2005] for an example of a stakeholder map of a major sport event's marketing group). It is important to consider not only organizations but also individuals, groups, and even inanimate entities, such as the environment. This could be the case if your organization was an outdoor adventure and travel company (Friedman et al., 2004).

The key is to determine who could have:

- A stake (equity, economic, or influencer; Freeman, 1984) in the organization's performance;
- Access to resources (time, money, or other) of interest to the organization, or are part of the industry structure, or part of the sociopolitical arena surrounding the organization (Post, Preston, & Sachs, 2002); or
- A moral obligation to the organization, or who can harm/benefit the organization (Phillips, 2003).

FIGURE 3.4   The stakeholder analysis process

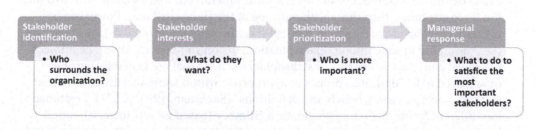

Step 2: stakeholder interests – what do they want?

Next, you need to figure out what each stakeholder needs and wants. You can determine this by understanding what the stake is (see above). You can also determine this by what types of interests the stakeholder has (Reichart, 2003):

- *Affiliative*: human relationships and the need to belong or associate with something/ someone;
- *Informational*: knowledge-based concerns;
- *Material*: gain or loss of tangible benefits;
- *Political*: distribution of political power and influence; and
- *Symbolic*: linked to symbols, image, reputation, and so forth.

For instance, Parent (2008) found that host governments of events are interested in material, political, informational, and symbolic aspects, while delegations are more interested in material and informational aspects in the case of major international multi-sport events.

You may likely find that stakeholders, even in the same group, can have differing interests, needs and wants, or issues they want addressed. This is called stakeholder heterogeneity. For example, Parent (2008) demonstrated that the various levels of host governments for a major international multi-sport event can have different interests: the federal government focuses on financial, visibility, politics, and participation issues; the provincial government focuses on financial, visibility, politics, and legacy issues; and the municipal government focuses on financial, visibility, participation, and legacy issues. In other words, do not assume that stakeholder groups are homogenous (see also Parent & Deephouse, 2007).

Step 3: stakeholder prioritization – who is more important?

At this point, you probably think you have too many stakeholders, and you are probably right. Therefore you need to prioritize them, as you do not have enough hours in a day or other resources (e.g., money) to address every stakeholder for every need. There are various ways to determine stakeholders' salience and prioritize them. Two popular means include:

- Clarkson's (1995) *primary versus secondary stakeholders*: primary stakeholders are those who are seen to be critical for the survival of the organization, and thus managerial attention should be focused on these stakeholders first. Secondary stakeholders are those who can influence the organization but are not essential for survival.
- Mitchell, Agle, and Wood's (1997) *power-legitimacy-urgency attribute typology*: this typology argues that the more a stakeholder has these attributes, the more salient the stakeholder is. In other words, stakeholders seen to have all three attributes are called definitive stakeholders and are the most salient, followed by those with two of the three attributes, then those with only one of the three attributes. Power can be coercive (i.e., the use of threat), utilitarian (i.e., the promise of rewards), or normative (i.e., the ability to use symbols, like reputation, to control; Etzioni, 1964). Legitimacy is a social construct referring to a stakeholder's actions that are generally perceived or assumed to be "desirable, proper or appropriate within some socially constructed system of norms, values, beliefs and definitions" (Suchman, 1995, p. 574). Legitimacy has different forms, including pragmatic legitimacy (based on self-interest); moral legitimacy (a positive normative evaluation of the organization and its activities); and

cognitive legitimacy (affirmative backing or "mere acceptance of the organization as *necessary* or *inevitable* based on some taken-for-granted cultural account"; Suchman, 1995, p. 582, emphasis in original). Finally, urgency is a more catalytic attribute, being linked to time sensitivity and the degree of impact (Mitchell et al., 1997). It is also about a willingness to act (Savage, Nix, Whitehead, & Blair, 1991). Often, activist organizations have urgency, but they may or may not have the other two attributes.

Parent and Deephouse (2007), for example, used Mitchell et al.'s (1997) typology to determine the salience of stakeholders surrounding a major international multi-sport event. Regardless of the approach you choose, stakeholder salience will depend on (Parent, 2008):

- You (the manager): your hierarchical level (top, middle, lower) and your cognitive perceptions of your environment; and
- The issue at hand and the timing of stakeholder assessment; any stakeholder can become critical at a particular time for a particular issue.

Step 4: managerial response – what to do to "satisfice" our most important stakeholders?

In this step, you must determine what needs to be done to ensure your salient stakeholders' needs are met. Ask yourself: how effective is the organization at meeting these needs currently? If gaps are found, then you need to modify the organization's policies, procedures, priorities, and so forth to meet the identified needs (Freeman, 1984). Ultimately, you want to satisfy and suffice (or "satisfice") your salient stakeholders.

One key is to manage the most salient stakeholders or those closest to the organization, for mutual benefit between the organization and the stakeholder, while decreasing or ensuring no harm and/or creating potential benefits for those less salient stakeholders.

Clarkson (1995) provided a stakeholder management strategies framework, called the Reactive-Defensive-Accommodative-Proactive (RDAP) Scale, which allows an organization to evaluate its corporate performance by characterizing managers' strategy/position in relation to a specific stakeholder group for one or more stakeholder issues. A *reactive* strategy suggests the organization should employ a "deny all responsibility and fight the stakeholder all the way" strategy; in other words, do less than is required by the stakeholder. A *defensive* strategy is seen when the organization admits responsibility but still tries to fight this responsibility by only doing the minimum required by the stakeholder. An *accommodative* strategy is seen when the organization accepts responsibility and does all that is required by the stakeholder; the organization can be seen as progressive in this case. Finally, a *proactive* strategy is seen when the organization wants to lead the industry by anticipating responsibility and doing more than is required by the stakeholders (McAdam, 1973; Carroll, 1979; Clarkson, 1995). Being proactive and accommodative results in better performance than being reactive or defensive (Clarkson, 1995).

▪ Summary

In summary, to survive, gain, and sustain a competitive advantage, the organization not only needs to understand its internal environment (strengths and weaknesses), but it must also have solid grasp of the trends in the external environment (opportunities and threats). The external environment includes the broader, general environment as well as the immediate task environment, with the stakeholders that can affect or be affected by the organization's actions.

The general environment can be broken down into seven sectors using the STEEPLE acronym: sociocultural, technological, economic, ecological/environmental, political, legal, and ethical. The task environment will vary depending on the nature of the organization. However, it can be analyzed using Porter's (1980) five forces model or using a stakeholder approach. Ultimately, the organization's salient stakeholders must be satisfied in order for the organization to survive and be successful.

CLOSING CASE: THE INTERNATIONAL OLYMPIC COMMITTEE RESPONDS TO GLOBAL TRENDS

The International Olympic Committee (IOC) is not immune to global trends. Like any organization, it must respond to changes and trends in its environment if it wants to survive.

For example, the rising costs of bidding and hosting the Olympic Games has led to many cities withdrawing from bidding, such as Bern (Switzerland), Budapest (Hungary), Hamburg (Germany), Krakow (Poland), Boston (United States), and Lviv (Ukraine), even previous Olympic cities such as Rome (Italy), Innsbruck (Austria), Calgary (Canada), and Oslo (Norway). Many of these cities cited costs as a major issue, with the local population often rejecting the idea of bids moving forward through referenda.

In response to this trend, the IOC put forth 118 recommendations on February 6, 2018, to decrease these costs. It also changed its managerial approach to bidding and organizing committees, primary stakeholders of the IOC, to being a partner instead of an oversight body (IOC, 2018).

A joint steering forum has been created between Tokyo 2020 key stakeholders – the IOC, the Organizing Committee for the Olympic Games (OCOG), the Japanese Government, and the Tokyo Metropolitan Government – to decrease costs to the order of USD 2.2 billion for the Tokyo 2020 Olympic Games. The 118 recommendations further suggest a potential reduction of USD 959 million for future Olympic Games and USD 527 million for future Olympic Winter Games (IOC, 2018).

At the same time, with Kodak and McDonald's dropping out as TOP sponsors, the IOC had an opportunity to align its TOP program and Olympic Movement processes with global trends, namely the digital era. The IOC did so by signing a long-term partnership with the Alibaba Group through 2028. Although Alibaba is not well-known in Europe or the Americas, it is actually the world's largest e-commerce (online and mobile) company, based in China (Alizila, n.d.). Alibaba's mission is to "build the future infrastructure of commerce," thereby reaching a target of two billion consumers served and lasting over 102 years (IOC, 2017).

When the partnership was announced, the IOC president, Thomas Bach, said:

> In this new digital world, Alibaba is uniquely positioned to help the IOC achieve a variety of key objectives outlined in Olympic Agenda 2020, while positively shaping the future of the Olympic Movement. This is a ground-breaking, innovative alliance, and will help drive efficiencies in the organisation of the Olympic Games through 2028, whilst also supporting the global development of digital opportunities including the Olympic Channel.
>
> (IOC, 2017, ¶1)

Alibaba will contribute to the Olympic Movement by developing best-in-class cloud computing infrastructure and services; developing and customizing the Olympic Channel for a Chinese audience; and creating a global e-commerce platform for Olympic stakeholders. The cloud computing component will also include support for big data analytics requirements.

As such, the IOC has taken note of various external environment sectors (sociocultural, economic, ecological/environmental, political, and technological) in these recent moves.

Chapter review questions

1   What are the external environmental aspects in the SWOT analysis? Describe what they mean.
2   Explain what the STEEPLE acronym means and provide an example for each dimension.
3   Pick an organization that you know and explain how globalization affects it.
4   Describe Porter's five forces model and use it to analyze a sport market that is of interest to you.
5   Pick an organization you know and conduct a stakeholder analysis of it.

Additional resources

- Websites
  - Differences between SWOT and STEEPLE analyses: http://pestleanalysis.com/difference-swot-pest-steep-steeple-analysis/
  - Big data analytics: What is it and why does it matter? www.sas.com/en_ca/insights/analytics/big-data-analytics.html
- Videos
  - The role of statistics in sport: www.soccermetrics.net/high-level-discussions/billy-beane-and-bill-gerrard-2
  - The big deal about big data: A lecture by Gary King: http://methods.sagepub.com/video/srmpromo/WZTNDG/the-big-deal-about-big-data-a-lecture-by-gary-king?utm_source=Adestra&utm_medium=email&utm_content=play&utm_campaign=Methods17Oct&utm_term=
- Books
  - Freeman, R. E., Harrison, J. S., Wicks, A. C., Parmar, B. L., & de Colle, S. (2010). *Stakeholder theory: The state of the art*. New York, NY: Cambridge University Press.
  - Lewis, M. (2003). *Moneyball: The art of winning an unfair game*. New York, NY: Norton.
  - Porter, M. E. (1980). *Competitive strategy*. New York, NY: Free Press.
  - Slack, T., & Parent, M. M. (2006). *Understanding sport organizations: The application of organization theory* (2nd ed., pp. 149–172). Champaign, IL: Human Kinetics.

References

Aguilar, F. J. (1967). *Scanning the business environment*. New York, NY: The Macmillan Company.

Alizila. (n.d.). *What we do*. Retrieved May 3, 2018 from www.alizila.com/about/

Andrews, K. R. (1980). *The concept of corporate strategy* (Revised ed.). Homewood, IL: Richard D. Irwin Inc.

Bonometti, R. J. (2012). Technology considerations for competing in the "big data"– social-mobile-cloud marketing space. *Competition Forum, 10*(2), 209–2014.

Byers, T., Slack, T., & Parent., M. (2012). *Key concepts in sport management*. London: Sage Publications Ltd.

Carroll, A. B. (1979). A three-dimensional conceptual model of corporate performance. *Academy of Management Review, 4*, 497–505.

Clarkson, M.B.E. (1995). A stakeholder framework for analyzing and evaluating corporate social performance. *Academy of Management Review, 20*(1), 92–117.

Davenport, T. H., & Dyché, J. (2013). *Big data in big companies.* Cary, NC: SAS Institute Inc.

Drucker, P. F. (1994, September/October). The theory of business. *Harvard Business Review,* pp. 95–104.

Etzioni, A. (1964). *Modern organizations.* Englewood Cliffs, NJ: Prentice Hall.

FCBEscola. (n.d.a). *International FCBEscola.* Retrieved May 1, 2018 from https://fcb-escola. fcbarcelona.com/international-fcbescola

FCBEscola. (n.d.b). *International FCBEscola: Where are we?* Retrieved May 1, 2018 from https://fcb-escola.fcbarcelona.com/international-fcbescola/location

Freeman, R. E. (1984). *Strategic management: A stakeholder approach.* Boston, MA: Pitman.

Friedman, M. T., Parent, M. M., & Mason, D. S. (2004). Building a framework for issues management in sport through stakeholder theory. *European Sport Management Quarterly, 4,* 170–190.

Gerrard, B. (2007). Is the Moneyball approach transferable to complex invasion team sports? *International Journal of Sport Finance, 2*(4), 214–230.

Hansen, G. S., & Wernerfelt, B. (1989). Determinants of firm performance: The relative importance of economic and organizational factors. *Strategic Management Journal, 10*(5), 399–401.

Hattery, M. (2017). Major League Baseball players, big data, and the right to know: The duty of Major League Baseball teams to disclose health modeling analysis to their players. *Marquette Sports Law Review, 28*(1), 257–283.

International Olympic Committee. (2017, January 19). *IOC and Alibaba Group launch historic long-term partnership as Alibaba becomes worldwide Olympic partner through 2028.* Retrieved May 3, 2018 from www.olympic.org/news/ioc-and-alibaba-group-launch-historic-long-term-partnership-as-alibaba-becomes-worldwide-olympic-partner-through-2028

International Olympic Committee. (2018, February 6). *The new norm: It's a game changer.* Retrieved May 3, 2018 from www.olympic.org/news/the-new-norm-it-s-a-games-changer

Kay, J. (1993). *Foundations of corporate success.* Oxford: Oxford University Press.

Lewis, M. (2003). *Moneyball: The art of winning an Unfair Game.* New York, NY: Norton.

Madden, P. (2016, September 14). Golfsmith files for bankruptcy, announces plans to sell golf town. *Golf.com.* Retrieved from www.golf.com/equipment/golfsmith-files-bankruptcy-announces-plans-sell-golf-town

Mason, D. S., & Foster, W. M. (2007). Putting Moneyball on ice? *International Journal of Sport Finance, 2*(4), 206–213.

McAdam, T. W. (1973). How to put corporate responsibility into practice. *Business and Society Review/Innovation, 6,* 8–16.

Merrilees, B., Getz, D., & O'Brien, D. (2005). Marketing stakeholder analysis: Branding the Brisbane Goodwill Games. *European Journal of Marketing, 39,* 1060–1077.

Mitchell, R. K., Agle, B. R., & Wood, D. J. (1997). Toward a theory of stakeholder identification and salience: Defining the principle of who and what really counts. *Academy of Management Review, 22,* 853–886.

Morden, T. (2007). *Principles of strategic management* (3rd ed.). London: Routledge.

Mumcu, C., & Fried, G. (2017). Analytics in sport marketing. *Sport Management Education Journal, 11*(2), 102–105.

Parent, M. M. (2008). Evolution and issue patterns for major-sport-event organizing committees and their stakeholders. *Journal of Sport Management, 22,* 135–164.

Parent, M. M., & Deephouse, D. L. (2007). A case study of stakeholder identification and prioritization by managers. *Journal of Business Ethics, 75*, 1–23.

Parent, M. M., & Smith-Swan, S. (2013). *Managing major sports events: Theory and practice.* London: Routledge.

Phillips, R. (2003). *Stakeholder theory and organizational ethics.* San Francisco, CA: Berrett-Koehler Publishers, Inc.

Play the Game. (2013). *Action for Good Governance in International Sports Organisations.* Retrieved October 20, 2015 from www.playthegame.org/theme-pages/the-sports-governance-observer/the-sports-governance-observer/

Porter, M. E. (1980). *Competitive strategy.* New York, NY: Free Press.

Porter, M. E. (1990). *The competitive advantage of nations.* London: Macmillan.

Post, J. E., Preston, L. E., & Sachs, S. (2002). *Redefining the corporation: Stakeholder management and organizational wealth.* Stanford, CA: Stanford University Press.

Reichart, J. (2003). A theoretical exploration of expectational gaps in the corporate issue construct. *Corporate Reputation Review, 6*(1), 58–69.

Rumelt, R. P. (1991). How much does industry matter? *Strategic Management Journal, 12*(3), 167–185.

Savage, G. T., Nix, T. W., Whitehead, C. J., & Blair, J. D. (1991). Strategies for assessing and managing organizational stakeholders. *Academy of Management Executive, 5*(2), 61–75.

Shekara, M. (2015, June 10). *Top 10 countries that dominate specific sports.* Retrieved May 1, 2018 from www.sportskeeda.com/sports/top-10-countries-that-dominate-various-sports

Shilbury, D., & Ferkins, L., (2015). Exploring the utility of collaborative governance in a national sport organization. *Journal of Sport Management, 29*, 380–397.

Stachura, M. (2012, May 14). Golf Town buys Golfsmith for $96 million in retail mega-merger. *Golf Digest.* Retrieved from www.golfdigest.com/story/golf-town-to-acquire-golfsmith

Stachura, M. (2016a, September 19). What Golfsmith's Chapter 11 filing really means – And which stores are closing. *Golf Digest.* Retrieved from www.golfdigest.com/story/what-golfsmiths-chapter-11-filing-really-meansand-which-stores-are-closing

Stachura, M. (2016b, October 21). Reuters: Dick's Sporting Goods buys up Golfsmith stores at bankruptcy auction. *Golf Digest.* Retrieved from www.golfdigest.com/story/reuters-dicks-sporting-goods-buys-up-golfsmith-stores-at-bankruptcy-auction

Suchman, M. C. (1995). Managing legitimacy: Strategic and institutional approaches. *Academy of Management Review, 20*, 571–610.

Torsiello, J. (n.d.). *Golfsmith continues its pattern of growth in the industry. The a position.* Retrieved from http://theaposition.com/torsmangolf/golf/520/golfsmith-continues-its-pattern-of-growth-in-the-industry

Transparency International. (2016). *Global corruption report: Sport.* London: Routledge.

Walker, M., & Parent, M. M. (2010). Toward an integrated framework of corporate social responsibility, responsiveness, and citizenship in sport. *Sport Management Review, 13*, 198–213.

Weimar, D., & Wicker, P. (2017). Moneyball revisited. *Journal of Sports Economics, 18*(2), 140–161.

Zeigler, E. F. (1985). Understanding the immediate managerial environment in sport and physical education. *Quest, 37*(2), 166–175.

4 Strategic leadership and governance

Introduction

This chapter examines strategic sport leadership and sport governance. While certainly interrelated, leadership within sport management is arguably a much broader concept than governance. In sport organizations, governance usually carries with it formal responsibilities including legal obligations. Meanwhile, in addition to formal positions of responsibility, leadership can occur informally throughout all layers of a sport organization or system of sport organizations (international, national, regional, local). Leadership can also occur in moments or "acts of leadership," depending on the lens through which leadership is viewed (Jackson & Parry, 2018). This chapter explores the multiple ways in which leadership can be viewed and how these intersect with the process of strategic sport management. We also offer a multifaceted view of sport governance, making the distinction between governance *of* a sport organization (role of the board) and governance that occurs *among* sport organizations (systemic governance). As with leadership, concepts of strategic sport management are woven throughout our discussion of sport governance as we examine the board's strategic role as well as the strategic concerns of governance across multiple organizations.

Strategic sport leadership: how lens matters

Leadership permeates a range of different contexts, levels, and layers within sport organizations and across multiple sport organizations that might be considered as sport systems. Leadership in the context of strategic sport management is perhaps most obvious in formally vested positions (e.g., CEO, event director, athletic director, chair, president). However, leadership can also occur informally (e.g., acts of leadership and influence) and often in the absence of a formal title (Marion, Christiansen, Klar, Schreiber, & Erdener, 2016). In capturing such variations in understanding leadership, Grint (2005) sets out four ways he considers leadership has been traditionally understood: person, results, position, and process. These four ways of viewing leadership are captured in Figure 4.1 and explained below.

First, leadership can be seen as a *person* – that is, *who* leaders are, and what enables them to lead (Grint, 2005). For example, Sebastian (Seb) Coe, former Olympic Gold medalist in the 1500 meters, has in recent times been active in advocating against corruption in sport, seemingly drawing on his moral compass and reputation for sense of fair play as his advocacy platform (albeit there are media reports challenging this in relation to some of his appointments; Ingle, 2017). Second, Grint (2005) explains that leadership can be seen via a *results* lens – that is, *what* leaders achieve is what actually makes them leaders. Using the example of Seb Coe, his outstanding success as an athlete, his work in leading a successful bid process for the London 2012 Olympics, and his "presenting" London 2012 to the world, points to perceptions of him as a high-profile and "successful" leader in sport.

FIGURE 4.1 Seeing leadership

Source: Adapted from www.samyoung.co.nz/2014/01/grint-lenses-of-leadership.html.
Thanks to Associate Professor Brigid Carroll Department of Management and International Business, The University of Auckland Business School Auckland, New Zealand for her work with past New Zealand Leadership Institute facilitators in creating Figure 4.1.

Third, leadership can be seen as a *position* (Grint, 2005) – that is, the hierarchical position in an organization *where* leaders operate from makes them leaders. In Seb Coe's case, his titles and positions include the title of "Lord" and "The Right Honorable" alongside his positions as president of the IAAF, chairperson of the British Olympics Association, chair of the London Organizing Committee of the Olympic and Paralympic Games, and president of the Organizing Committee for the Summer Olympic Games, to name a few. These titles play into this view of him as an influential leader. Fourth, Grint (2005) identifies leadership as a *process* – that is, *how* leaders get things done makes them leaders. Staying with the example of Seb Coe's role in IAAF governance, this might include how he interacts with the board to generate leadership among the group.

So of these multiple ways to view leadership, how might strategic leadership be described? If taking a person, results, and position view of leadership, then strategic leadership is focused on those who are responsible for consequential decisions and determining the long-term direction – for the whole of the organization or department – which has wide-reaching and long-term impact. The individual may need excellent communication skills and be considered charismatic in order to sell their vision and enable implementation of their decisions. Logically, this also directs us to the CEO and senior managers (for paid staff), and to the chairperson and directors/committee members in terms of voluntary and governance roles. This also leads us to consider the characteristics and behaviors of the individual, about which many leadership studies have focused (Jackson & Parry, 2018).

This view of leadership has fostered sport management research using a number of popular theories about leadership, based on the traits and behaviors of individual leaders, such as charismatic leadership, transactional leadership, and transformational leadership (Welty Peachey, Damon, Zhou, & Burton, 2015). However, as Burton (2014) explains in her article, such theories, developed to explain strategic sport leadership, were derived from a foundational bias in which white males were chosen as research participants or subjects for their high-level or strategic roles. Comparatively, very little research has investigated women leaders. This bias is a limitation in our understanding of leadership in that we have not necessarily generated leadership theories, and explanations of leadership in sport organizations, beyond this gender-biased view.

Strategic sport leadership as a process

A process view of leadership, however, focuses our attention differently. Alongside Grint's (2005) explanation of the four ways of thinking about leadership explained above, there has been growing interest in the idea of leadership as a *process*. This process view shifts leadership from an individual or person orientation to an influence *relationship* among leaders and followers (Jackson & Parry, 2018). This is a very different way of viewing leadership as, in many societies, we have been socially influenced to see leadership as the act of an individual leader (Jones, Wegner, Bunds, Edwards, & Bocarro, 2018). This is especially so in sport as often the media, in reporting on team sport performance, for example, single out the coach or the captain as the leader, and by omission exclude the contributions of others in the leadership dynamic. A process lens of leadership highlights the multiple interactions of people to create or generate leadership (Jackson & Parry, 2018). Seeing it this way shows how on-field acts of leadership in team sport do not just reside with the captain (one athlete/player). Rather, leadership can occur anywhere on "the field." This leads us to the distinction between formal and informal leadership, but it also helps us understand the collective nature of leadership.

How might this process view of leadership apply in a more off-field, organizational context? Well, in a sport organization context, collective contribution among leaders and followers is illustrated in the generation of leadership among the board of directors of a national governing body, rather than just via the chair or president. The idea that leadership is not necessarily about the individual leader, but instead is a social process that is co-generated among people or organizations, is potentially a helpful way to consider strategic leadership and governance (Ferkins, Shilbury, & O'Boyle, 2017). Intuitively, it makes sense that multiple people are involved in major, long-term, impactful decisions about the future direction of a sport organization. In this way, strategic leadership is about bringing people together to share a common purpose, rather than a more hierarchical approach to individual decision-making (Shilbury & Ferkins, 2015).

You may be able to pick up this distinction in the closing case about Jane, the newly appointed chairperson of a national governing body. While appreciating Jane's relational skills at first, eventually the board members found themselves pushing back, reacting negatively to the way Jane ultimately made decisions herself as chair, rather than the decisions being a reflection of the board as a whole. This tension relates to the adage used to describe a leader among leaders as "first among equals" (Ferkins, Shilbury et al., 2017). In contrast, a process view of leadership might mean that Jane would play the role of facilitator of board decisions as per a consensus decision-making approach around the boardroom table. Consensus decision-making within sport governance is an example of a collective leadership process, and is an important context within which strategic decisions are made by the board or senior management that potentially have long-term and wide-reaching impacts on the direction and functioning of the organization (Ferkins & Shilbury, 2015a). As you will see from the closing case about Jane, collective leadership is not necessarily an approach to leadership within sport governance that occurs as often as we might like.

In fact, the idea of collective leadership is relatively new in the conversation about leadership, whether it be within the boardroom context or at other levels and layers of a sport organization (Cullen-Lester & Yammarino, 2016). In many respects, this way of viewing leadership tips up conventional approaches as leadership has been strongly associated with individual leaders (O'Boyle, Murray, & Cummins, 2015). Another way of looking at this is to think about leadership *within* sport organizations (that is, the multiple people enacting leadership – who may not necessarily have the top title), rather than leadership *of* a sport organization. Grint (2005) describes the multiple contributions to leadership as putting the "ship" back into leadership. Using this approach, we suggest a definition of leadership that seems fitting for a new generation of sport management students and for the strategic sport management process, as *an influence relationship among leaders and followers who intend strategic change that reflects mutual purpose* (Jackson & Parry, 2018).

In picking up on the idea that leadership is something that is constructed through social interaction, rather than enacted by an individual, Ospina and Schall (2001) define leadership as "a social construct, as something that is created through dialogue among groups of people in a particular context" (p. 2). We like this definition as it captures the idea that leadership can be generated through social interaction (more than one person) as well as a concept that is socially made up (it doesn't just exist, we have created it)! The other reason we like it is because we think it creates greater access to leadership in sport management (Dee, Bryham, & Ferkins, 2018). For example, when we explain and discuss this way of viewing leadership with our students in our final year undergraduate class, those who by their own admission are shy and usually quiet in class tell us about their light bulb moment in realizing how they can be involved in leadership. We often hear from some students how they move from thinking they were not leadership material, and would never be a leader, to realizing how they can contribute to the leadership process of their respective sport organizations.

Coming back to our definition of the strategic sport management process – where organizations learn from their environments to "establish strategic direction, create strategies that are intended to help achieve established goals, and execute those strategies, all in an effort to satisfy key organizational stakeholders" (Harrison & St. John, 2014, p. 4) – how then does the notion of leadership fit into this? As per above, perhaps a person, results, and position view of leadership orientates us more toward the individual enacting strategic sport management, whereas a process view points us toward a collective or co-generated approach to strategic sport management. In this way, our lens certainly matters when viewing leadership (Ospina & Schall, 2001). Murray and Chua (2015) point out the evolving nature of leadership as they ponder how definitions of sport leadership are changing.

Critical thinking Box 4.1

So how might you define sport leadership? What does leadership mean to you? Write down your definitions, including key words that define a leader.

How might your meaning of leadership be different from say, that of your parents or the generation behind you? What has influenced your view of sport leadership?

The social construction of leadership: the influence of culture in strategic leadership

The exercise of working through what leadership means to you and what's influenced your view of sport leadership is part of a set of questions that we use in our research projects on leadership with sport organizations (see Dee et al., 2018; Ferkins, Dee, Naylor, & Bryham, 2017). We base this on a theoretical approach referred to as the *social construction of leadership* (Billsberry et al., 2018; Grint & Jackson, 2010; Meindl, 1995). As you read earlier, Ospina and Schall (2001) referred to leadership as a social construct, meaning it is something that is created through conversations. This idea that leadership is socially constructed is closely associated with the idea that your view of leadership has been, and will be, influenced by your life experiences (Dee et al., 2018; Kihl, Leberman, & Schull, 2010).

Another way of saying this is, how you have been socially constructed will influence how you view leadership. For example, if you grew up in a large family versus being an only child, this will likely have influenced your view of leadership – considering your parents may well be the most influential models of leadership you will encounter. Whether you played team sport, an individual sport, or no sport will also likely influence your view of leadership. Similarly, your religious and ethnic cultural experiences will also have shaped your beliefs and values that will no doubt permeate how you view leadership (Jackson & Parry, 2018).

Therefore, how strategic leadership is played out in sport organizations by individuals and leadership teams at all levels of the organization will also likely be heavily influenced by how people have been social constructed as well as how leadership is constructed through social interactions. Take again the example of Seb Coe and think about his background, his incredible experiences, and how his persona has been socially constructed. Such experiences will of course shape his current influence within the leadership of world sport. Also, consider the example of Jane (closing case) as the newly minted board chair, how she brings her experiences and backstory to the boardroom table, and how she is also potentially "constructing" leadership from among the board grouping. Finally, the story (opening case) of the newly appointed athletic director at the University of Hawaii was presented as creating "cultural collisions" in leadership where his cultural background was potentially quite different to the dominant ethnic group at the University of Hawaii. This leads us to consider the intersection between culture and leadership, or as the subtitle above indicates, the *influence* of culture in strategic leadership.

"Leadership is essentially a cultural activity – it is suffused with values, beliefs, language, rituals and artifacts" (Jackson & Parry, 2011, p. 71). In this statement, Jackson and Parry capture the significance of culture for leadership. Culture features heavily within the sport context and can be found not only on the field of sport but is also a significant element within clubrooms, headquarters, sport venues, and sport organization offices around the globe. Consider for example the memorabilia, trophies, and photographs that feature at world events or in major sport organization venues (Tour de France, Wimbledon, etc.). In this instance, we are generally referring to organizational culture, something that is passed down through the generations, often by those with leadership responsibilities (Maitland, Hills, & Rhind, 2015).

Another form of cultural influence within leadership is, of course, ethnicity (Ospina & Foldy, 2009). The story about the athletic director at the University of Hawaii being confronted by a culture different to perhaps what he may have been used to speaks to the challenge and opportunity of understanding cultural nuances and the diverse ways leadership is considered by different ethnicities, communities, or societies. As Hofstede (1991, p. 5) eloquently explains, culture is "the collective programming of the mind which distinguishes the members of one group or category from another." The strand of research undertaken on leadership and diversity tells us that there are cultural distinctions in how different ethnic communities perceive leadership (Chen & Mason, 2018; Ospina & Foldy, 2009; Palmer & Masters, 2010).

In their recent article about sport leadership, Chen and Mason (2018) offer a glimpse into what they describe as an Indigenous (non-Western) perspective of leadership. This view "conceptualizes leaders as community orientated" (p. 162) and heavily relationship based, which contrasts a Western view that would suggest "individualism and competition are the focus of human motivation" (p. 162). Chen and Mason contend that such cultural distinctions may heavily influence approaches to leadership. This may be what is at play within the University of Hawaii case where Indigenous perspectives are different from those of the athletic director. So in terms of the idea of strategic leadership, where *strategic* has been described as being long term, consequential, holistic, and taking into account internal and external environments, then understanding culture – both organization and/or ethnic – is an important foundation of both leadership and a strategic approach. That is to say, existing culture is potentially a barrier for major change, or an opportunity for major change. In the context of sport leadership, culture certainly seems to influence the lens through which leadership is viewed and undertaken (Chen & Mason, 2018).

◼ Strategic sport governance: boards and governing systems

In contrast to the dominant view of leadership, governance is usually considered a group, organization, or system-wide activity (Cornforth, 2012). It is rarely viewed in terms of individual qualities, nor does it focus on the act of an individual in the way that perhaps a discussion of leadership in sport might. This is certainly the case for the way that research on the two topics has evolved. This may be because leadership and governance have very different discipline foundations (Takos, Murray, & O'Boyle, 2018). The study of leadership has grown predominately from the discipline of psychology, where individual and interpersonal dynamics have been the primary interest (Erakovic & Jackson, 2012). Governance, in contrast, has its foundations in economic and legal interests, which have not traditionally been as people-oriented (Erakovic & Jackson, 2012). Having said that, in practice – particularly in terms of media coverage – it is often the president or chairperson that is singled out in terms of sport governance responsibilities when hard questions are being asked about issues or scandals. Perhaps unfortunately, it's probably not too hard for you to think of an example of a sport scandal where this has occurred!

Interestingly, while you would imagine that both are important topics in the context of strategic sport management, there are few studies to date that have considered leadership *within* sport governance (Ferkins, Shilbury et al., 2017). Instead, sport governance research has concentrated on the role and functioning of the board, as well as the governance relationships between organizations (O'Boyle & Shilbury, 2017). In this section we consider governance *of* a sport organization (work of the board) and governance that occurs *among* sport organizations (systemic governance) as we seek to demonstrate the important relationship between strategic sport management and sport governance.

There are many different types of organizations that make up the sport sector. In a governance sense, how a sport organization is legally constituted is an important place to start in terms of understanding the duties of governance. Such categories of legal constitution include private commercial (e.g., limited liability companies, partnerships), non-profit codes (e.g., those with either charitable or not-for-profit status), and public government agencies (e.g., taxpayer-funded local or central/federal government and related agencies). These types of organizations also vary according to the national context (e.g., the US sport system differs greatly from its neighbor, Canada, where there is more federal government involvement in funding and support and a sport system that features non-profit codes). In fact, in most Commonwealth countries (e.g., Australia, New Zealand, Canada, the United Kingdom) as well as many mainland European countries, the sporting landscape is dominated by non-profit and public sector sport bodies (O'Boyle & Bradbury, 2013).

Critical thinking Box 4.2

Investigate the sport organizations in your country. Are they predominantly non-profit and public sector sporting bodies? What is the governance structure of these organizations? Can you also identify other organizations that are for-profit or private commercial organizations? How are these organizations governed? Discuss the different governance structures of non-profit and private commercial organizations.

Defining sport governance as the work of the board

While the practice of governing sport is hundreds of years old (beginning with the establishment of sport bodies), a focused approach to understanding and developing sport governance practice via a research lens is only a relatively recent endeavor. Early researchers of sport governance began with a focus on the role of the board, seeking to clarify what boards do or should be doing (Inglis, 1997; Shilbury, 2001). Momentum was gained in the early 2000s with studies on board performance (Hoye & Auld, 2001) and board-executive relationships (Hoye & Cuskelly, 2003), reflecting the increasing number of paid positions being established to run sport organizations, especially within the context of sport codes and national governing bodies.

This period heralded an interesting dynamic that was emerging in practice between paid staff and voluntary board directors. Ferkins, Shilbury, and McDonald (2010) talked about the challenge of the "tail wagging the dog" in terms of the board being too passive and the paid CEO dominating direction and discussion. The relationship between senior paid staff and the board as *directors* of a sport organization is one area where strategic management and governance intersect. Carver (1997) offered a simple but useful distinction in explaining that the board's role is to create the future while the role of senior management is to "mind the shop." While in reality this relationship is perhaps not as arbitrary a distinction as that, it is a useful starting place in understanding the overlapping elements of strategic management and governance in sport organizations.

In their influential text, Hoye and Cuskelly (2007) drew on a definition proposed by the Australian Sports Commission (ASC) – now known as Sport Australia – that defined sport governance in a way that represented research and practice during this era (primarily for non-profit sport codes). The ASC proposed that sport governance is "the structure and process used by an organization to develop its strategic goals and direction, monitor its performance against these goals and ensure that its board acts in the best interests of the members" (Hoye & Cuskelly, 2007, p. 9). There are several key elements to this definition. The first is that sport governance is about *structure* and *process*. Indeed, governance carries with it formal, legal, and structural elements that are often described in the sport organization's constitution (search any non-profit national governing body website and you should be able to locate its constitution). Such structural elements might refer to voting structures, board composition structures, and the governing structure relating to affiliated entities (Ferkins, Shilbury, & McDonald, 2005). In this way, the structural elements of governance provide a more rigid framework within which fluid processes might flow. For example, sport board processes might include the way in which the agenda is established and a meeting is run. Or it might involve how a board member induction is carried out, or indeed the process around how collective or shared leadership is enacted (as per the situation with Jane in the closing case about the chair as first among equals).

The second element of Hoye and Cuskelly's (2007) definition is that sport governance is about *strategic direction*. It is now well established in practice documents, such as the Australian Sports Commission's (2015) Mandatory Sports Governance Principles, that the board's role is more than compliance and monitoring and that sport boards need to be active in designing the strategic direction of the organization (Ferkins & Shilbury, 2015a). A series of action research studies by Ferkins and Shilbury (2010, 2012, 2015a) also established the need for board involvement in strategy and strategic direction by exploring how boards of national sport organizations can develop their strategic capability.

The third element identified by Hoye and Cuskelly (2007) is *monitoring* of performance and compliance. This aspect is probably the most established element of a board's role and responsibilities in any sector and is no less critical for sport boards. This element is about ensuring that the CEO and organization is functioning according to agreed policies, processes, and strategies (e.g., adhering to an athlete selection policy) as well as complying with legal requirements (e.g., government legislation). Finally, Hoye and Cuskelly (2007) note the need for accountability to *stakeholders*. One of the difficult questions within sport governance is discerning precisely whom the board is acting on behalf of. As you can imagine, there are many individuals and organizations that claim to have a stake in any given sport organization.

Consider for example, South African Rugby, the national governing body for rugby in South Africa. Among its stakeholders are players, coaches, officials, clubs, provinces, the government, media companies, sponsors, stadium trusts, and fans, to name a few. You might also imagine that some strategic and resource allocation decisions that its executive council (the governing group) might need to make could be competing (e.g., commercial decisions might challenge aspirations for community participation). On what basis might the executive council make these decisions? Who is it governing on behalf of, and who is it primarily responsible to? These are vexed questions for sport governance and the subject of several studies that have used stakeholder theory to help shed light on this issue (see Ferkins & Shilbury, 2015b; Senaux, 2008). As Hoye and Cuskelly (2007) signal in their definition above, perhaps the priority stakeholder is the members; that is, the group of organizations (e.g., provinces or clubs) or individuals nominated in the constitution as those who make up the membership. Ferkins and Shilbury (2015b) referred to these stakeholders (again, in the context of non-profit entities) as "stakeowners." These governance "ownership" arrangements described above contrast commercial sport organizations (sport event companies, sport marketing companies, private sport teams, etc.), where the owners are the shareholders of the business who have a financial interest in the company/team and, for the most part, are seeking some kind of financial return.

Another definition of sport governance was later offered by Ferkins et al. (2009) who stated that sport governance is "the responsibility for the functioning and overall direction of the organization and is a necessary and institutionalized component of all sport codes from club level to national bodies, government agencies, sport service organizations and professional teams around the world" (p. 245). Here, Ferkins et al. (2009) go some way to capturing the different types of sport organizations where governance plays a significant part, as well as signaling the institutionalized or "embedded" nature of governance for sport.

As noted above, governance has been around as long as sport has; but even so, there is no universally agreed definition of sport governance and, as with sport leadership, we are evolving our understanding of this relatively new field of scholarly and practice endeavor.

There is little doubt, however, as to the importance of the institution of governance for sport organizations and its relationship with strategic sport management. As Pye (2004, p. 65) eloquently described, "Boards are identified theoretically as the crucial lynchpin at the head of the organization. . . . In practice, they are also the point at which the buck stops."

Placing the definition of the strategic sport management process alongside conceptions of sport governance, we can see clear overlaps in terms of the responsibility for direction setting/steering on behalf of stakeholders, stakeowners, and owners. To remind you, we have established the definition of strategic sport management as

> the process through which organizations analyze and learn from their internal and external environments, establish strategic direction, create strategies that are intended to help achieve established goals, and execute those strategies, all in an effort to satisfy key organizational stakeholders.
>
> (Harrison & St. John, 2014, p. 4)

Finally, another helpful way to think about sport governance in the context of the work of the board was offered by Ferkins and Kilmister (2012) when they described the board's role as "foresight" (i.e., direction setting), "oversight" (i.e., monitoring and control), and "insight" (i.e., the wisdom, experience, and understanding of the sport environment to make informed and effective decisions) on behalf of their "stakeowners." Each of these ideas could also be associated with the strategic sport management process outlined above.

Systemic sport governance and collaborative governance directions

Both of the definitions discussed above come at governance from an individual organization viewpoint (e.g., an international, national, or local governing body, such as the International Tennis Federation, Swiss Tennis, and Geneve Tennis, respectively). As with our understanding of sport leadership, our theoretical and practical understanding of sport governance is also evolving. Cornforth (2011), an influential researcher in non-profit governance, has encouraged other researchers to consider a broader approach to the study of governance in response to "the changing context in which many non-profit organizations operate" (p. 2) as well as the complexity of governance arrangements where there are often multiple organizations involved in governance. This idea fits the sport system of most Commonwealth countries (noted above) where there are multiple legal entities involved in governing just one sport code. For example, consider again South African Rugby, the NSO for rugby in South Africa. Examples of its affiliates with some responsibility for governing rugby include World Rugby, as well as the provinces and clubs in South Africa. If we take these multiple organizations together, it becomes evident that governance is both organization-based and systemic (a system of organizations responsible for the governance of the sport).

From this view, a helpful definition offered by Rosenau (1995) expands on an organizational view of governance. Here, Rosenau conceives governance as a formal or institutionalized process in which an organization, a network of organizations, or a society steers itself, allocates resources, and exercises control and coordination. This definition (developed to capture governance in the public or government sector) has influenced how researchers have come to define sport governance (Ferkins & Shilbury, 2015a). In fact, Henry and Lee (2004) first made the distinction between governance *of* a sport organization and governance *between* sport organizations (systemic governance). Interestingly, a bit like the way sport leadership is evolving, sport governance is also being conceived beyond the individual organization.

Here is how Shilbury, Ferkins, and Smythe (2013) describe this evolution in seeing governance beyond the individual organization: "sport governance is, therefore, a system that does not rely on a specific organization, but on the associations or inter-organizational relationships between organizations responsible for the shared governance of the sport" (p. 251). While the examples used previously have been largely drawn from non-profit sport, the notion of a governing system or shared governance could also be applied to a commercial sports league or sport events where there might be multiple commercial (and public/non-profit) entities involved. Parent, Rouillard, and Naraine (2017) explore the multiple organizations involved in the governance of events. Their article focuses on network governance of a Winter Olympics and captures the multi-level, multi-sectoral nature of this sport event.

In considering the intersection between systemic sport governance and strategic sport management, how sport organizations work together to govern an event, league, or sport code is potentially a critical strategic issue. Responses to the changing environment (noted by Cornforth, 2011), including the challenge of limited resources and the evolving understanding of sport governance as something beyond the individual organization, has led sport managers and researchers to consider a more system-wide and collaborative approach to sport governance (Shilbury & Ferkins, 2015). The idea of collaborative governance is something that seems to be increasingly used by governance and businesses that are seeking to take on large and complex tasks, which may not be able to be fulfilled by a lone entity (Vangen, Hayes, & Cornforth, 2015).

Shilbury, O'Boyle, and Ferkins (2016) considered that the idea of collaborative governance might be well suited to the sport setting, whereby "collaboration between parties who, by working together, may achieve common goals and more optimum outcomes than by working in isolation" (p. 479). Despite this, to share control and power with another entity in the governance of sport is an idea that potentially challenges many sport organizations (Shilbury et al., 2016). Imagine the IOC or FIFA, for example, formally and constitutionally sharing their power and control with another entity. Nonetheless, collaborative sport governance seems to offer some promising ways forward for ways of governing within a sport system.

Summary

This chapter has explored ideas of leadership and governance within the setting of sport organizations and how the two elements intersect with strategic management. Referred to as *sport leadership*, a key message from this section is the idea that there are multiple ways to view leadership and that, potentially, how we have been socially constructed strongly influences how we might perceive sport leadership. Grint (2005) offers a helpful way to explain this in identifying four lenses through which leadership might be viewed: leadership as a person, leadership as a position, leadership as results, and leadership as a process. This discussion led to establishing a definition of leadership that seems fitting for a text on strategic sport management: *sport leadership is an influence relationship among leaders and followers who intend strategic change that reflects mutual purpose* (Jackson & Parry, 2018).

The discussion on strategic sport governance traversed both the work of individual sport boards as well as sport governance across a system of organizations. Here, we highlighted the evolutionary nature of sport governance conceptions (i.e., how the meaning of sport governance has evolved from an individual organization view to include a systemic view). A useful definition of sport governance seen in a contemporary light, which also seems fitting for a text on strategic sport management, is therefore established as follows: *sport governance is a formal and institutionalized process in which a sport organization, or network of sport organizations, steers itself, allocates resources, and exercises control and co-ordination* (Rosenau, 1995). In placing sport leadership alongside sport governance, we noted that sport governance carries with it formal responsibilities and legal obligations, whereas leadership can occur both formally *and* informally throughout all layers of a sport organization or sport system. Both, however, are important considerations for the strategic management of sport organizations, as both leadership and governance are concerned with how sport organization managers learn from their environments to establish strategic direction, and execute those strategies in an effort to satisfy key organizational stakeholders (Harrison & St. John, 2014).

CLOSING CASE: THE CHAIR AS FIRST AMONG EQUALS – LEADERSHIP COLLISIONS IN SPORT GOVERNANCE

A new chair was appointed to a national governing body in the United Kingdom. She is the first woman to be appointed in a sport that is popular with both men and women. The media release that promoted Jane's appointment detailed her corporate background involving CEO positions with major multinational corporations. She was first appointed to the board as an independent director because of her commercial acumen and strategic orientation, and the move to the chair's position was unanimously supported by all board members. Jane's appointment was also very well received by the sport's members, among whom she had developed a strong reputation for building good relationships and promoting a more collaborative approach among counties and affiliates within the sport. At first, Jane's style of chairing the board was highly favored by the remaining six other board members; she facilitated discussion, asked good questions, and summed up the board debate with precision. Twenty months on from her appointment, there is unrest within the board. Quietly at first, members have expressed their concern that while their views are being heard, Jane is making all the decisions. One board member remarked, "She is running the board like a CEO rather than a chair." Another reflected, "The chair should be first among equals, not the decision maker on all occasions. Jane takes our views into account but then makes her own judgment. What happened to consensus decision making?"

Chapter review questions

1 Explain how you have come to understand leadership after reading this chapter.
2 Can you explain the difference between the notion of "a leader" and "leadership"?
3 What does collective leadership mean to you?
4 What is the difference between organizational governance and systemic governance? Use examples from sport to support your answer.
5 Identify a sport you are interested in. Now map out the governance of this sport from the grassroots through to international levels.
6 Why do you think governance is important for sport organizations?
7 There are many issues embedded within the closing case study that highlight the opportunities and challenges of leadership and governance. What are your interpretations of what is happening in this case? If you were to pull out three talking points for discussion, what would they be?

Additional resources

- Websites – leadership
  - Centre for Creative Leadership: www.ccl.org/
  - www.samyoung.co.nz/2014/01/grint-lenses-of-leadership.html
- Websites – governance
  - www.sportaus.gov.au/governance
  - https://sportnz.org.nz/managing-sport/search-for-a-resource/news/governance-mark-for-sport-and-recreation-launched

References

Australian Sports Commission, (2015). *Mandatory sports governance principles.* Canberra: Australian Government.

Billsberry, J., Muller, J., Skinner, J., Swanson, S., Corbett, B., & Ferkins, L. (2018). Reimagining leadership in sport management: Lessons from the social construction of leadership. *Journal of Sport Management, 32,* 170–182.

Burton, L. (2014). Underrepresentation of women in sport leadership: A review of research. *Sport Management Review, 18,* 155–165.

Carver, J. (1997). *Boards that make a difference: A new design for leadership in nonprofit and public organisations* (2nd ed.). San Francisco, CA: Jossey-Bass Publishers.

Chen, C., & Mason, D. (2018). A postcolonial reading of representations of non-western leadership in sport management studies. *Journal of Sport Management, 32,* 150–169.

Conway, S. (2016). *The Ohana way report: An introduction to shaping the culture of community.* Amazon Digital Services LLC.

Cornforth, C. (2011). Nonprofit governance research: Limitations of the focus on boards and suggestions for new directions. *Nonprofit and Voluntary Sector Quarterly, 41*(6), 1116–1135.

Cornforth, C. (2012). Nonprofit governance research: Limitations of the focus on boards and suggestions for new directions. *Nonprofit and Voluntary Sector Quarterly, 41,* 1116–1135.

Cullen-Lester, K., & Yammarino, F. (2016). Collective and network approaches to leadership: Special Issue introduction. *The Leadership Quarterly, 27,* 173–180.

Dee, K., Bryham, G., & Ferkins, L. (2018). Advancing leadership in sport management: Revealing the significance of emotional intelligence. *International Journal of Sport Management, 19,* 82–109.

Erakovic, L., & Jackson, B. (2012). Promoting leadership in governance and governance in leadership: Towards a supportive research agenda. In A. Davila, M. Elvira, J. Ramirez, & L. Zapata-Cantu (Eds.), *Understanding organizations in complex, emergent and uncertain environments* (pp. 68–83). Basingstoke: Palgrave Macmillan.

Ferkins, L., Dee, K., Naylor, M., & Bryham, G. (2017). *Navigating two worlds: Report for New Zealand Rugby on Pacific Island involvement in non-playing rugby activities.* Auckland: New Zealand Rugby.

Ferkins, L., & Kilmister, T. (2012). Sport governance. In S. Leberman, C. Collins, & L. Trenberth (Eds.), *Sport business management in New Zealand and Australia* (pp. 137–159, 3rd ed.). Melbourne: Cengage Learning Australia Pty Ltd.

Ferkins, L., McDonald, G., & Shilbury, D. (2010). A model for improving board performance: The case of a national sport organisation. *Journal of Management & Organization, 16*(5), 633–653.

Ferkins, L., & Shilbury, D. (2010). Developing board strategic capability in sport organisations: The national-regional governing relationship. *Sport Management Review, 13,* 235–254.

Ferkins, L., & Shilbury, D. (2012). Good boards are strategic: What does that mean for sport governance? *Journal of Sport Management, 26,* 67–80.

Ferkins, L., & Shilbury, D. (2015a). Board strategic balance: An emerging sport governance theory. *Sport Management Review, 18*(4), 489–500.

Ferkins, L., & Shilbury, D. (2015b). The stakeholder dilemma in sport governance: Toward the notion of "stakeowner". *Journal of Sport Management, 29*(4), 93–108.

Ferkins, L., Shilbury, D., & McDonald, G. (2005). The role of the board in building strategic capability: Towards an integrated model of sport governance research. *Sport Management Review, 8*(3), 195–225.

Ferkins, L., Shilbury, D., & McDonald, G. (2009). Board involvement in strategy: Advancing the governance of sport organizations. *Journal of Sport Management, 23*(3), 245–277.

Ferkins, L., Shilbury, D., & O'Boyle, I. (2017). Leadership in governance: Exploring collective board leadership in sport governance systems. *Sport Management Review, 21*(3), 221–231.

Grint, K. (2005). Problems, problems, problems: The social construction of "leadership". *Human Relations, 58*(11), 1467–1494.

Grint, K., & Jackson, B. (2010). Toward "socially constructive" social constructions of leadership. *Management Communication Quarterly, 24*, 348–355.

Harrison, J.S. & St. John, C.H. (2014). *Foundations in strategic management* (6th Ed.). Mason, OH: Thomson South-Western.

Henry, I., & Lee, P. C. (2004). Governance and ethics in sport. In J. Beech & S. Chadwick (Eds.), *The business of sport management* (pp. 25–41). Essex: Pearson Education.

Hofstede, G. (1991). *Cultures and organizations: Software of the mind.* London: McGraw-Hill.

Hoye, R., & Auld, C. (2001). Measuring board performance in nonprofit sport organisations. *Australian Journal of Volunteering, 6*(2), 109–116.

Hoye, R., & Cuskelly, G. (2003). Board-executive relationships within voluntary sport organisations. *Sport Management Review, 6*, 53–74.

Hoye, R., & Cuskelly, G. (2007). *Sport governance.* Sydney: Elsevier.

Ingle, S. (2017, February 1). *Sebastian Coe faces increasing scrutiny over what he knew at IAAF.* Retrieved from www.theguardian.com/sport/2017/feb/01/sebastian-coe-increasing-scrutiny-iaaf-athletics-nick-davies

Inglis, S. (1997). Roles of the board in amateur sport organisations. *Journal of Sport Management, 11*, 160–176.

Jackson, B., & Parry, K. (2011). *A very short, fairly interesting and reasonably cheap book about studying leadership* (2nd ed.). London: Sage.

Jackson, B., & Parry, K. (2018). *A very short, fairly interesting and reasonably cheap book about studying leadership* (3rd ed.). London: Sage.

Jones, G., Wegner, C., Bunds, K., Edwards, M., & Bocarro, J. (2018). Examining the environmental characteristics of shared leadership in a sport-for-development organization. *Journal of Sport Management, 32*, 82–95.

Kihl, L. A., Leberman, S., & Schull, V. (2010). Stakeholder constructions of leadership in intercollegiate athletics. *European Sport Management Quarterly, 10*, 241–275.

Maitland, A., Hills, L. A., & Rhind, D. J. (2015). Organisational culture in sport – A systematic review. *Sport Management Review, 18*, 501–516. https://doi.org/10.1016/j.smr.2014.11.004

Marion, R., Christiansen, J., Klar, H., Schreiber, C., & Erdener, M. (2016). Informal leadership, interaction, cliques and productive capacity in organizations: A collectivist analysis. *The Leadership Quarterly, 27*, 242–260.

Meindl, J. R. (1995). The romance of leadership as a follower-centric theory: A social constructionist approach. *The Leadership Quarterly, 6*(3), 329–341.

Murray, D., & Chua, S. (2015). What is leadership? In I. O'Boyle, D. Murray, & P. Cummins (Eds.), *Leadership in sport* (pp. 9–18). London: Routledge.

O'Boyle, I., & Bradbury, T. (Eds.). (2013). *Sport governance: International case studies*. London: Routledge.

O'Boyle, I., Murray, D., & Cummins, P. (Eds.). (2015). *Leadership in sport*. Oxon: Taylor & Francis.

O'Boyle, I., & Shilbury, D. (2017). Comparing federal and unitary models of sport governance: A case study investigation. *Managing Sport and Leisure, 21*, 353–374.

Ospina, S., & Foldy, E. (2009). A critical review of race and ethnicity in the leadership literature: Surfacing context, power and the collective dimensions of leadership. *The Leadership Quarterly, 20*(6), 876–896.

Ospina, S., & Schall, E. (2001). *Leadership (re)constructed: How lens matters*. Washington, DC: APPAM Research Conference. Retrieved from http://leadershiplearning.org/system/files/LEADERSHIP%20(RE)CONSTRUCTED.pdf

Palmer, F., & Masters, T. (2010). Maori feminism and sport leadership: Exploring Maori women's experiences. *Sport Management Review, 13*, 331–344.

Parent, M., Rouillard, C., & Naraine, M. (2017). Network governance of a multi-level, multi-sectoral sport event: Differences in coordinating ties and actors. *Sport Management Review, 20*, 497–509.

Pye, A. (2004). The importance of context and time for understanding board behavior. *International Studies of Management & Organization, 34*, 63–89.

Rosenau, J. (1995). Governance in the twenty-first century. *Global Governance, 1*(1), 13–43.

Senaux, B. (2008). A stakeholder approach to football club governance. *International Journal of Sport Management and Marketing, 4*, 4–17.

Shilbury, D. (2001). Examining board member roles, functions and influence: A study of Victorian sporting organisations. *International Journal of Sport Management, 2*, 253–281.

Shilbury, D., Ferkins, L., & Smythe, L. (2013). Sport governance encounters: Insights from lived experiences. *Sport Management Review, 16*, 349–363.

Shilbury, D., O'Boyle, I., & Ferkins, L. (2016). Toward a research agenda in collaborative sport governance. *Sport Management Review, 19*, 479–491.

Takos, N., Murray, D., & O'Boyle, I. (2018). Authentic leadership in nonprofit sport organization boards. *Journal of Sport Management, 32*, 109–122.

Vangen, S., Hayes, J. P., & Cornforth, C. (2015). Governing cross-sector, inter-organizational collaborations. *Public Management Review, 17*(9), 1237–1260.

Welty Peachey, J., Damon, Z. J., Zhou, Y., & Burton, L. J. (2015). Forty years of leadership research in sport management: A review, synthesis, and conceptual framework. *Journal of Sport Management, 29*(5), 570–587.

Wright, B. (2017, April 10). Wright on: For better or worse, unsettling times at UHH. *Hawaii Tribune-Herald*. Retrieved from http://hawaiitribune-herald.com/sports/local-sports/wright-better-or-worse-unsettling-times-uhh

5

Strategic direction

OPENING CASE: TENNIS IN NEW ZEALAND STRATEGIC FRAMEWORK (ADAPTED FROM TENNIS NEW ZEALAND [2018] *STRATEGIC FRAMEWORK FOR TENNIS IN NEW ZEALAND*)

It is an exciting but challenging time for tennis in New Zealand (NZ). Tennis faces a decline in participation alongside some other traditional sports. Responding to demographic shifts and busy lifestyles, the tennis community needs to work together on fresh approaches to spread the love of tennis around Aotearoa (the Indigenous name for New Zealand). We cannot ignore the slow but steady decline in participation.

A second major challenge for tennis is that 75% of those participating are not club members. Tennis needs new avenues for engaging these players and bringing commercial sustainability to the custodians of tennis facilities. New approaches can be developed. Using consumer data, a better understanding of people's needs and motivations can inform new tennis offers. Digital technology is another opportunity and we already see the emergence of platforms for booking courts and finding partners.

Tennis New Zealand, with significant input from around the country, has developed a *new strategic framework* for "Tennis in New Zealand." This framework is designed to engage the efforts of everyone involved in tennis: from clubs, coaches, and diverse tennis communities to our affiliates, associations, and regional bodies as well as Tennis NZ itself. The framework will also serve to engage with external stakeholders as we look for greater innovation and collaboration to develop the sport.

Many plans across the grassroots of tennis in New Zealand already reflect components of this framework. By working together on these priority goals over the coming years we can make more difference than by working alone. Our last strategic plan focused on the rollout of national programs such as Tennis Hot Shots, the coach development framework, coach and community play at clubs. These are excellent foundations on which we can build for the future. With the present framework, Tennis New Zealand's role is to lead and monitor progress against the strategic framework. This will involve directly developing and delivering national initiatives and playing a support and facilitation role with other tennis actors working on local priorities. Here are some further facts and figures about Tennis in New Zealand, which supports the need for our newly established strategic framework:

Club member insights

- 90% of club members plan to rejoin next year, but only 44% of new members are satisfied with their joining experience (Neilsen survey)
- Tennis is seen as having great coaches compared to other sports (Neilsen survey)
- 50% of lapsed members still play tennis and 80% want "pay for play" options
- 75% of club members support casual hire at off-peak times (Northern survey)

Insights from Sport New Zealand (the government agency for sport in New Zealand)

- Between 1997/98 and 2013/14 tennis participation has declined 45% with the biggest drop in young men
- In addition to time availability, barriers to playing include cost, others to play with, the need to be a club member and having tennis equipment
- Sports on a growth trajectory rate highly on fitness and convenience – participants rate tennis below average on these dimensions
- Of all tennis participants, 22% belong to a club
- Tennis participation is skewed to high income New Zealand Europeans

Tennis community views

- Over 90% of clubs want to attract more players and 50% want to make court access easier for casuals
- 98% of clubs see an opportunity for stronger relationships with schools
- Over 80% of clubs want new ideas for membership options and social play formats and 50% are interested in greater collaboration between clubs.

(Tennis New Zealand, 2018)

Introduction

Embedded within the narrative above are signals about the changing environment for tennis in New Zealand, both internally and externally. The "demographic shifts" and "busy lifestyles" are indicative of the changing sociocultural elements of New Zealand society and the opportunity of digital technology to support platforms for booking courts and finding partners makes reference to the rapidly evolving technological environment. There is also reference to the internal environment in terms of capacity, partnerships, and financial sustainability. You will also note that Tennis New Zealand (as a national sport organization [NSO]) encompasses its affiliated entities and casual participants (regions, clubs, individuals, etc.) within its strategic framework (i.e., Tennis *in* New Zealand). The bullet points of facts and figures about tennis in New Zealand also offer some insight into the potential case for change, the need to do things differently in order to keep pace with its changing environment.

What does this mean for its strategic direction? What elements encompass a strategic direction? Does this mean tennis should reinvent its purpose? What kind of vision is needed for tennis in New Zealand that might sustain the sport for the next five years? How does an NSO like Tennis New Zealand go about designing its strategic direction?

This chapter begins by explaining the *key foundation stones of strategic direction* for sport organizations. The concept of strategic direction is as relevant in commercial sport settings as it is for non-profit sports. We begin with discussing different terminology used in establishing a strategic direction (vision, mission, objectives, goals, strategy, policy, values, philosophy, policy, etc.) and explaining the notion of "hierarchy" involved in strategic direction setting. We also discuss how strategic thought has evolved from deliberate strategy evident in the idea of a strategic plan to a more emergent style of design that is more dynamic and responsive to ongoing feedback and evaluation. After key foundation stones of strategic direction are discussed, the next section explores the *process of designing and creating strategic direction*, the need for stakeholder engagement, and the role of leadership in creating strategic direction. We conclude with the challenges and benefits of alignment in strategic direction and why sport organizations are compelled to undergo what are often resource-intensive and costly processes in order to establish and articulate their strategic direction.

◼ The foundation stones of strategic direction

As with leadership and governance, *strategic direction* is a concept central to the strategic management of sport organizations. In terms of the strategic management process presented in Chapter 1, it falls broadly within the bounds of strategy formulation and encompasses the major element of strategy such as purpose and vision (Hoye, Smith, Nicholson, & Stewart, 2018). The establishment of the major elements of strategic direction also guides what comes next in terms of the more specific objectives and statements of action. This idea is evident in the definition of strategic management that we are using throughout this book, as the "process through which organizations analyze and learn from their internal and external environments, establish strategic direction, create strategies that are intended to help achieve established goals, and execute those strategies, all in an effort to satisfy key organizational stakeholders" (Harrison & St. John, 2014. p. 4). The Tennis New Zealand case indicates how the organization has gone about analyzing and learning from its internal and external environment in order to establish its strategic direction. The case detail is just a small summary of the much more comprehensive analysis undertaken by the Tennis New Zealand board and CEO, which formed the platform for establishing its strategic direction (Tennis New Zealand, 2018).

While there are many interpretations of *strategic direction*, for our purposes and to align with the context of sport organizations, we suggest that an interpretation of strategic direction is most closely aligned with established definitions of strategic *thinking*. Henry Mintzberg is one of the most well-known proponents of strategic thinking and its application into the organizational setting. He considered that strategic thinking is about synthesis, or in other words, a process of "connecting the dots." He argued that it is about capturing learning from multiple sources and then bringing together that learning into a vision for the direction of the organization. Mintzberg and his colleagues also argued that strategic thinking is a central element of formulating strategy (Mintzberg, Ahlstrand, & Lampel, 1998).

We suggest that strategic thinking is the activity needed to be able to establish the sport organization's strategic direction. In drawing on Mintzberg et al. (1998), we therefore propose the following definition of strategic direction for sport organizations: *capturing learning from multiple sources to articulate a shared purpose, vision, objectives, and values to guide the long term future of the sport organization and/or sport system*. In the next section we "unpack" the key foundations of strategic direction, and later we discuss *who* in sport organizations undertakes strategic thinking and direction setting and *how* it is/could be done (i.e., the process).

Mission, vision, objectives, and values and all else in between

Many sport organizations make their strategic direction, strategic framework, or strategic plan publicly available. Such documents are often readily accessible and sit on their websites for easy download. This is particularly the case for non-profit sport organizations that act on behalf of and/or are accountable to their membership, participants, and stakeholders. This can be distinct from commercial sport organizations that might focus more on publicizing their story, brand, product range, and/or profile statement. Many commercial entities also now clearly articulate a mission or purpose. For example, a visit to the adidas website reveals that its mission is "to be the best sports company in the world" (adidas, n.d.).

Alternatively, International Management Group (IMG) offers its story within which sits elements of its purpose and positioning. It begins with its origins: "Founded in 1960 with a single deal that would prove the advent of modern-day sports marketing, IMG is now a global leader in sports, events, media and fashion, operating in more than 30 countries" (IMG, n.d.). Coming back to the world of tennis, the International Tennis Federation (ITF), recognized as the international governing body for tennis, has 210 member nations as of January 1, 2018, including Tennis New Zealand (International Tennis Federation, n.d.). Sitting on its website under "Role" is its articulation of strategic direction (ITF2024). As detailed on the website (www.itftennis.com/about/organisation/role.aspx), the ITF uses the terminology of *why* (encompassing ambition and purpose), *what* (encompassing priorities, objectives, and key performance indicators [KPIs]), and *how* (encompassing values). In contrast, Tennis New Zealand, after articulating the case for change in the first two pages (noted above), it then chooses *vision* and *mission* as the headline concepts/terminology for its strategic framework. Refer to Fig. 5.1 for common terminology associated with strategic direction.

Critical thinking Box 5.1

Check out your favorite sport and see if you can locate its official governing body, whether it be worldwide (e.g., FIFA) or in country (e.g., Brazilian Football). From there, see if you can find the organization's strategy, strategic plan, or strategic direction. Such documents are located in a multitude of places on the official website (sometimes under "About Us," sometimes under "Structure," etc.). You will note from this exercise that a range of terminology is used to articulate the strategic direction of the sport organization or sport system (collection of sport organizations) that it encompasses. Such terms can include *vision, mission, purpose, goals, strategic priorities*, and so forth.

FIGURE 5.1   A selection of the array of terms used in strategy terminology in relation to strategic direction

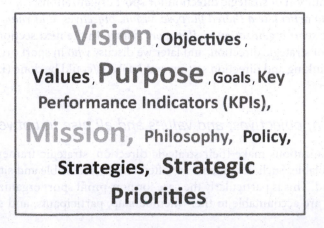

Carter, Clegg, and Kornberger (2010) helpfully point out that, as students, "it is important to be able to read and understand the language of strategy. Especially if you are an ambitious student of [sport] management! The reason is simple: strategy occupies the commanding heights of the organization" (p. 2). As you will see from your web search and the examples above, strategy and (as we refer to it in this chapter) strategic direction do indeed occupy a central role of any organization's explanation of itself. This is largely because it provides those who wish to know a sense of what the organization is, its reason for existence, where it is heading, how its leadership intends to get there, and how they seek to be held to account. In fact, these are the key elements of strategic direction, which can also be rephrased as questions that help to unpack the key foundation stones of strategy. That is, strategic direction is in essence about asking:

1   Why do we exist?
2   Where are we now?
3   Where are we heading?
4   How do we get there?
5   How do we know when we have arrived?

These five questions also help to guide us with regards to the myriad terms used to portray strategic direction. Wheelen and Hunger (2010) help to define the range of terms used as follows:

- *Mission*: organization's reason or purpose for existence
- *Vision*: desired state of what the organization wishes to achieve or where it wants to be
- *Values*: guiding beliefs and principles to underpin actions
- *Policies*: guidelines for behavior/decision-making
- *Philosophy*: a stance or approach to a particular problem/issue/topic/subject
- *Objective/goal*: a more specific desired future state.

A good way to understand these terms is to turn them into personal questions. So, what do you want to achieve, say, in the next three to five years? Why – what is your purpose/mission? What matters to you most? What are your guiding values, beliefs, and principles? What are the things you need to do in order to achieve your vision?

Personalizing these questions of strategic direction can help to reveal the key foundation stones of strategic direction. Hoye et al. (2018) also help orientate us as to which of the array of foundation stones for strategic direction might be most relevant for the sport management context. To begin, they argue that strategic direction influences the long-term direction of a sport organization and sets out what the organization wants to achieve. Hoye and his colleagues, therefore, suggest the key terms are *mission, vision*, and *objectives*. We also consider that a central part of strategic direction is understanding and articulating *why* the sport organization's leadership wants to set sail in that direction and what are the underlying principles and values that guide such aspirations. For this reason, our preferred foundation stones of strategic direction include *purpose or mission* (i.e., the why), *vision* (i.e., the aspiration going forward), *values* (i.e., the underlying principles that guide desired behavior) and *strategic priorities* that might break down the overall vision into three or four key areas, which sit alongside *indicators of performance*. These are captured in Figure 5.2. In the next section, we discuss the interaction between these foundations and suggest that a certain hierarchy exists in their use.

FIGURE 5.2   Foundation stones of strategic planning

Purpose/Mission,
Vision, Values,
Strategic Priorities,
Performance Indicators (KPIs)

The hierarchy of strategic direction – why the "Golden Circle"?

While the formulation or development of strategic direction is, as we have argued, central to the strategic management of sport organizations, sadly there have been few research studies that have focused on this topic. David Shilbury, one of our leading scholars in sport management globally, lamented this in his keynote address at the North American Society for Sport Management (NASSM) conference in 2012. He said:

> To date, strategy research has not been tackled with the centrality it deserves. Managing competitive forces on and off the field is central to the task of management, and therefore, if competition is the heart and soul of sport management, then strategy research is the conduit to the spirit and character of our field.
>
> (Shilbury, 2012, p. 9)

In this, Shilbury links strategy with competition, as we have done in previous chapters, and is clear about the need for future sport management research to target strategy as a topic area. Of the studies that have considered strategy in sport management, fewer still have focused on strategic direction or the development of strategic direction. What we do know formally in a research sense has come largely from studies that have looked at the strategic capacity or strategic planning in the context of national sport organizations (e.g., Robinson & Minikin, 2011; Thibault, Slack, & Hinings, 1993, 1994). There is also a series of studies about the development of strategic capability within boards of NSOs (Ferkins, Shilbury, & McDonald, 2005, 2009; Ferkins & Shilbury, 2010, 2012, 2015a, 2016) that is useful to draw from in our discussion of formalized knowledge about the development of strategic direction. Of course, this sits beside current practice and how major sport entities such as the ITF present their strategy. The Tennis New Zealand case study threaded throughout this chapter also gives us some insight into how this is being done in practice.

In addition to these sources, which help to inform current practice in the development of strategic direction within sport organizations, another source of wisdom on the topic is available from the work of Simon Sinek. Sinek, an author, motivational speaker, and organizational consultant, offers a very compelling argument for why organizations need to start with *why* in their endeavors to create strategic direction. As we also suggest above, it helps to personalize these ideas. Sinek (2017) argues that every person has a why. He says that your why is the cause, purpose or belief that will inspire you. If you know your why, it provides a filter to make life choices and will enable greater fulfillment in everything you do (Sinek, 2017). Sinek argues that people and organizations can easily explain *what* they do, as well as *how* they do it, but few people or organizations fully grasp *why* they do what they do.

Critical thinking Box 5.2

Resources on Simon Sinek's thinking are readily accessible via websites, YouTube, and TED Talks as well as books (https://startwithwhy.com). Do a search for Sinek's work and engage with these resources to learn more about *why* it might be important to start with *why*! How would you apply what you have learned to a sport organization's efforts to set its strategic direction?

This argument also forms the basis of another suggested principle in the development of strategic direction, which is that a hierarchy exists in the interaction of the key foundation stones. Sinek (2009) referred to this as the "Golden Circle," which, in his depiction, begins with why (see https://startwithwhy.com). Our studies in the sport management context also tell us that the strategic process for sport boards involves setting the organization's mission, vision, and objectives (Inglis, Alexander, & Weaver, 1999), and that the mission (i.e., why) is one of the first and foremost roles (Ferkins et al., 2005; Inglis, 1997). In seeking to determine how boards can develop their strategic capability, Ferkins et al. (2009) asked the board and CEO of New Zealand Football about their expectations of what strategic direction should encompass. Their responses indicated the importance of giving purpose to the organization (mission) and, significantly, providing a united purpose for all stakeholders.

They also said strategic direction is about providing a roadmap (vision and objectives) and emphasized the need for broad key performance indicators within that (Ferkins et al., 2009).

The Tennis New Zealand Strategic Framework (2017–2022) provides a good example of the hierarchy involved in the key elements of strategic direction. It sets out the mission and vision first, which provides the foreground for subsequent objectives. As noted earlier, prior to the mission and vision statements, Tennis New Zealand also highlight elements of a changing environment, setting out the summary of its environmental analysis. The three objectives are then supported by more specific outcome statements signaling, in essence, key performance indicators (Tennis New Zealand, 2018). Interestingly, Tennis New Zealand's mission statement tackles the idea of the role of tennis within New Zealand society, articulating its mission as "building community through tennis" (Tennis New Zealand, 2018). Implicit in this statement is how Tennis New Zealand sees its mission in terms of a higher purpose, something bigger than the development of the sport. Its vision (i.e., what is aspires to achieve) is articulated as "tennis – accessible and thriving" (Tennis New Zealand, 2018). This statement essentially slots underneath its higher purpose statement, which answers the question, why does Tennis New Zealand want to be accessible and thriving? What purpose will this serve? As its mission states, if we can achieve the outcome of tennis being a sport that is accessible and thriving, then we can build community through tennis.

Underneath the mission and vision statements in Tennis New Zealand's strategic framework sit its three objectives: "enable," "win," and "secure." These objectives and the accompanying outcome statements that contribute toward achievement of the vision (what) and, ultimately, if achieved are designed to help fulfill its purpose (why). Figures 5.3a and 5.3b set out a visual representation of the key foundation stones of Tennis New Zealand's strategic direction. More details on this document can be found at http://tennis.kiwi/news/a-strategic-framework-for-tennis-in-nz.

FIGURE 5.3A–B Strategic framework for Tennis New Zealand

Source: Tennis New Zealand (2018).

> ### Critical thinking Box 5.3
>
> It would be a useful exercise to visit the websites of other national tennis organiza-
> tions including the ITF site (www.itftennis.com/about/organisation/role.aspx) to see
> how they compare with Tennis New Zealand. Is there a focus just on the develop-
> ment of the sport, or is there a statement of higher purpose? What other foundation
> stones have been identified in their strategic direction? Both Tennis Australia (www.
> tennis.com.au/) and the ITF, for example, include values statements. For Tennis Aus-
> tralia, it has identified its values (guiding beliefs and principles to underpin actions)
> as excellence, humility, loyalty, and teamwork. The ITF has identified its values as
> innovative, proactive, inclusive, and accountable. In these examples, can you identify
> the variation in the choices made by sport organizations as to how they frame their
> respective strategic directions?

Why *process* is critical in creating strategic direction

Just as the section above set outs out many ways sport organizations choose to go about articulating strategic direction, so too does this section offer different ways to consider the *process*
of strategic design. One view of the strategic design process, as explained by Carter et al.
(2010, p. 84), is "one of negotiation, learning and exploring opportunities as they unfold.
The process is less analytical and more creative, allowing for 'trial and error' and the playful
exploration of ideas." The authors consider that this way of viewing strategic design is futur-
istic, as design is essentially focused on generating a state that does not yet exist. It is "simply a way of addressing the future – speaking about missions and visions, hopes and fears,
opportunities and threats" (p. 90). This way of viewing strategic design is also known broadly
as the "emergent" school of thought on strategy (Mintzberg, 1994; Mintzberg et al., 1998);
this emergent approach contrasts a more historical view of strategic design that emphasized
"rational planning," or a deliberate approach to strategic planning (Ansoff, 1965; Carter et al.,
2010; Mintzberg & Waters, 1985).

Many non-profit sport organizations in the 1990s went through a period of becoming
increasingly formalized as they moved from voluntary-based organizations to an increasing
number of paid staff (Shilbury & Ferkins, 2011). During this time, those sport systems with
government sport agencies (e.g., Canada, Australia, the United Kingdom, New Zealand),
saw many NSOs engaged in producing strategic plans in order to secure government funding (Thibault et al., 1994). In many respects, these efforts could potentially be described as
rational planning, as many NSOs used deliberate approaches to strategic planning (Thibault
et al., 1994). As the process of strategic design has evolved, contemporary thought promotes
a more dynamic approach to the development of strategic plans and strategic direction
(Carter et al., 2010). This encompasses both the idea that organizations need to be strategically agile and that strategic plans need to be highly responsive to changing environments.
This way of looking at strategic design also tends to value *the way* in which the mission,
vision, values, and objectives were created, and who was engaged in the process, as much as,
if not more than, the strategic statements produced as an outcome. As T. S. Eliot, a famous
poet of the 20th century, once wrote: "The journey, Not the destination matters" (Eliot, n.d.).

Stakeholder engagement in the process

Those research studies that have been undertaken about the strategic design process in sport organizations affirm that stakeholder engagement in the process of direction setting is a key element (Ferkins & Shilbury, 2012; Ferkins & Shilbury, 2015a). As Carter et al. (2010) argue, the process of strategy-making needs to be undertaken from both the "bottom up" as well as the "top down" and potentially all else in between. They go on to explain that valuable insights may reside in the heads of those who are "on the ground," implementing as much as in the heads of those formally charged with design. In a non-profit sport organization, those charged with designing strategic direction are usually identified as the board and CEO (Australian Sports Commission, 2015). However, as discussed in the previous chapter on leadership and governance, there is much evidence to indicate the benefits of multiple contributions into the strategic design process (Shilbury & Ferkins, 2015).

In fact, there is a strong body of knowledge that has established the central role of stakeholders in organization business (Fassin, 2012). This work often refers to the early work of Freeman (1984), a vigorous proponent of the centrality of stakeholders in organizational strategy. Freeman (2010) defines stakeholders as "any group or *individual* who can affect or is affected by the achievement of the organisation's objectives" (p. 25). This definition casts the net wide in terms of who the stakeholders might be for the purposes of strategic design for a sport organization. For example, consider the global reach of adidas and its potential stakeholders, which might include its owners, senior leadership, staff, suppliers, retailers, and customers, to name a few. Consider the complexity of the task when a company like adidas seeks to involve its stakeholders in designing its strategic direction!

In building on the work of Freeman (1984), Fassin (2009) introduced terminology that breaks down different stakeholder groups. That is, there might be those stakeholders who "hold the stake, the stakewatcher who watches the stake and the stakekeeper who keeps the stake" (p. 128). Inspired by Fassin's (2012) later work, Ferkins and Shilbury (2015b) introduced the term "stakeowner" to describe the "members" of an NSO. These members are primarily made up of the regional or state bodies (e.g., Tennis Auckland in New Zealand, Punjab State Lawn Tennis Association in India, or Tennis British Columbia in Canada). In a governance sense, it is the stakeowners that the NSO has primary responsibility to, that is, the NSO is set up to govern on behalf of (Ferkins & Shilbury, 2015b). This thinking offers sport organizations a way of differentiating between stakeholders or stakeholder groups, particularly when considering their involvement in strategic design.

For Tennis New Zealand, the board and CEO *facilitated* the strategic design process. This involved ten months of collaboration and consultation with the "tennis community" including national, regional, and local workshops, a survey, trend analysis, the preparation of draft documents, feedback, and multiple iterations of ideas as the thinking underpinning the document was formulated. The tennis community included the national body, its staff beyond senior management, its regional (stakeowners) and association entities, clubs and participants. The work undertaken in the analysis of participation trends in sport was designed to capture the non-participant and to understand the barriers and enablers for those who do not currently participate in tennis (Tennis New Zealand, 2018).

This type of process that encompasses many months of consultation, workshops, and analysis is designed to engage the community that the strategy will most impact and who will also play an important role in the implementation of the strategic framework and resulting plans. Seen this way, it makes sense to engage as many people as possible. As Carter et al. (2010) notes, such a process brings people together and can motivate and animate an organization by asking people to think about where they are and where they want to go, together. Such a process, however, takes a great deal of effort, and uses valuable organizational resources (financial, human, etc.). It is much easier for senior management to determine the strategic direction themselves, and this often happens (Carter et al., 2010). To press the point further, we draw from Hamel (1996) and Carter et al. (2010), who offer a list of key considerations in the strategic design process:

- *Watch out for the bottleneck at the top.* "Normally, senior managers define strategy. The normal organizational hierarchy is based on experience . . . [but] successful past experience can become the obstacle to tomorrow's success" (Carter et al., 2010, p. 90). This approach needs to be supplemented with "a hierarchy of imagination, which might be inversely distributed compared to the formal hierarchy" (p. 90).
- *Change is not necessarily the challenge, engagement is.* Change is often viewed as a word for routine attempts to restructure an organization. However, "it is more important to engage people, especially revolutionaries, in a discourse about the future and create commitment" (Carter et al., 2010, p. 91).
- *The end is not visible from the beginning.* A strategy process that is emergent and open-ended can lead to surprises. "The new cannot be judged on the premises of the old because it follows different rules . . . a really open process leads to a future that cannot be predicted as it unfolds because people explore new avenues" (Carter et al., 2010, p. 91).
- *Top down or bottom up are not the only options.* It is not either/or, rather it is a question of facilitating communication among those who have the formal responsibility and expertise, and those people who bring a change in perspective, creative ideas, energy to engage and care about the future (Carter et al., 2010).

The role of leadership in the process

Some of the above principles and considerations are evident in the Tennis New Zealand example given above. Its design process indicates a power-sharing approach by the national body that sought to work with its member bodies (the regions) and, in turn, their member bodies (i.e., the associations and, in turn, the clubs) to collectively design the strategy for tennis in New Zealand. As well as engaging this formal chain of governing entities (which also includes affiliated bodies such as Tennis New Zealand Umpires Association), Tennis New Zealand sought feedback from other stakeholder groups such as coaches, players, and administrators at social, competitive, and high-performance levels. More difficult, was canvassing firsthand thinking from non-participants or future participants as well as the casual participant, an aspect where insight was sought using existing data on participation trends in sport (Tennis New Zealand, 2018).

Throughout this process, Tennis New Zealand's intent was to engage in a strategic design process to produce a strategic framework that was *for* tennis in New Zealand, rather than solely for the direction of the NSO (Tennis New Zealand, 2018). Therefore, its members (through the governing chain) were involved in the design work in recognition of the collective role needed in implementing the strategic direction. Such a collectivist process is not easy to achieve, and often its success lies in the process of facilitating the generation of ideas in forums and workshops, summarizing the thinking, prioritizing ideas, feeding back progress to those who have contributed, and driving the next steps. Figure 5.4 summarizes

FIGURE 5.4   Strategic planning process for Tennis New Zealand
Source: Tennis New Zealand (2018).

the many process steps used in the design of the Tennis in New Zealand strategic framework. Indicated within Figure 5.4 is the efforts made by the board of the NSO to engage in facilitative leadership (O'Boyle, Murray, & Cummins, 2015), that is, to drive the process, but to do so in collaboration with its stakeowners and stakeholders. As O'Boyle et al. (2015, p. 3) affirm in regards to NSOs, "the CEO or board members, are often required to enact facilitative leadership to ensure there is cohesion and shared understanding . . . to unify the direction of the sport they are charged with leading."

Summary

This chapter has highlighted the key foundation stones of strategic direction for sport organizations and explained the sequence or hierarchy of thinking that is useful in strategic design. Specifically, in the process of direction setting, once management sufficiently understands its external environment, we argue the need to begin with why the sport organization exists (i.e., mission). Next comes an articulation of where the sport organization is heading (i.e., vision), which is then "chunked" into its major strategic priorities (objectives). Some sense of values is also helpful in this high-level articulation of strategic direction (Wheelen & Hunger, 2010). In this discussion, we also recognize the diversity of thinking that exists in understanding strategic direction, including the myriad terms used to describe different elements of strategic direction. The chapter has also discussed the importance of *process* in the design of strategic direction for sport organizations, and who, why, and how stakeholders might be engaged in the direction setting process. There are many challenges to stakeholder engagement in an effort to create alignment in strategic direction. Such processes can be resource intensive/costly and take many months, if not years. The diversity of stakeholder groupings and their connection to the sport also pose challenges in the engagement process. Sifting, sorting, and mapping types of stakeholder groups and their centrality for the sport (e.g., stakeowners) is also a key part of engagement. Nonetheless, the benefits of such a process are potentially evident when considering the collective contribution needed to implement strategic priorities, particularly when dealing with non-profit sport organizations.

CLOSING CASE: EMBEDDING VALUES INTO STRATEGIC DIRECTION – THE NEW HIRE

A new head of performance is appointed to direct the high-performance program for a South African national sport association (equivalent to an NSO). He comes from a European country and was attractive to the board and CEO of the NSO, who made the decision to appoint him because of his expert knowledge. The high-performance program had been a success for the sport, but a new strategic objective was to grow this success with greater reach across the whole country. However, six months into his tenure, tensions were evident between the new appointee and existing staff within the high-performance division, including with the national coach.

The first official complaint was received by the CEO shortly thereafter by the national coach on behalf of the high-performance division. After several months of discussions and mediation with matters unresolved, the CEO decided to escalate the situation to the board to seek its counsel on the situation. As the CEO explained to the board, the issue seemed to be about how the head of performance communicated with his team. According to staff members, their boss was rude to them, belittling, and sometimes they were subject to his angry and demanding outbursts. They provided examples of this for the CEO. The CEO outlined to the board that while the head of performance brought expert knowledge about high-performance systems, he had been unable to foster positive relationships with his staff, and as a consequence, several staff were considering resigning.

Following questioning and discussion with the board, it became clear that the nub of the issue was a different set of expectations and understanding of organization values between the new appointment and the NSO he had joined. Prior to this appointment, the CEO and staff had evolved a working culture of commitment and hard work but also respect and appreciation for each other's efforts on behalf of the athletes they served. This friendly, warm, and supportive culture had progressed over time in an informal way and they all enjoyed each other's company, which helped to drive motivation for the demands of their high-performance work. The style of the new appointee was in stark contrast to this set of values and culture that had evolved. The new head of performance believed that high performance was derived from a strict, severe culture and a demanding attitude toward others. As the CEO described this to the board, a board member asked how the new appointee might have known about the existing values that were embedded within the team. The CEO responded that while their strategic direction had a clear mission (purpose) and vision (direction), they had not sufficiently articulated the organization's aspired values to the new appointment.

Chapter review questions

1   What is the difference between vision and mission in the context of strategic direction?
2   Look up the mission statements of ten sport organizations. Discuss any common termi-
    nology you come across. Why do you think these types of words and sentiments might
    be common across mission statements?
3   "Not all sport organizations have mission and vision statements, yet they survive." Dis-
    cuss this statement in terms of the function that mission, vision, and clearly articulated
    strategic direction serves for a sport organization.
4   Which particular foundation stones would you choose if you were planning your own
    strategic direction? Explain your reasoning.
5   Draw a quick sketch of the Golden Circle as promoted by Simon Sinek. Now,
    explain why you think the *why* might be critical to setting strategic direction for
    sport organizations.
6   What is the difference between a stakeowner and a stakeholder for an NSO?
7   Why do you think it might be important for sport organizations to reach beyond the
    involvement of top management in the design of strategic direction?
8   The closing case highlights the need to be explicit in articulating values that guide
    expectations about how people treat each other and the centrality of this to achieving
    strategic direction. Why do you think the new appointee may have brought a differ-
    ent set of values than existed within the NSO team depicted in the case? If you were a
    board member of this NSO, what might you suggest as a course of action for the CEO to
    resolve this situation?

Additional resources

* Websites
  o   Simon Sinek: https://startwithwhy.com/find-your-why
  o   International Tennis Federation: www.itftennis.com/about/organisation/role.aspx
  o   Tennis Australia: www.tennis.com.au/
  o   Tennis New Zealand: www.tennis.kiwi/About/Strategic-Plan
* Books
  o   Carter, C., Clegg, S. R., & Kornberger, M. (2010). *A very short, fairly interesting
      and reasonably cheap book about studying strategy*. Thousand Oaks, CA: Sage.
  o   Wheelen, D., & Hunger, J. (2010). *Strategic management and business policy* (12th
      Ed.). Upper Saddle River, NJ: Pearson/Prentice Hall.

References

Adidas. (n.d.) *Profile*. Retrieved January 22, 2019 from www.adidas-group.com/en/group/
    profile/
Ansoff, I. H. (1965). *Corporate strategy: An analytical approach to business policy for growth
    and expansion*. New York, NY: McGraw-Hill.
Australian Sports Commission. (2015). *Mandatory sports governance principles*. Canberra:
    Author.

Carter, C., Clegg, S. R., & Kornberger, M. (2010). *A very short, fairly interesting and reasonably cheap book about studying strategy*. Thousand Oaks, CA: Sage.

Eliot, T. S. (n.d.). *Wikipedia*. Retrieved January 23, 2019 from https://en.wikipedia.org/wiki/T._S._Eliot

Fassin, Y. (2009). The stakeholder model refined. *Journal of Business Ethics, 84*, 113–135.

Fassin, Y. (2012). Stakeholder management, reciprocity and stakeholder responsibility. *Journal of Business Ethics, 109*, 83–96.

Ferkins, L., & Shilbury, D. (2010). Developing board strategic capability in sport organisations: The national-regional governing relationship. *Sport Management Review, 13*, 235–254.

Ferkins, L., & Shilbury, D. (2012). Good boards are strategic: What does that mean for sport governance? *Journal of Sport Management, 26*, 67–80.

Ferkins, L., & Shilbury, D. (2015a). Board strategic balance: An emerging sport governance theory. *Sport Management Review, 18*(4), 489–500.

Ferkins, L., & Shilbury, D. (2015b). The stakeholder dilemma in sport governance: Toward the notion of "stakeowner". *Journal of Sport Management, 29*(4), 93–108.

Ferkins, L., & Shilbury, D. (2016). Developing a theory of board strategic balance. In G. Cunningham, J. Fink, & A. Doherty (Eds.), *Routledge handbook of theory in sport management* (pp. 114–131). New York, NY: Routledge.

Ferkins, L., Shilbury, D., & McDonald, G. (2005). The role of the board in building strategic capability: Towards an integrated model of sport governance research. *Sport Management Review, 8*(3), 195–225.

Ferkins, L., Shilbury, D., & McDonald, G. (2009). Board involvement in strategy: Advancing the governance of sport organizations. *Journal of Sport Management, 23*(3), 245–277.

Freeman, R. E. (1984). *Strategic management: A stakeholder approach*. London: Pitman Press.

Freeman, R. E. (2010). *Strategic management: A stakeholder approach*. Cambridge: Cambridge University Press.

Hamel, G. (1996, July–August). Strategy as revolution. *Harvard Business Review*, pp. 69–82.

Harrison, J., & St John, C. (2014). *Foundations of strategic management* (6th ed.). Mason, OH: Cengage Learning.

Hoye, R., Smith, A., Nicholson, M., & Stewart, B. (2018). *Sport management principles and applications* (5th ed.). New York, NY: Routledge.

IMG. (n.d.). *Our story*. Retrieved January 22, 2019 from http://img.com/story

Inglis, S. (1997). Roles of the board in amateur sport organisations. *Journal of Sport Management, 11*, 160–176.

Inglis, S., Alexander, T., & Weaver, L. (1999). Roles and responsibilities of community nonprofit boards. *Nonprofit Management and Leadership, 10*(2), 153–167.

International Tennis Federation. (n.d.). *Structure*. Retrieved January 22, 2019 from www.itftennis.com/about/organisation/structure.aspx

Mintzberg, H. (1994, January–February). The fall and rise of strategic planning. *Harvard Business Review*.

Mintzberg, H., Ahlstrand, B., & Lampel, J. (1998). *Strategy safari: A guided tour through the wilds of strategic management*. New York, NY: The Free Press.

Mintzberg, H., & Waters, J. A. (1985). Of strategies, deliberate and emergent. *Strategic Management Journal, 24*, 257–272.

O'Boyle, I., Murray, D., & Cummins, P. (2015). Framing leadership in sport. In I. O'Boyle, D. Murray, & P. Cummins (Eds.), *Leadership in sport* (pp. 1–6). London: Taylor & Francis.

Robinson, L., & Minikin, B. (2011). Developing strategic capacity in Olympic sport organisations. *Sport, Business and Management: An International Journal, 1*(3), 219–233.

Shilbury, D. (2012). Competition: The heart and soul of sport management. *Journal of Sport Management, 26*(1), 1–10.

Shilbury, D., & Ferkins, L. (2011). Professionalisation, sport governance and strategic capability. *Managing Leisure, 16*, 108–127.

Shilbury, D., & Ferkins, L. (2015). Exploring the utility of collaborative governance in a national sport organization. *Journal of Sport Management, 29*(1), 380–397.

Sinek, S. (2009). *Start with why: How great leaders inspire everyone to take action.* New York, NY: Penguin.

Sinek, S. (2017). *Find your why: A practical guide for discovering purpose for you and your team.* New York, NY: Penguin Random House.

Tennis New Zealand. (2018). *Strategic framework for tennis in New Zealand (2017–2022).* Retrieved January 22, 2019 from www.tennis.kiwi/About/Strategic-Plan

Thibault, L., Slack, T., & Hinings, B. (1993). A framework for the analysis of strategy in nonprofit sport organizations. *Journal of Sport Management, 26*, 25–43.

Thibault, L., Slack, T., & Hinings, B. (1994). Strategic planning for nonprofit sport organizations: Empirical verification of a framework. *Journal of Sport Management, 8*, 218–233.

Wheelen, D., & Hunger, J. (2010). *Strategic management and business Policy* (12th ed.). Upper Saddle River, NJ: Pearson/Prentice Hall.

6 Multi-level strategy formulation

OPENING CASE: RESORT LATITUDE ZERO
(With Matt and Jenny Cruden)

The sport of surfboard riding has enjoyed increasing popularity in recent times. With inclusion in the 2020 Tokyo Olympic Games, this upward trend in participation looks set to continue. While Olympic inclusion could potentially stimulate new pockets of participation growth around the world, currently the majority of the global surfing population resides in the mature economies of the United States, Australia, Brazil, Japan, and Western Europe. This means that most surfers practice their sport in urban areas where crowding and its associated negative social behaviors is now a major concern in the sport. Meanwhile, surfing and travel have always been intertwined as surfers continue to search for high-quality, uncrowded surf breaks. The advent of online communication technologies, social media, and budget airlines has only accelerated surfers' appetite for travel in recent decades.

Barbieri and Sotomayor (2013) contend that surf tourism is now a sector of economic and social significance that demands increasing scholarly attention. Most of the sector's growth has been in remote corners of developing countries as time-poor, cash-rich surfers from mainly Western nations seek to escape their overcrowded home locations. Today, there are thriving surf tourism sectors in the Maldives, the Philippines, Taiwan, and Papua New Guinea; South American nations like Mexico, Brazil, Costa Rica, Nicaragua, and Chile; South Pacific Island nations like Samoa, Tonga, Fiji, and Tahiti; and especially in the island chains of Indonesia (O'Brien & Ponting, 2013; Ponting & O'Brien, 2014, 2015; Towner, 2016). In fact, Indonesia is a magnet for surfers from around the world, who are drawn to its many island chains that offer consistent, high-quality, warm-water surf combined with unique cultural experiences.

In the 1990s, the islands around northern Sumatra, Indonesia, saw innumerable small surf tourism operations emerge to cater to increasing demand from traveling surfers. Some operations were simple home stays while others offered capacity for up to 20 surfers, but all operations stayed very basic with shared facilities and often little or no electricity or running water. Another popular surf tourism choice to emerge in the region was the all-inclusive, live-aboard open ocean charter vessels catering to up to a dozen surfers. These operations were still very small, and while quality varied, the overwhelming majority offered all-inclusive seven- to ten-day packages for budget-minded young males, typically traveling in groups of 6 to 12. By 2009, the market was cluttered with comparable budget-oriented packages, until one charter operator decided to do something different.

The Mentawai Islands off the coast of Sumatra, Indonesia, have been described as Nirvana for surfers (Ponting & O'Brien, 2015). Matt and Jenny Cruden ran one of the original charter operations in the Mentawais with their vessel, the *Mangalui Ndulu*. After 15 years of successful operation, the Crudens identified an unsatisfied niche in the market and established a land-based surf resort in the nearby Telo Island chain called Resort Latitude Zero. Resort Latitude Zero, so named due to its location near the equator, is a boutique water sport resort set on its own private island. The accommodation consists of two pole-constructed timber houses with six additional high-end, open plan bungalows, and all with 270-degree ocean views and premium levels of service. Each bungalow is set in its own private garden with high ceilings, air conditioning, fans, flat screen TV, Wi-Fi and en suite bathrooms. All bedrooms can be tailored to suit individuals, groups, private couples, or families with children. Families are especially catered to, with a wide array of children's activity options and a babysitting service. Guests have access to a central 7-meter by 14-meter infinity swimming pool, a library/chill-out area, massage tables, a small gymnasium, and a host of water sport activities. Figures 6.1 and 6.2 depict some of the facilities at Resort Latitude Zero and the epic waves that surfers enjoy there. Guests also enjoy unlimited transfers to a plethora of high-quality surfing and fishing options on a fleet of six speedboats, each with experienced and qualified local surf guides. The *Mangalui Ndulu* charter vessel also remains an option for groups of up to 12 surfers wanting seven- to ten-day charters around the archipelago on top of their stay at the resort.

FIGURE 6.1   Resort Latitude Zero facilities

Source: Photograph by Simon Williams with permission of Matt Cruden and Resort Latitude Zero.

FIGURE 6.2   Surfers flock to Indonesia to ride waves like this

Source: Photograph by Danny O'Brien.

Clearly, rather than offering budget accommodation for twentysomething, mainly male surfers, Resort Latitude Zero offers a premium product that targets both male and female surfers who are most likely older, have a higher disposable income, and possibly want to bring family members. And, reflecting the owners' commitment to local communities and the environment, Resort Latitude Zero is one of only a handful of surf tourism operations globally to have achieved "Benchmark" status with "STOKE Certified" – the surf tourism industry's only sustainability certification program (O'Brien & Ponting, 2018). Not surprisingly, in the years since opening, Resort Latitude Zero has become the "bucket list" fantasy surf trip for surfers the world over.

Introduction

By this stage of the strategic management process, we've analyzed our internal and external environments and our organizational leadership has articulated a mission and vision and the values central to us achieving both. What we need to do now is consider the various strategic options available to us as we progress the sport organization toward fulfilling that mission and achieving competitive advantage. This is an exciting, though perilous process in the life of a sport organization. There are times where uncertainty reigns and senior executives copy the strategies of their leading competitors, somewhat akin to confused children in a classroom who blindly "follow the leader." While that may seem like a safe option, the fact of the matter is that we will never stand out when we look like everyone else. And competitive advantage is about standing out – in a good way! The opening case illustrates that sometimes it can be beneficial to think more laterally and seek to position your organization completely differently to your competitors. Equally, there may be times where we seek aggressive growth or, alternatively, to steady the ship and consolidate. These types of decisions relate to the multiple levels of strategy and the related decisions about strategic directions and appropriate strategic methods with which to achieve them.

Multiple levels of strategy

Sport organizations operate at three main levels of strategy: functional, business, and corporate levels. At the functional level, decisions revolve around the various functions required for day-to-day operation. So in a professional football club, for example, these functional areas might include marketing, membership services, corporate development, finance, risk, community outreach, human resources, and the various aspects of on-field production such as strength and conditioning, medical, psychological, talent identification, player welfare, and coaching functions. While these functional areas are an important part of strategy *implementation*, they are more *operational* than *strategic* in nature. What we are more concerned with in this section is strategy *formulation*. To that end, in this chapter we address the formulation of strategy at both the business and corporate levels.

Business-level strategy deals with how a sport organization positions itself relative to its perceived competitors (Clegg, Schweitzer, Whittle, & Pitelis, 2017). The word "perceived" is important here because not all managers perceive their competition exactly the same. For example, in the opening case, a surf charter operator in the Mentawai Islands may perceive his or her competition as being limited to other Mentawaian surf charters. Meanwhile, Matt and Jenny Cruden perceive their competition very differently. They see their competition as not only other North Sumatran charter operators but also the land-based operations in the region and further afield throughout Indonesia and beyond. They also recognize that the profile of surf tourists and their related consumer behavior has changed and is now much more diverse, and that opportunities and competitive advantage lay in taking a more flexible approach to business.

Clearly, the Crudens' approach is very strategic in that they seek to create a dramatically different value proposition for their guests, thus positioning Resort Latitude Zero for competitive advantage. In this chapter, we examine the generic business-level strategies, originally proposed by Michael Porter (1980), by which sport organizations go about positioning themselves relative to their competitors: low-cost leadership, differentiation, and focus.

When we move one rung up the strategy-making ladder to multi-business, diversified sport organizations, we are addressing corporate-level strategy. Whereas single-business sport organizations like Resort Latitude Zero plan for competition in one distinct industry environment, the task becomes more complex as organizations pursue growth and one organization becomes two or several strategic business units (SBUs), often seeking to compete in multiple business environments. In the case of Catapult Sports in this chapter's closing case, the organization now consists of multiple SBUs that compete in different sport technology markets. Thus, executive management's task is to align strategy in each individual SBU with the overall corporate-level strategic direction. This is the essence of corporate-level strategy, where senior executives leave business-level strategies to the heads of each individual SBU and seek to coordinate these in an overarching corporate-level strategy to guide the corporation as a whole. The aim is to create "a rational whole out of its diversified collection of individual businesses" (Thompson, Peteraf, Gamble, & Strickland, 2018, p. 215).

Regardless of whether a sport organization is a single-business organization or a diversified corporation, all senior managers need to consider strategic direction and whether they seek growth, stability, or a period of defensive strategies. Meanwhile, they must also decide how they plan to achieve these ambitions, which refers to strategic method. Our discussion of business-level strategy will subsequently be placed into the context of strategic direction and strategic method, as will our entire exploration of corporate-level strategy.

Generic business-level strategies

As mentioned earlier, Porter's (1980) generic business-level strategies for single-business organizations consist of low-cost leadership, differentiation, and focus. We will now explore each one in turn.

Low-cost leadership

The low-cost leadership generic business-level strategy involves sport organizations staking out a territory in which they are the recognized lowest-cost providers of a chosen good or service. The challenge for low-cost leaders is to work out how to maintain such a position while still remaining profitable. Where a sport organization pursues low-cost leadership, it aggressively seeks reductions in production costs – from logistics, raw materials and procurement, through to research and development, manufacturing, marketing, and distribution.

Larger sport organizations can achieve cost savings from economies of scale, which refers to the cost savings that derive from being large. For example, Dick's Sporting Goods is a Fortune 500 sporting goods retailing corporation with over 600 stores across the United States, including specialty golf, running, and outdoor retail chains within its portfolio. Its sheer size enables Dick's to procure stock in massive amounts, which compels suppliers to offer them cheaper prices. These procurement savings allow the company to pass savings on to customers, thus selling goods of equal quality but at a cheaper price than the competition – true cost leaders.

Such a position often requires a low-margin/high-volume approach to business. That is, while the profit margin on each individual unit may be small, if enough units are sold, the gross outcome is hopefully one of profitability. In the opening case, for example, by keeping overheads down with "no-frills" offerings and minimal added services, most Mentawaian surf tourism operators pursued low-cost leadership. As the word implies, though, there can only be one "leader," thus not every organization pursuing low-cost leadership is actually a "leader." But therein lies a potential drawback of low-cost leadership, because in periods of intense competition, a "race for the bottom" can ensue where less competitive organizations may find themselves struggling for survival.

Differentiation

Quite the opposite of low-cost leaders, sport organizations pursuing differentiation seek to position themselves as unique and pursue consumers who are willing to pay a premium price for this uniqueness. Successful differentiators know their customers intimately and strive to be first to market with innovations. This requires a great deal of attention to research and development, both in terms of market research to gain a clear picture of consumers' behavior, needs and trends; and technical research into more effective ways to develop market leading products and services. The qualifications, training, and experience of researchers and the high-end equipment involved in the research and development process do not come cheaply, nor do the raw materials that go into producing high-quality products and services. So while sport organizations employing differentiation pay a high price to be perceived as unique, they pursue a market that is willing and able to pay a premium price for their goods and services. Meanwhile, low-cost leaders wait for the differentiators' products to be proven in the market and then simply imitate them as best they can without the high costs associated with research and development. Herein lies a major problem of differentiation: being "out-differentiated" by competitors.

Therefore, the sport organization pursuing differentiation must find a delicate balance between the higher production costs associated with creating an aura of uniqueness while still offering a product that is affordable to a market of sufficient size to sustain the business. Traditionally, many golf clubs have pursued differentiation by positioning themselves as "exclusive" and "unique." The Grand Golf Club, in the hinterland of the city of Gold Coast, Australia, is one such club. With the tag line, "Private, exclusive, and only available to a privileged few," The Grand Golf Club limits its membership to 555 members and offers members a sense of exclusivity with personalized locker spaces, valet service, international cuisine, and wine lists as well as, of course, access to the course at any time with no bookings required (The Grand, 2018). This strategy presents a risk because superior quality comes at a premium price. The sunk costs in the unique architecture, high-end infrastructure, succulent cuisine, and other premium services are significant. To recoup these costs, a higher per unit price must be passed on to the consumer. This means that a key consideration for the sport organization pursuing differentiation is establishing exactly how much consumers are willing to pay for uniqueness. The marketing function is critical here in communicating to the target market the value proposition such that the high quality of the offering is explained and the aura of uniqueness is accentuated. Failure to achieve this can result in the product looking overpriced in comparison to competitors, thus challenging the very viability of the business.

Focus

The third main generic business-level strategy is known as focus. When a sport organization stakes out a very narrow target market and structures its activities around satisfying that particular niche, it is pursuing a focus strategy. While firms pursuing low-cost leadership and differentiation strategies target much broader markets, firms pursuing a focus strategy aim only at a carefully chosen consumer group that is defined by its own very distinctive preferences. Thus, the key difference between firms pursing low-cost leadership and differentiation on the one hand, and those pursuing focus on the other, is one of market size: firms pursuing a focus generic business-level strategy have opted to pursue a much smaller niche market. The basic assumption here is that the focus strategy allows the firm to specialize its activities in ways that firms pursuing broader low-cost leadership or differentiation strategies cannot.

For a focus strategy to work, the sport organization must carefully select a niche whose needs are not currently being sufficiently met by the market. Often, such niches may be too small, too dynamic, or just plain unattractive to larger, more broad-scope firms. Thus, because of the small niche size, a focus strategy requires the sport organization to develop an intimate knowledge of the chosen segment so that it can be first to market when tastes or market conditions change. Ideally, such an approach will engender loyalty and repeat purchase from consumers who, over time, become knowledgeable about the sport organization's offerings (Clegg et al., 2017).

Focus may be pursued in two main ways: focus through differentiation and focus through low-cost leadership. All of the sources of competitive advantage discussed earlier with respect to differentiation and low-cost leadership strategies also pertain to the focused sport organization, just at the level of niche market rather than mass market. In the opening case, Resort Latitude Zero focuses on a small, high-yield niche within the wider global surf tourism sector, which is itself a niche with the overall tourism industry. With their deep knowledge gained through decades of experience in the international surf tourism market, the Crudens pursued focus differentiation to develop a product of dramatically superior quality to anything previously in the market.

Meanwhile, in terms of focus low-cost leadership, the recent rise in the popularity of health clubs has seen some operators targeting the budget-conscious consumer who is happy to forsake personalized service and high-end equipment for a no-frills, leaner approach to traditional gym membership. EasyGym, with 17 franchises throughout the United Kingdom, pursues exactly this strategy of low-cost leader focus. Clearly, they are not the only operators who have noticed this trend; Washtell (2017) reports that 46% of the new gyms in Central London are classed as "budget" gyms, with membership plans costing less than £50 a month. She quotes Ross Kirton, head of UK leisure at the global real estate advisers Colliers International: "Budget gym operators have cast aside concerns of rent affordability in London and are catering to the large number of customers who are keen to swap expensive monthly memberships in favor of no frill concepts" (Washtell, 2017, ¶5). The apparent popularity of this focus low-cost leader strategy in the London fitness market illustrates that one of the main dangers of low-cost leadership – that "race for the bottom" among competing firms – is also a key danger at the smaller niche market level.

Strategic directions

So far in this chapter, we have explored generic business-level strategies that sport organizations choose in order to competitively position themselves in relation to rivals. Now we turn to the various strategic directions they may pursue at the business level, and we'll also incorporate the corporate level of strategy. Essentially, managers may choose from three main strategic directions: growth, stability, or defensive. We will now explore each of these strategic direction options, beginning with growth, which we explore at both the business and corporate levels.

Business-level growth strategies

Igor Ansoff's (1957) product-market strategies for business growth alternatives provided the basis for a widely accepted approach to understanding strategic growth directions at the business level. Table 6.1 shows an adapted version of Ansoff's work that separates into new and existing product and market variables, with added levels of comparative risk: market penetration, market development, product development, and diversification. As with all strategy, risk is a key consideration. Ansoff's matrix works on the premise that entering new markets and developing new products are inherently risky, thus the options are presented from least risky in market penetration, then with product development and market development at similar levels, through to the strategic direction with the highest level of risk, diversification.

Market penetration

The primary goal of a market penetration strategy is to grow market share within existing markets using existing products. This will involve investment in additional marketing and promotional capacity but, largely because there is no introduction of a new product, and the market is one that is already understood by the firm, other expenses are comparatively minimal. For this reason, market penetration is considered the least risky of Ansoff's growth strategies. A personal trainer just starting out in her business has to work out ways to penetrate the existing market – just as a professional sport team seeking to build its local fan base must ascertain how best to position itself to win over new, or possibly win back former, fans. They may choose to compete on price with low-cost leadership, or they may try to differentiate themselves from their opposition.

TABLE 6.1 Product market strategies for business growth alternatives

Strategy	Markets	Products	Comparative risk
Market Penetration	Existing	Existing	Lower
Market Development	New	Existing	Intermediate
Product Development	Existing	New	Intermediate
Diversification	New	New	Higher

Source: Adapted from Ansoff (1957, p. 114).

Product development

Product development entails introducing a new product to your existing market. One trend in world sport that has been gathering pace over the last decade is the emergence of shorter versions of established sports. Largely produced with a broadcast market in mind, sports such as cricket, tennis, rugby union, rugby league, netball, track and field athletics, and Australian rules football have all engaged in product development with shorter format versions of their respective sports. While these new versions of "old favorites" may horrify purists, their aim is simple enough – product development to offer existing consumers something new to engage with while potentially attracting new consumers.

Another example of product development in sport is the Association of Tennis Professionals (ATP) – the world governing body for men's professional tennis – launch of the ATP Cup concept. The ATP Cup, launched for the first time in January 2020, is contested by teams of four players from 24 nations, so it will be somewhat similar in format to the Davis Cup. However, the Davis Cup is not owned by the ATP, but is an International Tennis Federation (ITF) product. Where the WTC will differ from the Davis Cup will be the USD 15 million prize money and 750 ATP tour ranking points at stake. At the time of writing, the ITF was considering sweeping changes to the Davis Cup's structure and timing as well as introducing USD 20 million prize money (Martin, 2018). However, the ATP Cup's key differentiator of 750 tour ranking points is something that ITF cannot replicate. The ATP executive chairman and president, Chris Kermode, described the ATP's new product this way:

> The ATP Cup fits perfectly with our strategy to innovate and look towards the future. We know from our extensive discussions with the players that the ATP Cup will provide a great way for them to open their season – bringing together the world's best for a major team event that compliments existing scheduling, provides highly-coveted ATP Ranking points and clearly links to the Australian Open.
>
> (Association of Tennis Professionals Tour, 2019, ¶4)

Market development

Instead of developing new products, market development involves bringing an existing product to a new geographic, demographic, or psychographic market. It is now quite common to see professional sport leagues sending season openers, all-star matches, or even regular season games to overseas locations far away from their core markets. For example, since 2013 the American sports venture firm, Relevant Sports, has run the International Champions Cup (ICC), in which European Association football clubs play matches in the United States, Canada, Australia, China, Mexico, and across Europe. In 2018, the inaugural ICC Women's tournament was launched featuring four women's European and American clubs. Obviously, for Relevant Sports, this is a commercial opportunity, but for European Association football, it is about spreading their product to new and potentially lucrative international markets.

Interesting work by Kunkel, Doyle, and Funk (2014) explored the sport brand development potential of market penetration, market development, and product development strategies in Australia's premier-level football league, the A-League. Kunkel and his colleagues found that the use of these strategies, both by the A-League as a whole and by individual clubs, strengthened the level of involvement of existing A-League fans while also building connections with new consumers. What was particularly interesting was that the authors explored the complexity of managing strategy in a context where, despite the A-League employing its own growth strategies, consumers actually build their connection with the league through the individual clubs, which each engage their own individual market penetration, market development, and product development strategies. Building consistency between the overarching league brand and individual club brands is a crucial and ongoing challenge and speaks to why strategic management is so important!

Diversification

The last of Ansoff's growth strategies is diversification. Diversification involves a sport organization investing in a new business area or product line to reach a new market. It carries the highest risk of Ansoff's strategies because it involves development of both new products and markets simultaneously. Diversification can be of two types: related or unrelated. These will be explored in detail in the next section.

Corporate-level growth strategies

At the corporate-level, firms may pursue growth through three main means: concentration, diversification, and vertical integration.

Concentration

The majority of organizations, especially in sport, begin by operating in a single market with a small group of product offerings. For example, Skydive Dubai in the United Arab Emirates concentrates exclusively on the skydiving market. The company offers individual, tandem, and group skydives with different products for beginners through to more proficient skydivers (Skydive Dubai, 2018). Concentration strategies allow managers to direct all of their resources toward doing one thing well and, as explored earlier, may involve cost leadership, differentiation, or focus strategies at the individual business level. Concentration does not preclude growth; for example, rather than competing with a key competitor, management may decide to engage in *horizontal integration* by actually acquiring that competitor. For example, when, the owner of the Australian surfsport brand Quiksilver acquired rival brand Billabong in early 2018, this was horizontal integration and a continued concentration in surfsports. adidas' purchase of its competitor Reebok in 2006 was also a high-profile example of this. Such a strategy can sometimes be profitable as managers invest profits directly back into building proficiency in that one particular business environment.

Ideally, the intimate market knowledge that concentration relies upon for success enables the organization to be agile and react swiftly to any changes in consumer tastes or other market conditions. However, having all of the sport organization's eggs in one basket is also fraught with risks posed by product obsolescence, altered market conditions, and internal changes triggered by patchy cash flow, uneven profitability, or key personnel leaving (Harrison & St. John, 2014). Often, if the organization has achieved growth through a successful concentration strategy, it will eventually saturate its current market. At this point, further growth in this one market area becomes problematic, and management may seek to spread the organization's risk profile by considering other markets to diversify into.

Diversification

Think of any of the world's major sport apparel and equipment companies, like Nike, adidas, Li-Ning, Hurley, Callaway, and so forth. One thing they all have in common is that they all started by concentrating in one particular product and/or market area. For example, Callaway started out in 1983 focused purely on manufacturing golf clubs in Carlsbad, California, where the company's founder, Ely Callaway, could be found selling clubs from the back of his Cadillac. Today, Callaway is the world's biggest manufacturer of golf clubs, but it has also diversified into general golf lifestyle products with golf-specific apparel, shoes, bags, headwear, watches, rangefinders, practice aids, and travel gear.

Thus, diversification involves management spreading the organization's risk profile by growing into other business areas; this growth may be by various methods such as internal development, acquisitions, mergers, or joint developments, all of which we will explore later. The new business areas may be related or unrelated to the original business domain.

Callaway's diversification involved acquisitions of other companies in the golf equipment industry, such as Strata Golf Clubs, Odyssey Sports, Top-Flight Golf, and Ben Hogan Golf.

The type of diversification Callaway pursued is referred to as *related* diversification, because it stayed focused within the golf equipment industry. But you'd be forgiven for wondering how the competencies required for the design and manufacture of golf clubs could bear any semblance to those required for rangefinders and watches. How could these be described as "related?" This is where the line between what is labeled "related" versus "unrelated" diversification can become blurry. However, relatedness does not simply refer to end products; it also includes similarities in resource conversion processes and end-user markets of the focal businesses. Ideally, similarities in these areas can result in *synergy*, where the whole becomes greater than the sum of its parts. The task for management is to decipher where these potential synergies lay, and which resources and capabilities are competitively valuable and can be combined or transferred from one business to another to reduce production and/or distribution costs. What makes Callaway's golf clubs and watches "related" from a diversification standpoint is clearly their common market base, but it could also be excellent research and development engineers, or something less tangible but equally powerful, such as the Callaway brand name itself.

Quite different to related diversification, unrelated diversification does not rely on synergies or common value chain activities. It is exactly as it sounds: expansion into industries that have nothing to do with the core business. For example, the Gold Coast Suns is an Australian rules football club that plays in the AFL. As a professional sport club, the Suns' core business is providing a high-quality sport entertainment product and generating revenue through membership, ticket sales, sponsorship, corporate hospitality, and match broadcasts. However, in 2019 the Suns are planning to establish an early learning center and childcare industry training college on the site of their home ground at Metricon Stadium. The Suns' general manager of media and marketing, Stephen Wilson, said:

> Like the majority of sporting clubs around the globe, we need to identify additional revenue streams to stay competitive at the top level. We looked at ways as to how we could use Metricon Stadium, others stadiums have gyms, cafes, medical practitioners based in their stadiums. We challenged ourselves to identify opportunities that provided social or community benefits, one of those was a childcare facility, which we also think can help us with our community programs and growing our fan base.
>
> (Boswell, 2018, ¶¶6–8)

So for the Gold Coast Suns, despite having no expertise in the childcare sector, the opportunity to diversify into an unfamiliar business area – unrelated diversification – was assessed on its merits to supplement the club's traditional sources of revenue generation such as ticket sales, membership, sponsorship, broadcasting, and so forth. On a much larger scale, Richard Branson, with his Virgin brand, has been a "poster child" for unrelated diversification, building companies for over 50 years in everything from student magazines to record companies to airlines to telecommunications and fitness centers. Branson remains the only person to have built eight billion-dollar companies in eight different industries, and still has more than 60 active Virgin companies operating globally (Buss, 2017). Branson believes his Virgin brand name can apply to almost any business area, as he stated somewhat lightheartedly:

> We got lucky. About the only one we came unstuck on was Virgin Brides, there wasn't a market for them. But generally, (the Virgin name) works well with just about anything you can do. Virgin Condoms also had some issues.
>
> (Buss, 2017, ¶6, parentheses in original)

The concept of diversification is also relevant to the public sector's strategic involvement in sport. For example, from regional to national levels, it is common for public sector agencies responsible for economic development to seek to diversify their respective local economies in order to spread risk and decrease reliance on one or a few specific sectors. Such strategies typically include aspects of both related and unrelated diversification. For example, in the Brittany region of France, the region's key economic drivers include agriculture, fishing, food processing, car manufacturing, and interestingly, shipbuilding. Gerke, Desbordes, and Dickson (2015) explore the strategic development of a "cluster" of sport businesses in Brittany related to ocean racing marine yachting equipment. This sport cluster is designed to capitalize on the competencies and reputation of Brittany's shipbuilding sector by encouraging development of a sport business cluster related to the construction, processing, distribution, and the actual sport practice of ocean racing yachts. So in Brittany, while prosperity is sought across a diversified local economy, within specific industrial sectors, related diversification is a key tool for regional economic development.

Vertical integration

Madison Square Garden is an iconic sport and entertainment facility located in midtown Manhattan, New York, owned by Madison Square Garden Company (MSGC). The same company also owns other sport properties such as the New York Knicks (NBA), New York Liberty (WNBL), Westchester Knicks (NBA G-League), New York Rangers (NHL), and Westchester Wolf Pack (AHL). Each of these professional sport franchises plays their respective home games at Madison Square Garden. As with any sport and entertainment facility, Madison Square Garden relies upon sport teams, athletes, and entertainers to supply products that attract customers who pay for tickets, sponsorship rights, and broadcast fees, which generate significant revenue for the company. By actually owning some of its key suppliers – the sport franchises listed above – MSGC is employing *vertical integration*. Vertical integration occurs when an organization controls steps in the value chain of a core product or service. The term "value chain" refers to the journey products and services undergo from raw materials to processing to distribution to end-user consumers.

Thus, when a firm extends its operations up or down its value chain, it is engaging in vertical integration. This can be of two main types: *backward* vertical integration, where the firm moves "upstream" into sources of supply or raw materials; or *forward* vertical integration, where the firm extends its operations "downstream" in the distribution of core products or services to consumers. Why would an organization do this? Well, one of the core functions of management is to reduce environmental uncertainty, and we know that the costs involved at each point along the value chain, from resource access through to distribution of end products, represent key sources of uncertainty. Thus the logic for vertical integration is founded upon *transaction cost economics*, which posits that vertical integration is more efficient than paying for goods and services in the marketplace when open market transaction costs become excessive. However, when a vertically integrated corporation becomes too large, the costs of managing internal transactions in a big bureaucracy may become more excessive than simply purchasing the required goods externally, which would actually defeat the purpose of vertically integrating in the first place. In such a case, *outsourcing* – sourcing goods and services from the open market – would become the preferred option over vertical integration (Hunger & Wheelen, 2011).

Referring back to MSGC, by owning some of its key suppliers – the professional sport teams listed above – the company has vertically integrated backwards to reduce uncertainty around its access to a key resource: high-quality sport entertainment. Meanwhile, major sport apparel companies like Nike choose to sell their products in Nike-branded retail outlets in major shopping malls. While Nike still sells in generic sport stores alongside its competitors, by vertically integrating forward with Nike-branded retail stores, this ensures Nike's products are free from the clutter of competitors' products and presented in precisely the manner the company wishes them to be presented. Thompson, Peteraf, Gamble, and Strickland (2018) sum up the potential advantages of, and appropriate conditions for, vertical integration:

> Under the right conditions, a vertical integration strategy can add materially to a company's technological capabilities, strengthen the firm's competitive position, and boost its profitability. But it is important to keep in mind that vertical integration has no real payoff strategy-wise or profit-wise unless the extra investment can be justified by compensating improvements in company costs, differentiation, or competitive strength.
>
> (p. 163)

Critical thinking Box 6.1

Consider the discussion of the Madison Square Garden Company (MSGC) above. In August 2016, MSGC bought a major stake in Townsquare Media, a radio, digital media, entertainment, and digital marketing solutions company (InsideRadio, 2018). Search the web for information on this deal. Identify the specific type of vertical integration MSGC was pursuing with its acquisition of Townsquare Media and explain why you think management chose this particular growth path.

Stability strategies

When it comes to sport, many people intuitively think that bigger is better and all sport organizations naturally seek growth. But it might surprise you that this is not at all the case. In fact, while the definition of a small business differs by country and industry, it is safe to say that most sport organizations fit this category and are quite happy to remain as small businesses. Many sport organizations start out as devotees' hobbies that gradually turn into small businesses; but the motivation is equal parts hedonic and economic, which can sometimes run counter to traditional notions of neoliberal-style aggressive growth (O'Brien & Ponting, 2018). In such a scenario, growth brings the burden of debt, shared ownership, and the dilution of the founder's original levels of high control over the sport organization that they brought into being.

Even for large sport organizations, growth is sometimes undesirable due to ambiguity around consumer taste or changes in legislation, tax laws, government, or any other combination of environmental uncertainty. This all means that not all sport organizations seek unfettered growth, all of the time. Rather, there may be periods where management considers it more prudent to pursue *stability strategies* – that is, to maintain current activities without any major change in direction (Evans, Campbell, & Stonehouse, 2003). As Evans and his colleagues note, pursuing a stability strategy is not "doing nothing"; rather, stability requires protective actions in order to preserve the current market position from competitors.

Hunger and Wheelen (2011) propose three types of stability strategy: a pause/proceed-with-caution strategy, a no-change strategy, and a profit strategy. A pause/proceed-with-caution strategy is typically a temporary rest period in which management waits for the environment to become more hospitable. This may be, for example, at the end of an Olympic funding cycle for a national sport organization (NSO) or in the lead-up to national elections for a major sport event organizing committee. For many sport organizations, seasonality plays a major part in their annual strategic planning. Hinch and Higham (2011) note that seasonality is typically treated as a burden by sport tourism operators, but they argue that off-seasons and shoulder seasons are actually ideal times for auditing, training, equipment upkeep, and otherwise consolidating the business – prime examples of a pause/proceed-with-caution strategy.

A no-change strategy is rarely articulated as a formalized strategy, but simply refers to management's decision to not commence any new strategic initiatives in the near term. Such a position may evolve where a sport organization has found a comfortable niche that encourages management to follow a no-change strategy, "in which the future is expected to continue as an extension of the present" (Hunger & Wheelen, 2011, p. 95). This is desirable in encouraging certainty for stakeholders but may be dangerous if complacency sets in and managers fail to note environmental changes. Last, a profit strategy is when, in a hostile economic environment, management attempts to artificially support falling profits by reducing investment and short-term discretionary expenditures in areas like maintenance, research and development, marketing, and so on. Such a strategy is at best, only a temporary measure, as management seeks to ride out a difficult period of environmental uncertainty before pursuing further growth or, alternatively, embarking on defensive strategies.

Defensive strategies

Defensive strategies are necessary when the sport organization is in a weak competitive position and the environment is forecast to remain unfavorable for the use of growth or stability strategies. Parent and Slack (2006) identify three types of defensive strategy: turnaround, divestiture, and liquidation.

When a sport organization has problems with its competitive position or other key indicators of success, but the problems are not yet of a critical nature, it may embark on a *turnaround* strategy. Turnaround strategies are typically two-pronged attacks where the first stage "stems the bleeding" with staff layoffs and other cost cutting, followed by a period of consolidation with programs to stabilize the now leaner organization (Hunger & Wheelen, 2011). When the situation is too dire for turnaround, *divestiture* of a whole business or parts thereof may be necessary. For example, Chinese sportswear giant Li-Ning emerged in August 2018 from a turnaround strategy that saw it divest (sell off) 10% ownership in one of its top performing brands, the Double Happiness table tennis company. The divestiture allowed the management of both Li-Ning and Double Happiness brands to better focus on their respective businesses.

For Li-Ning, divestiture was one part of its overall turnaround strategy, which saw Li Ning himself step in as the interim CEO, as the company closed loss-making stores and renovated inefficient ones, at the same time expanding its sales network to reach more customers. As a result of this turnaround strategy, Li-Ning positioned itself to take advantage of more favorable market conditions in 2018, and first-half profits rose 42% over 2017 (Inside Retail Asia, 2018).

When sport organizations face difficult environments that they are unable to successfully navigate using turnaround or divestiture strategies, *liquidation* is sometimes the only option remaining. Liquidation refers to closing down an organization and selling off its assets (Parent & Slack, 2006), and may (or may not) come after other defensive strategies have been attempted. For example, Welch Sports was a family-run sports retailer that operated five stores in Ireland. However, Welch Sports found it difficult to compete with the rise of online shopping, and market share and profit began to dwindle. Despite reducing the size of its workforce and divesting three stores in 2016 and 2017 as part of a turnaround strategy, by August 2018 it became necessary to liquidate its remaining two stores and all of its assets in order to pay creditors. So after 22 years, Welch Sports was officially out of business (Shanahan, 2018).

This section has covered a lot of territory – from growth strategies at business and corporate levels, through stability strategies, and finishing off with defensive strategies. Many of the concepts you will no doubt have heard of, but may not have actually known exactly what they meant in a strategic sense. It is important that you understand these concepts because while the discussion so far has centered on strategic direction, we now turn to strategic method – that is, *how* we actually propose to move the sport organization in our preferred direction.

Strategic method

In the previous section, we made the point that there are certain times in the life cycle of sport organizations where it is just not appropriate to pursue growth. Now it's time to switch gears again, because in this section we are addressing periods where growth is indeed the strategic direction of choice. And, as we established earlier, at the business level of strategy formulation, there are various growth options available to the firm including market penetration, product development and market development, while at the corporate level, we explored growth options of concentration, diversification, and vertical integration. Whether at the individual business or corporate level, if you think of these as the direction in which the sport organization wishes to travel, what we now need to know is our method of transport – that is, by what *strategic method* will we achieve our growth ambitions? To address this question, we will now explore three strategic growth methods: internal growth, mergers and acquisitions, and joint developments.

Internal growth

In October 2018, the Indian Premier League (IPL) franchise, Rajasthan Royals, established its first grassroots cricket development academy called "Royal Colts." The Royals established the academy to "unearth fresh talent and provide them an opportunity to make a mark in the cricketing world" (Gulf News, 2018, ¶1). The initiative is an example of *internal growth*, also referred to as organic growth, where business growth is resourced through the organization's own resources and capabilities rather than sourcing these externally through an alliance, merger, or acquisition. Such an option relies on the sport organization's capacity to develop its own internal resources and capabilities.

As we explored in Chapter 2, the first part of a situation analysis requires an assessment of the organization's core competencies. An internal growth strategy would ideally leverage these core competencies to expand current operations or, more aggressively, pursue a green-field investment; that is, where a new business is started from scratch. For the Rajasthan Royals, the franchise has core competencies in talent identification and development, which they sought to build on in undertaking this venture. As the franchise's head of cricket, Zubin Bharucha, explained: "At the Rajasthan Royals, we are passionate about developing talent. Since the start of the IPL, we have invested in youth and subsequently launched many players onto the international stage" (Gulf News, 2018, ¶3).

The main advantage of an internal development approach is that it is less disruptive to the organization as a whole because there is no need to seek compatibility in cultures, systems, and processes with any partner organizations. In addition, all learning and competence development – not to mention return on investment – is kept within the focal organization. However, this raises a key disadvantage, in that start-up businesses are notoriously resource-hungry, and with internal development, all of the cost and risk of the venture must be borne internally. Therefore, if the environment shifts unexpectedly and the internal growth venture does not make a return on investment – or worse, results in significant losses – the focal organization has no option but to bear these losses in revenue and, quite possibly, reputation.

Mergers and acquisitions

Rossignol is a well-known French manufacturer of alpine sports equipment and accessories and was one of the first companies in the world to introduce plastic skis. Like most highly innovative organizations, Rossignol has a history of developing strong brand equity around its reputation for innovative product development. In 2018–2019, Rossignol announced plans to become an "all-year brand" by diversifying into new product lines for trail running and cycling – sports that are popular in ski areas outside of Rossignol's core business of winter ski season products (Jans, 2018a).

So, with Rossignol's management setting the strategic direction of growth by related diversification, they now had to choose a suitable *strategic method*. One option would be internal growth – to develop the necessary resources and capabilities internally. This would entail employing specialist research and development technicians to initially develop the products, and then buying in the required manufacturing, warehousing, logistics, and distribution capabilities to actually get the products to market. While internal growth would keep all proprietary knowledge and intellectual property in-house, and would be culturally and politically easier to manage, it would also require massive investment in resources and time. Alternatively, Rossignol could acquire a company that already had all of the necessary competencies and resources to achieve its related diversification goals. This would enable Rossignol to be in the market quicker than if it was to develop these competencies on its own.

However, the real world of strategic management is somewhat messier than the neat boxes and arrows in your lectures and textbooks (like this one!). The strategic method Rossignol ultimately chose was a bit of both: it used internal growth to develop a mountain bike range, but an acquisition strategy to develop high-end road and triathlon bikes. Bruno Cercley, the Rossignol CEO, explained the company's strategy:

> This is why we decided to acquire Time Sport and Felt Bicycles, really good brands, especially with the development of carbon framing products. We bought these two brands, because we needed to acquire competences we didn't have. What we are trying now, is to put Felt Bicycles, Time Sport and Rossignol each in a strong position within the market: Rossignol means mountain bikes, Time Sport stands for high-end road bikes and Felt Bicycles' core competence is in triathlon.
>
> (Cercley, as quoted in Jans, 2018b, ¶27)

In the example above, note that when Rossignol acquired Time Sport and Felt Bicycles, these companies were incorporated as subsidiaries under the overall Rossignol corporate umbrella. Sometimes acquisitions like this are not possible, and rather than one company being subsumed under another, as was the case with Time Sport and Felt under Rossignol, the organizations actually merge into one. In a *merger*, the owners (whether they be shareholders or private owners) of separate organizations come together – most often willingly – to share the goals and resources of the expanded (merged) organization; thus, owners from both sides of the merger agree upon goals and conditions and become mutual owners in the new organizational entity (Evans et al., 2003). For example, in April 2018, the International Mixed Martial Arts Federation (IMMAF) and the World Mixed Martial Arts Association (WMMAA) announced a merger that saw the global unification of the sport of mixed martial arts (MMA). In this merger, both parties shared mutual goals to achieve the inclusion of MMA into the Olympic Games, recognizing the impossibility of this if they remained separate entities. As the president of the WMMAA, Vadim Finkelchtein, explained:

> I truly believe that the coming amalgamation will give a huge boost to the global development of MMA as a sport and it will bear positive influence even in those countries in which MMA is still forbidden. Joining forces will provide us with an opportunity to achieve recognition for MMA at every official level and to subsequently enter the Olympic Movement. I'm pleased that our organizations have similar goals and a shared vision for the acceptance of MMA into the Olympic Games for 2024–2028. This would not be possible without our cooperation, which I believe will be fruitful to the benefit of our beloved sport.
>
> (immaf.org, 2018, ¶6)

Mergers are quite common in sport. In recent decades, many national and provincial sport governing bodies throughout the world that were previously separated based on gender undertook mergers into single entities. In 1997, the federal government agency responsible for sport funding in Australia, the Australian Sport Commission (ASC), which has now rebranded to Sport Australia, released a report titled the Amalgamation Guidelines for Recreation and Sporting Organizations (ASC, 1997) which recommended the merger of those sports with separate gender-specific national governing bodies. The implicit message was that NSOs should restructure if they wished to access government funding. As a result, sports like golf, hockey, cricket, and lawn bowls, among numerous others, sought to merge their separate gender-based NSOs. While many of the mergers worked well, it must be said, not all were structured equally. For example, Women's Cricket Australia (WCA) and the Australian Cricket Board (ACB) merged to form Cricket Australia (CA) on July 1, 2003. However, it was a decade before CA had a woman director on its board. To this day (at the time of writing), CA states on its website (under the section "Our History") that "the organization changed its name in 1973 to the Australian Cricket Board, then on July 1st 2003, it became Cricket Australia" (CA, n.d., ¶4). All of CA's past chair*men* are also listed, but the history of women's cricket in Australia is completely ignored. With mergers remaining such a prevalent aspect of the sport environment, and the continued growth and recognition of women's participation in traditionally "male" sports throughout the world, paying attention to the equitable and transparent navigation of merger processes and outcomes has never been more critical.

Critical thinking Box 6.2

Consider the closing case on Catapult Sports. How would you characterize Catapult Sports' choice of (a) strategic direction and (b) strategic method? Discuss what you think are the key considerations for Catapult Sports in pursuing this strategic path.

Joint development

Joint development strategic methods for growth include *strategic alliances* and *joint ventures*. These terms are often used synonymously, but they actually have quite different meanings. Strategic alliances are bonds between organizations intended to realize an objective sooner or more efficiently than if either entity attempted to do so on its own. Organizations of all shapes and sizes, including those involved in sport, are increasingly allying with other organizations for purposes that include entering new markets, learning new technologies or skills, and developing new products (Pitts & Lei, 2006). For example, Kennelly and Toohey (2014) examined strategic alliances in sport event tourism and demonstrated how alliances between NSOs and sport tour operators can facilitate and often accentuate the potential for positive sport, tourism, and economic and social development outcomes from hosting major sport events.

Critical thinking Box 6.3

Go to: https://asunow.asu.edu/20170612-asu-news-adidas-global-partnership-shape-future-sport

Discuss the nature of the partnership between adidas and Arizona State University. List the resources each partner in the alliance might be seeking to gain access to. What might be some independent goals of each respective alliance partner? Suggest what you consider would be some mutual goals for the alliance.

Like strategic alliances, *joint ventures* are also formed to capitalize on complementary resources, learn new technologies and processes, or to otherwise achieve mutual goals; but they differ from strategic alliances in that joint ventures involve the creation of a separate organizational entity. That separate entity is the actual joint venture, which will include two or more partner organizations in a legally binding arrangement in which each has mutually agreed percentages of ownership in the venture. For example, ONE Championship is Asia's (and perhaps the world's) largest martial arts event. In 2019, ONE Championship formed a joint venture with Dentsu Inc., Japan's largest global advertising agency. The joint venture is called ONE eSports and has the aim to become the world's largest global eSports championship series (ONE Championship, 2018). Each partner brings unique resources and capabilities to the joint venture that complement those of the other partner. As Shuntaro Tanaka, director of the Content Business Design Center of Dentsu, stated:

> We are pleased to announce this partnership with ONE Championship as we look to further develop the rapidly growing eSports industry in Japan and the rest of Asia. We recognize good synergy between martial arts and eSports, making this a fantastic opportunity for both ONE Championship and Dentsu to participate in this growing segment in Asia, as well as leverage multiple content platforms for additional sales and business opportunities. ONE Championship has been a terrific partner and Dentsu is happy to move forward with ONE in this eSports venture.
>
> (ONE Championship, 2018, ¶5)

As can be seen from the discussion so far, whether talking about mergers, acquisitions, strategic alliances, or joint ventures, the overriding concern is the presence of synergy – the notion that two partners can operate more effectively together than they would separately (Hunger & Wheelen, 2011). A two-driver rally team is a good way to think about synergy; one team member drives while the other navigates. The alliance gets them through the course in the most efficient way possible. If each partner worked independently, they would each be trying to drive and navigate simultaneously, which would not only be inefficient but also unsafe. Therefore, to be considered successful, the chosen strategic method must exploit synergies in unique capabilities and resources and add value in terms of higher profit or stronger market position. Clegg et al. (2017) further break down the notion of synergy by referring to complementary and supplementary fit. *Complementary fit* refers to the sharing of distinct resources – for example, in the ONE eSports example, where each partner has unique resources that the other partner seeks access to. Meanwhile, *supplementary fit* refers to the pooling of matched resources by partners who, for example, mutually seek to meet high costs and improve efficiencies.

◼ Summary

In this chapter, we explored the formulation of strategy at the business and corporate levels and placed both in the context of strategic direction and strategic method. Business-level strategy, that is, how an individual sport organization positions itself relative to its competitors, was explored in terms of Porter's (1980) generic business-level strategies of low-cost leadership, differentiation, and focus. We then discussed strategic direction and identified growth, stability, and defensive strategies as the major strategic options. Within the growth strategic direction, we discussed applications of Ansoff's (1957) work on market penetration, market development, product development, and diversification at the business level. At the corporate level, growth direction strategies include concentration, diversification, and vertical integration. In terms of stability as a strategic direction, we identified three options: pause/proceed-with-caution, no-change, and a profit strategy. We then explored three types of defensive strategy: turnaround, divestiture, and liquidation. Finally, we identified that where growth is the preferred strategic direction, we much also make decisions around three categories of strategic growth method: internal growth, mergers and acquisitions, and joint developments.

CLOSING CASE: CATAPULT SPORTS

Catapult Sports is a sport technology company headquartered in Melbourne, Australia, that specializes in wearable athlete tracking devices. The company was founded in 2006 by Shaun Holthouse and Igor van de Griendt, and emerged from a partnership between Cooperative Research Centers (CRC) and the Australian Institute of Sport. With a resolute focus on elite sport performance, the company has grown from a humble Australian start-up to be a global category leader in elite sport technology. Catapult Sports now supplies its devices to 1,638 teams in 35 sports across 61 countries, with around 16% market penetration of the roughly 10,000 elite teams globally that are the targeted customers of wearable products (Lemire, 2018). By 2023, this market is estimated to be worth USD 15.5 billion, up from USD 764.3 million in 2016 (Research and Markets, 2017).

In 2018, Catapult Sports was in the midst of an ambitious growth strategy to penetrate further into the sport technology market. While the company dominates the elite professional sport market, the new strategy sought to penetrate the subelite category, that is, individuals and sport clubs that may not be full-time professional. The CEO of Catapult's Americas division, Matt Bairos, explained the company's ambitions:

> Catapult isn't a wearable company. It has wearable products, but it's a platform. Our mission is to own the technology performance stack for all teams. On the planet. That means wearables, it means video, it means anything that directly ties back to player performance, and that's either through organically developed products, potential acquisitions and good partnerships.
>
> (Lemire, 2018, ¶¶10–12)

In order to realize its ambitions of penetrating the subelite sport technology market, Catapult is seeking to develop a product that is more user-friendly and doesn't require a team of data analysts and sport scientists to interpret. As part of this strategy, acquisitions began in 2014 with the purchase of GPSports, then in 2016 came the acquisition of the market leader in video-based sport performance technology, XOS Digital, and also the Irish company, PlayerTek (Catapult Sports, 2018). While Catapult's traditional customer base of professional sport franchises have access to qualified data analysts who process the mountains of data produced by their wearable technology devices, Catapult's new target market of subelite teams are typically not as resource-rich. PlayerTek was founded on the principle of delivering tracking data to teams that lack the analytical and sport science support of elite clubs. Thus, by purchasing PlayerTek, this saved Catapult the time and expense of developing its own subelite (or what they call "prosumer") product. To complement the PlayerTek acquisition, in August 2017 Catapult also acquired the SportsMed Elite and Baseline athlete management systems, which are essentially cloud-based platforms that store team data and information, including player wellness metrics, injury and medical records, wearable data, and video (SMG, 2017).

Catapult is initially targeting subelite football players with its prosumer product, a market it estimates at 270 million players worldwide, of which their initial target demographic is around three million players (Lemire, 2018). The Catapult executive charged with bringing the prosumer product to market, Benoit Simeray, explained the challenge ahead:

How do we build as much of that sport science into the tech and content that we provide to those prosumers? It's got to be really insightful. It's got to be a terrific user experience. It's got to be aligned to the particular sporting code that we're focused on, and we need to make that as easy to use and as interactive as possible. That absolutely is a key part of our challenge to take to market.

(Lemire, 2018, ¶30)

Chapter review questions

1   Think of a sport organization that pursues a focus business-level strategy. Explain the manner in which the organization focuses – as a low-cost leader, or as a differentiator? Analyze the characteristics of the market being focused upon and explain why you think management has chosen this strategy and whether you think it was the appropriate choice.

2   Referring to Figure 6.1, discuss an example of a sport organization that has pursued one of these strategic growth options. Name the organization, the strategic growth option, and why you believe that in this case management did not pursue the other three options.

3   Discuss with a colleague a case where a sport organization has pursued one or more of Ansoff's four strategic growth directions. In the pursuit of that growth, dig deeper and identify any business-level strategies that were employed. So you might end up, for example, with an organization pursuing market development using low-cost leadership.

4   Think of a multi-business sport organization that you are familiar with. Identify the corporate-level strategic direction(s) this organization pursues. In so doing, also identify the strategic method(s) the organization employs. Explain how effective you think this strategy has been and the rationale for your answer.

5   You have been asked to advise a sport organization on a suitable strategy to grow into a new city. A much smaller competitor has already proven there is demand in that city for your service. You know that a competitor is considering an internal development growth initiative into this city, so speed of entry is very important for your client. Work through the strategic options available to your client and explain the rationale for your final advice.

6   Identify a joint development arrangement in the sport industry and articulate the nature of the arrangement as either a strategic alliance or a joint venture. Analyze the arrangement and identify where and how there are complementary and supplementary fits.

Additional resources

- Journal articles
    o   Boone, C., Lokshin, B., Hannes, G., & Belderbos, R. (2019). Top management team nationality diversity, corporate entrepreneurship, and innovation in multinational firms. *Strategic Management Journal, 40,* 277–302.

- o Ferkins, L., & Shilbury, D. (2012). Good boards are strategic: What does that mean for sport governance? *Journal of Sport Management, 26*, 67–80.
- o Huff, J. O., Huff, A. S., & Thomas, H. (1992). Strategic renewal and the interaction of cumulative stress and inertia. *Strategic Management Journal*, 13, 55–75.
- Websites
  - o OnStrategy: https://onstrategyhq.com/resources/strategic-implementation/
  - o Strategic management: Formulation and implementation: www.strategy-implementation.24xls.com/en101
  - o 5 structural elements of strategy: www.entrepreneur.com/article/196932
  - o Sport Techie: www.sporttechie.com/
- Videos
  - o The five competitive forces that shape strategy: An interview with Michael Porter (Harvard Business Review): www.youtube.com/watch?v=mYF2_FBCvXw
  - o Porter's generic strategies – Choosing your route to success: www.mindtools.com/pages/article/newSTR_82.htm
  - o GoPro corporate strategy 720: www.youtube.com/watch?v=BgWuFpd40TY
  - o Nike – The rise of a billion-dollar brand: www.youtube.com/watch?v=Gi7Vy_2B_D8

References

Ansoff, H. I. (1957). Strategies for diversification. *Harvard Business Review, 35*(5), 113–124.

Association of Tennis Professionals Tour. (2019). *ATP Cup confirms Sydney and Brisbane as hosts for 2020*. Retrieved January 21, 2019 from www.atptour.com/en/news/atp-cup-confirms-sydney-and-brisbane-as-hosts-for-2020

Australian Sports Commission, (1997). *Amalgamation guidelines for recreation and sporting organisations*. Canberra: Australian Sports Commission.

Barbieri, C., & Sotomayor, S. (2013). Surf travel behavior and destination preferences: An application of the serious leisure inventory and measure. *Tourism Management, 35*(April), 111–121.

Boswell, T. (2018). Gold Coast Suns in talks to establish early learning centre as part of plans to become financially stable. *Gold Coast Bulletin*. Retrieved January 23, 2019 from www.goldcoastbulletin.com.au/sport/afl/gold-coast-suns-in-talks-to-establish-early-learning-centre-as-part-of-plans-to-become-financially-stable/news-story/2f2dcf22d260a4292f27ccd27ac6c5e0

Buss, D. (2017). Richard Branson on the Virgin brand – And the future of travel. *Brandchannel*, October 19, 2018. Retrieved November 5, 2018 from www.brandchannel.com/2017/10/19/richard-branson-101917/

Catapult Sports. (2018). *Our story*. Retrieved May 25, 2018 from www.catapultsports.com/about

Clegg, S., Schweitzer, J., Whittle, A., & Pitelis, C. (2017). *Strategy: Theory and practice* (2nd ed.). London: Sage.

Cricket Australia (n.d). *Our history*. Retrieved January 20, 2019 from: https://www.cricketaustralia.com.au/about/our-history

Evans, N., Campbell, D., & Stonehouse, G. (2003). *Strategic management for travel and tourism*. Burlington, MA: Butterworth-Heinemann.

Ferkins, L., & Shilbury, D. (2012). Good boards are strategic: What does that mean for sport governance? *Journal of Sport Management, 26*, 67–80.

Gerke, A., Desbordes, M., & Dickson, G. (2015). Towards a sport cluster model: The ocean racing cluster in Brittany. *European Sport Management Quarterly, 15*, 343–363.

The Grand. (2018). *Private, exclusive, and only available to a privileged few.* Retrieved May 3, 2018 from www.thegrandgolfclub.com.au/

Gulf News. (2018). *Rajasthan Royals to launch grassroots development programme: IPL franchise will be holding trials from October 11.* Retrieved November 8, 2018 from https://gulfnews.com/sport/cricket/india/rajasthan-royals-to-launch-grassroots-development-programme-1.2284883

Harrison, J. S., & St. John, C. H. (2014). *Foundations in strategic management* (6th ed.). Mason, OH: Thomson South-Western.

Hinch, T., & Higham, J. (2011). *Sport tourism development* (2nd ed.). Bristol: Channel View Publications.

Hunger, J. D., & Wheelen, T. L. (2011). *Essentials of strategic management* (5th ed.). Upper Saddle River, NJ: Prentice Hall.

IMMAF.ORG. (2018). *World MMA Association (WMMAA) and International (IMMAF) unite in one bid for sport recognition.* Retrieved November 10, 2018 from www.immaf.org/mma-world-governing-bodies-amalgamate/

Inside Radio. (2018). MSG, attracted by events biz, buys 12% Townsquare Stake. *Inside Radio: The Most Trusted News in Radio.* Retrieved November 2, 2018 from www.insideradio.com/msg-attracted-by-events-biz-buys-townsquare-stake/article_cc1e3256-6477-11e6-9782-6f12e41e16b6.html

Inside Retail Asia. (2018). Li Ning's profit soars on turnaround strategy. *Inside Retail – Asia.* Retrieved November 15, 2018 from https://insideretail.asia/2018/08/13/li-nings-profit-soars-on-turnaround-strategy/

Jans, G. (2018a). Rossignol wants to become an all-year brand: "This is a sea change for the Rossignol Group". *Ispo.com.* Retrieved May 11, 2018 from www.ispo.com/en/companies/rossignol-wants-become-all-year-brand

Jans, G. (2018b). Bruno Cercley: Rossignol is performing better than the market. *Ispo.com.* Retrieved November 8, 2018 from www.ispo.com/en/companies/bruno-cercley-rossignol-performing-better-market

Kennelly, M., & Toohey, K. (2014). Strategic alliances in sport tourism: National sport organizations and sport tour operators. *Sport Management Review, 17*(4), 407–418.

Kunkel, T., Doyle, J., & Funk, D. (2014). Exploring sport brand development strategies to strengthen consumer involvement with the product – The case of the Australian A-League. *Sport Management Review, 17*, 470–483.

Lemire, J. (2018, March 6). Catapult Sports broadens strategy, "Isn't a wearable company" anymore. *Sport Techie.* Retrieved May 25, 2018 from www.sporttechie.com/catapult-sports-broadens-strategy-isnt-wearable-company-anymore/

Martin, R. (2018, November 22). Tennis: Davis Cup could merge with ATP for unified event – Costa. *Reuters.* Retrieved January 21, 2019 from www.reuters.com/article/us-tennis-daviscup-interview/tennis-davis-cup-could-merge-with-atp-for-unified-event-costa-idUSKCN1NQ23W

O'Brien, D., & Ponting, J. (2013). Sustainable surf tourism: A community centered approach in Papua New Guinea. *Journal of Sport Management, 27*, 158–172.

O'Brien, D., & Ponting, J. (2018). STOKE Certified: Initiating sustainability certification in surf tourism. In B. McCullough & T. Kellison (Eds.), *Handbook on sport, sustainability, and the environment* (pp. 301–316). Oxford: Routledge.

ONE Championship. (2018). ONE Championship launches Asia's largest eSports
    championship series. *Press Releases*, November 7, 2018. Retrieved November 12, 2018
    from: www.onefc.com/articles/one-championship-launches-asias-largest-esports-
    championship-series/

Parent, M. M., & Slack, T. (2006). *Understanding sport organizations: The application of
    organization theory* (2nd Ed.). Champaign, IL: Human Kinetics.

Pitts, R. A., & Lei, D. (2006). *Building and sustaining competitive advantage* (4th Ed.).
    Mason, OH: Thomson.

Ponting, J., & O'Brien, D. (2014). Liberalizing Nirvana: An analysis of the consequences
    of common pool resource deregulation for the sustainability of Fiji's surf tourism
    industry. *Journal of Sustainable Tourism, 22,* 384–402.

Ponting, J., & O'Brien, D. (2015). Regulating "Nirvana": Sustainable surf tourism in a
    climate of increasing regulation. *Sport Management Review, 18,* 99–110.

Porter, M. E. (1980). *Competitive strategy: Techniques for analyzing industries and
    competitors*. New York, NY: The Free Press.

Research and Markets. (2017). Sports player tracking and analytics: Market shares,
    strategies, and forecasts, worldwide 2017–2023. *Research and markets: The World's
    largest market research store*. Retrieved May 25, 2018 from www.researchandmarkets.
    com/research/mjwfkj/sports_player

Shanahan, C. (2018). Family-run retailer Welch Sports shuts after 22 years. *Irish Examiner*.
    Retrieved November 16, 2018 from www.irishexaminer.com/breakingnews/ireland/
    family-run-retailer-welch-sports-shuts-after-22-years-865508.html

Skydive Dubai. (2018). *About us*. Retrieved October 23, 2018 from www.skydivedubai.ae/
    about-us.html

SMG. (2017). *World's most advanced athlete management systems acquired*. Retrieved May
    25, 2018 from www.smg-corporate.com/blog/sportsmed-elite-baseline-acquired-by-
    catapult/

Thompson, A., Peteraf, M., Gamble, J., & Strickland, A. (2018). *Crafting and executing
    strategy: The quest for competitive advantage, concepts and cases* (21st ed.). New York,
    NY: McGraw-Hill Education.

Towner, N. (2016). Community participation and emerging surfing tourism destinations: A
    case study of the Mentawai Islands. *Journal of Sport & Tourism, 20,* 1–19.

Washtell, F. (2017). Central London bulked up on budget gyms last year with 46 per cent
    of new openings in the low-cost sector. *City AM*. Retrieved May 1, 2018 from www.
    cityam.com/256482/central-london-bulked-up-budget-gyms-last-year-46-per-cent

7

Strategy evaluation and selection

OPENING CASE: NATIONAL STRATEGY SELECTION FOR SUCCESSFUL HIGH PERFORMANCE SPORT
(By Richard I. Toomer)

A country, just like an organization, needs its leadership to determine strategic objectives for the attainment of targeted, in this case, national outcomes. The development of public policy is simultaneously a key influence on and reflection of these national objectives and, in terms of objectives related to the sport industry, it is with a national sport policy. The Commonwealth nations of Canada and Jamaica have both formulated and implemented national sport policies.

Canada introduced its sport policy in 2002, which was revised in 2012; and Jamaica first introduced its sport policy in 1994, with a revision in 2013. Both sport policies inform sport development from the grassroots level in each respective nation. However, significant differences exist for the development of elite-level sport, with Canada selectively funding high-performing sports while Jamaica employs a much more broad-based approach.

The Sport Policy factors Leading to International Sporting Success (SPLISS) model (De Bosscher, De Knop, van Bottenburg, & Shibli, 2006) suggests that nations influence elite sporting success through policies at the meso-level (actions and decisions by national government). SPLISS recommends that using financial support (inputs) and funding channeled into sport development processes (throughputs) should lead to desired results (outputs) from international high performance sport.

Using the Olympic Games as a point of reference, both Canada and Jamaica have competed in Winter and Summer Games and have attained various successes. Between the years 1900 to 2018, Canada amassed 501 medals: 302 at the Summer Games and 199 at the Winter Games (International Olympic Committee, n.d.). Conversely, Jamaica has competed since 1948, amassing 77 medals between 1948 and 2018, all at the Summer Games, with 76 coming from the sport of athletics and one from cycling (in 1980). Interestingly, since 2002 and the introduction of its sport policy, Canada amassed 72 of 302 medals from multiple sports at the Summer Games, representing 23.84% of total medals received, and 121 of 199 medals from multiple sports at the Winter Games, representing 60.80% of total medals. For Jamaica, 53 of its 77 medals were received after the introduction of its sport policy in 1994, and represented 68.83% of the country's total medals.

Although these results are positive, direct attribution to the respective sport policy in each nation cannot be substantiated at this time. Therefore, it is important to understand the different strategic approaches these two nations took toward the attainment of their respective sporting successes.

In Jamaica, the Sports Development Foundation, a government agency established in 1995 to receive and distribute the Jamaican Lottery funds for the development of all sporting activities, spearheads the funding of sport (Toomer, 2015). Furthermore, Jamaica does not have any centralized institution for the advancement of high-performance sport, and funding support goes directly to the 42 autonomous national sport organizations (NSOs) to use as they see fit. Each NSO can either request additional funding for special circumstances or seek private support for high-performance sport development. While the outputs indicate a successful nation at the Olympic Games, there is no documentary support to show a clear link between the financial support from government to national sport organizations, leading to successful results at these Games. In fact, the opposite may be true, whereby the success of Jamaican athletics is more a result of personal training and the involvement of private actors working in collaboration with educational institutions (see Robinson, 2009). While there may be a link to government through these institutions, no strategic link is seen attributable to any identifiable sport policy. It is the established structure of athletics that allows Jamaica to be successful in high-performance sport, as opposed to any of the other 41 funded sports.

For Canada, Own the Podium (OTP), a non-profit sport organization initially created ahead of the 2010 Vancouver Olympic Winter Games to enhance Canada's chances of winning medals (especially gold medals) on home soil, works with Sport Canada (the federal government department responsible for driving sport in the country), the 32 Olympic sport-related NSOs, and the Canadian Olympic and Paralympic committees as well as the sport institute network to advance the government's national strategy for targeting sporting excellence in high-performance sport (Own the Podium, 2017). OTP makes recommendations to funding parties by incorporating an evidence-based, expert-driven, targeted, and collaborative approach to the investment strategies for high-performance sport.

From the strategic approaches of Canada and Jamaica, it is evident that financial resources and the structure of the sport delivery systems in each respective country dictate the evaluation and selection of investments in high-performance sport. Jamaica's decision to undertake a broad-based approach, which respects the autonomy of the NSOs, provides minimal funding support to all organizations, but it also allows for the sport discipline with a competitive advantage to be sustainable without government intervention. For Canada, a targeted approach gives control to the government via Sport Canada, which in turn, provides funding to select NSOs, based on an assessment of past high-performance success at the Olympics, Paralympic Games, and world championships.

Introduction

From reading the chapters in this book so far, you know the importance of assessing your organization's internal and external environments, as well as determining a strategic direction and formulating potential strategies, with a view to gaining a competitive advantage. As this chapter's opening case illustrates, there is no one best choice of strategy and some choices are not ideal fits for a particular situation – they just don't provide the outcome management is seeking.

As such, properly evaluating your strategy options and selecting the best strategy for your sport organization's situation and desired goals is critical for gaining and/or sustaining a competitive advantage. This chapter will provide you with an overview of the process of and considerations related to strategy evaluation and selection, as well as some tools to help you in this process.

Strategy evaluation and selection

As Evans, Campbell, and Stonehouse (2003) note, it is not easy to make important decisions. Choosing the right solution is critical for the survival and success of the organization. You need to know where you have been and where you want to go. Hubbard, Rice, and Galvin (2015) propose five key questions to guide the (strategic) choice process:

1   Do you want to grow the organization?
2   What products/services do you plan to offer?
3   What geographic and customer markets do you plan on targeting?
4   What basic strategy do you plan to use to position your organization in a unique manner compared to your competitors?
5   What position do you plan on taking in the future?

Remember, this is about making strategic decisions, not operational ones. Strategic decisions are high-level decisions looking at the organization overall, its strategic business units (SBUs), and how they are and should be positioned in terms of their products/services and competitors.

Important decisions are never easy. To make the appropriate choice, you should (Evans et al., 2003):

1   Gather all the relevant information, notably through a SWOT analysis (see Chapters 2 and 3);
2   Know all the options available to you (see Chapters 4 through 6);
3   Evaluate each option using a consistent set of criteria; and,
4   Select your strategy based on the outcome of your evaluation.

In this chapter, we address steps 3 and 4 in particular.

For non-profit sport organizations specifically, Thibault, Slack, and Hinings (1993) developed six imperatives to use when analyzing potential strategic options. Table 7.1 details these imperatives, which are grouped into two dimensions:

- Program attractiveness: the ability to provide services and programs to members; and,
- Competitive position: the ability to attract and retain members.

Below, we provide three additional approaches for evaluating strategic options, approaches that can be applied to all types of sport organizations: (1) the suitability-feasibility-acceptability-competitive advantage approach, (2) the strategic options grid, and (3) portfolio analysis.

TABLE 7.1   Six strategic choice imperatives for non-profit sport organizations

Program attractiveness	Competitive position
Fundability: stability of funding and ability to attract new external funding	*Equipment costs*: the extent of costs participants need to incur for equipment so they can compete in the sport at an introductory level
Size of client base: number of members of the organization	*Affiliation fees*: costs associated to participating in a sport, mainly membership fees required to access coaching, training facilities, and competitions
Volunteer appeal: ability to attract volunteers, be they administrators, coaches, officials or other	
Support group appeal: degree of media exposure/visibility and awareness of the sport by the general public	

Source: Based on Thibault et al. (1993).

Approach 1: suitability-feasibility-acceptability-competitive advantage

As we have seen in Chapter 6, managers are not confined to one or two ways to achieve the sport organization's mission; there exist a bewildering array of potential strategies to choose from. Many will have merit depending on environmental conditions at the time. So there's no one "right" way to "do" strategy. And, we can't do everything, so we do indeed have to make strategic choices. The choice that you make for your sport organization is the one that, based on your assessment, you hope will give you the best chance of gaining or sustaining a competitive advantage.

So if we have to make an assessment of the best strategy for our sport organization, what criteria should we use? Evans et al. (2003) proposed the general criteria contained in the Suitability-Feasibility-Acceptability (SFA) analysis as positive way to make informed strategic choices. They also added a fourth criterion: will the option enable the organization to achieve competitive advantage? We will now work through each criterion of the Suitability-Feasibility-Acceptability-Competitive-Advantage (SFACA) analysis:

- *Suitability*: This refers to the degree to which the option can actually help the sport organization reach its strategic goals and objectives. If the option is unlikely to help us reach our strategic goals, then it should be rejected. Most options, however, will fall in a range of suitability. So scoring each option from 1 = low suitability to 5 = high suitability can help. To determine suitability, use the outcome of your SWOT analysis (see Chapters 2 and 3) and evaluate the degree to which the given option:
  - Capitalizes on identified strengths and/or addresses or avoids weaknesses;
  - Exploits identified opportunities and/or decreases or avoids threats;
  - Meets stakeholder expectations; and, of course,
  - Helps achieve organizational goals.
- If any option is deemed unsuitable, that is, it received a low suitability score across the above criteria, it should be screened out of the process and rejected. However, if the opposite is true, then we can move to the next step: determining whether the option is feasible.
- *Feasibility*: Feasibility refers to the extent to which the option is "doable." Again, you can score each option on a scale from 1 = not feasible to 5 = highly feasible. To determine feasibility, you can undertake a feasibility study and/or examine whether the organization has the necessary:
  - Internal factors (resources, skills, capabilities, capacity, and culture) to undertake the given option; and,
  - External factors (support or acceptance from stakeholders, potential competitive reactions, and approvals from government/regulatory bodies, if needed) to facilitate the implementation and success of the given option.

At this point, if the option is indeed feasible, then we move on to the next step in the SFACA analysis: acceptability.

- *Acceptability*: This is the degree to which your (primary) stakeholders (see Chapter 3) will see merit in your chosen strategy. For example, will the board of directors and employees commit to the strategy? To what degree will customers like your new offering? To determine the degree of acceptability, three aspects are often considered:

- o   Return on investment (ROI), such as through a financial and non-financial cost-benefit analysis (e.g., size of potential customer base, equipment costs, impact on brand and reputation, or labor costs);
- o   Degree of risk, such as through a risk analysis of implementation and potential outcomes/expectations; and,
- o   Stakeholder reactions, such as through a stakeholder analysis of their salience, needs, and wants.

- •   Comparing the ROI with the potential risks and favorable/unfavorable stakeholder reactions will determine the degree of acceptability of the option. Again, scoring could be done on a 1 to 5 scale.
- •   *Competitive advantage*: The end goal of this analysis, of course, is to choose the option that exhibits the highest potential to deliver a competitive advantage to the sport organization (see Chapter 2). The strategy should generate value (financial or other) for the organization. Ultimately, if the option cannot help the sport organization gain or sustain a competitive advantage, it should be rejected. Based on the final cumulative score of the SFACA analysis, strategic options can be compared, opportunity costs can be considered, and a final, informed strategic choice can be made.

Critical thinking Box 7.1

The Chikara Tennis Academy (CTA)[1] is a small but growing chain of tennis coaching academies in Tokyo, Japan. The organization is seeking to grow and the CEO has narrowed down the strategic options to two choices. She has asked you to use the SFACA set of criteria to evaluate the following growth options available to CTA and to recommend a preferred strategic choice.

1   Develop a new CTA in Osaka as a joint venture (JV) with a local operator; or
2   Grow CTA's current market by adding another SBU to its three existing ones in Tokyo.

The Japanese word *chikara* means "power" in English, and CTA has been operating for three years very successfully using an aggressive growth strategy. It is now a market leader in Tokyo. The existing SBUs are in the premium category and targeted at the high socioeconomic end of the market. CTA has two core competencies that it strives to sustain at all costs: (1) a reputation for innovation and (2) exceptional customer responsiveness. The major investor strongly supports aggressive growth, and organizational goals revolve around improving market position and maintaining a "cutting-edge" reputation. Figure 7.1 provides further information for your evaluation.

SFACA CTA analysis questions

1   Identify the strategic direction and method of both options identified in the case.
2   Work through each criterion in the SFACA analysis to fully evaluate both strategic choices to arrive at a final selection of the best option.
3   Finally, identify and briefly justify your recommendation of the best strategic choice.

FIGURE 7.1 SWOT analysis for Chikara Tennis Academy

Strengths include:	**Weaknesses** include:
Vibrant, innovative organizational culture;	Low operating capital;
Exceptional service reputation;	Chronic inability to pay suppliers on time;
Excellent customer responsiveness;	Poor market knowledge beyond Tokyo.
Good brand awareness in Tokyo;	
Two males who have made the top 100 on the ATP Tour; and three females who have made top 100 on the WTA Tour.	
Strong marketing skills.	
Opportunities include:	**Threats** include:
Prospective Osaka JV partner is keen to reach agreement, and has strong operating capital;	Forecasts predict economic slowdown in Japan with property development costs increasing dramatically;
Asia is now recognized as tennis' biggest growth market;	Continued uncertainty over interest rates and family consumer spending;
Japanese professional tennis players performing particularly well on both men's and women's world tours.	Prospective JV partner in Osaka is third in market, and lags behind competitors in customer responsiveness and service quality.

1 Chikara Tennis Academy is a pseudonym.

Approach 2: strategic options grid

The strategic options grid (see Grundy, 2018) is another way to evaluate your strategic options. Here, your evaluation is based on the degree of fit and attractiveness of your options with the established set of criteria (Grundy, 2018; Morden, 2007). Table 7.2 provides an overview of various criteria that can be used to determine strategic option fit and attractiveness.

You can create a strategic options grid of the criteria versus the set of options and evaluate the option for each criteria, giving a score of 1 = low attractiveness or fit, 2 = medium attractiveness or fit, and 3 = high attractiveness or fit (Grundy, 2018). Table 7.3 provides a template of this strategic options grid, which you can adapt to your needs. Grundy suggests focusing on one option at a time, going through all criteria for the option and determining its overall score before moving on to the next, to minimize bias.

TABLE 7.2   Criteria for evaluating strategic options

	Criteria	Description/example
Attractiveness	Strategic attractiveness	Attractiveness of the chosen market and relative competitive position. This can be determined using drivers of growth, Porter's five forces model, and the external environmental analysis.
	Financial attractiveness	Potential short- and long-term returns for the given option. This can be determined using economic profit/net cash flow relative to investment.
	Implementation difficulty	Sum of difficulty to reach the strategic goals over time through the given option. This includes the length of time to implement the option and the extent of change (structural, human resources, etc.) required to implement the option.
	Uncertainty and risk	Degree of volatility (or lack thereof) of the assumptions made for the given option.
	Stakeholder acceptability	Extent of stakeholder favor, neutrality, or disfavor for the given option.
Fit	With external environment (stable vs. changing)	If the organization finds itself in a volatile or constantly changing market, the chosen strategy will need to be flexible/adaptable to changing conditions without requiring a full, new strategic planning process.
	With critical success factors and key performance indicators	The strategy must help meet the organization's chosen success factors and performance indicators.
	With internal resources, capacity, and capabilities	The organization must have the resources (financial, material, etc.), capacity, and capabilities (see Chapter 2) to undertake the given option. This criterion also includes constraints, such as cost considerations to implement the given option.
	Offer value generation and competitive advantage	The given option must demonstrate the ability to provide value to the organization and gain or sustain a competitive advantage (see Chapters 2 and 3).

Source: Based on information in Grundy (2018) and Morden (2007).

TABLE 7.3   Criteria for evaluating strategic options

Criteria	Option 1	Option 2	Option 3	Option 4
Strategic attractiveness				
Financial attractiveness				
Implementation difficulty				
Uncertainty and risk				
Stakeholder acceptability				
External environment				
Critical success factors and key performance indicators				
Internal resources, capacity, and capabilities				
Source of value generation and competitive advantage				
Other criteria . . .				
Total score:				

Approach 3: portfolio analysis – the Boston Consulting Group (BCG) matrix

In the previous chapter, much of the discussion was around growing the sport organization by implementing various strategic directions and methods for growth. Obviously, as a sport organization grows and diversifies into two or more businesses (or SBUs) making strategic choices becomes more complex. With multiple product lines and/or SBUs, senior management must work out how best to utilize these to boost the sport organization's overall corporate performance.

One means to aid strategy making in a multi-business organization is portfolio analysis, which simply refers to analyzing the corporation's mix of businesses with a view to balancing risk and opportunity across the portfolio. There are a number of portfolio analysis techniques, but the original technique and the one from which most others derived, is the Boston Consulting Group (BCG) Matrix, also known as the Growth/Share Matrix (Henderson, 1970). As the latter name indicates, this tool was designed by Bruce Henderson for BCG to evaluate a company's product/service activity or SBU portfolio and make decisions for long-term growth.

The BCG Matrix is based on two factors: industry growth rate and relative market share. Industry growth rate is decided in relation to whether the SBU's industry is growing quicker than the wider economy (Slack & Parent, 2006). Where growth rates are recorded above the economy's average, they are considered high; and when below the economy's average, they are considered low. Industry growth rate is represented on the vertical axis of the BCG Matrix.

Meanwhile, relative market share is calculated as the size of the focal SBU's market share divided by that of the largest other competitor. Using this calculation, a market share above 1.5 defines the market leader. Diagrammatically, relative market share is represented on the horizontal axis of the BCG Matrix.

The vertical (industry growth rate) and horizontal (relative market share) axes of the BCG Matrix create four quadrants in which all of the sport organization's SBUs can be plotted as Stars, Question Marks (also known as "Problem Children"), Cash Cows, and Dogs. The line dividing areas of high and low relative market share is set at 1.5 times. A product or SBU needs relative market share at or above this level to be considered a Star or Cash Cow; those below 1.5 are considered to have low relative market share and are categorized as Question Marks or Dogs. Figure 7.2 displays an adapted BCG Matrix with the strategic considerations that accompany SBUs placed in each respective quadrant.

As can be seen in Figure 7.3, each SBU or product line is represented by a circle, with the size of the circle signifying the "relative significance of each business unit or product line to the corporation in terms of assets used or sales generated" (Hunger & Wheelen, 2011, p. 97). Stars are positioned as high growth rate and high market share, and are obviously very desirable in a corporate portfolio. However, because they are in high growth markets, they require a high level of investment to maintain market share. When the growth rate of their market decreases, if they maintain market share, Stars can become Cash Cows. Cash Cows generate more profit than they need investment, with the analogy being that they can be "milked" – that is, the profits redirected elsewhere in the organization to fund research and development, marketing, and other functions to support Stars and Question Marks.

In Figure 7.3, we have a BCG Matrix with one SBU in each quadrant of Star, Question Mark, Cash Cow, and Dog. This is an ideal type – we rarely see SBUs categorized so

FIGURE 7.2   BCG Matrix strategic choice considerations

Relative Market Share

		HIGH	LOW
Market Growth Rate	**HIGH**	**Stars** Although high investments are required, they are market leaders in high growth markets and may provide higher ROI than other SBUs. Recommendation: Build, develop, and invest in maintaining market leadership.	**Question Marks (Problem Children)** Require high investments to increase market share to become Stars, but uncertainty reigns. Careful analysis is warranted. High growth market is attractive. Recommendation: Carefully build; invest "experimental" funds to see if SBU can become a Star.
	LOW	**Cash Cows** Typically mature products/services in mature markets that generate high ROI with low investment. Recommendation: Hold and harvest; "milk the cow" as long as it can survive and use capital to invest in Stars or Question Marks.	**Dogs** These are a drain on resources with market share in low growth market. Recommendation: Divest and redirect capital to Stars and Question Marks (unless servicing a lucrative niche market, in which case, treat same as Cash Cow due to low growth market).

FIGURE 7.3   Portfolio analysis – the BCG Matrix

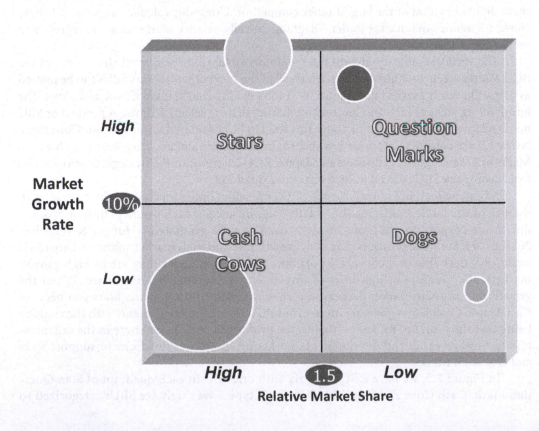

neatly in the real world! But for the sake of developing our understanding of portfolio analysis, let's explore this figure. The sport organization depicted in Figure 7.3 would be advised to divest themselves of their Dog SBU and use any capital generated to support growth in their Star and Question Mark SBUs. SBUs that fit the Question Mark category are often in new, high growth markets with a large number of competitors, so we may need to invest heavily in marketing and competency development to "shake out" competitors, create loyal customers, increase our market share, and hopefully, become a Star. Star SBUs may be market leaders, but again, they are in high growth markets with significant competition – so here too, we need to invest heavily to maintain market leadership and to survive the inevitable shake-out of competitors as market growth eventually slows. Meanwhile, Cash Cows may be market leaders (or close to) but exist in low growth markets. This makes heavy investment in further marketing somewhat pointless. In this case, we would employ a strategy of consolidation and use the high profits generated to fuel our growth in Star and Question Mark SBUs.

Question Marks are also known as Problem Children because although they are in high growth markets, they do not yet have high relative market share, at which point they would become a Star. Conversely, if a Question Mark does not gain market share and its industry growth rate slows, it can potentially become a Dog – the least attractive type of business, with low relative market share and low growth rate. It was originally thought that the only course of action for Dogs was divestiture, so that capital could be redirected to high-performing Stars or budding Question Marks. However, this is not necessarily the case – some organizations may have strategic reasons for keeping a Dog in their portfolio when, for example, it completes a product line, or it fills an attractive industry niche without being too much of a drain on overall corporate resources.

The BCG Matrix, with its reliance on only two indicators – relative market share and industry growth rate – has been criticized for being too simplistic. Other, more complex tools such as the General Electric Business Screen take into account a greater number of indicators, but predictably, they require commensurably far more data input and analyses. Thus, the simplicity of the BCG Matrix is both its strength and a source of criticism.

Nevertheless, the BCG Matrix can help senior managers make strategic choices regarding resource allocation and cash flow as well as to plan strategy around stability, acquisition, and divestiture. The idea is to maintain a balance of risk and opportunity in the overall corporate portfolio such that there are Cash Cows funding exciting opportunities in Stars and Question Marks and, only if resources allow, there may be a Dog servicing a lucrative niche market. With this balance of opportunity and risk, "the firm can be self-sufficient in cash and always work to harvest mature products in declining industries to support new ones in growing industries" (Hunger & Wheelen, 2011, p. 99).

Although, like approaches 1 and 2 noted above, the BCG Matrix was developed for organizations outside the sport industry, it can be used as is or adapted for sport organizations. Figure 7.4 provides an example of how the BCG approach can be adapted for sport organizations undertaking strategic planning (LeBlanc, 2018).

Clegg et al. (2017) maintain that taking a portfolio approach is a key consideration in approaching the future of strategy. They state that "the focus is on competitive advantage but such advantage never lasts long; rather than a single strategy that unfolds, a portfolio of competitive opportunities should be continuously under revision in terms of goals and environments" (Clegg et al., 2017, p. 495).

FIGURE 7.4   Adapting the BCG Matrix

Big Prize (High ROI)

	Quick Wins	Big Wins that Differentiate	
Easy to Do	Easy implementation and highly positive impact = go for it!	Implementation difficulty and high cost means you may only be able to pick one of these strategies to undertake.	**Hard to Do**
Cheap To Do	**Small Wins**	**Time Wasters**	**Expensive to Do**
	Easy but low impact = could be politically good to have some small wins, but may be rejected if resources are limited.	Low ROI and high cost = reject this strategy.	

Small Prize (Low ROI)

Critical thinking Box 7.2

You have been asked to conduct a portfolio analysis for *South East Fitness*[1] and present the results of your analysis in the form a BCG Matrix, with recommendations, to your board of directors. Relevant data for each of South East Fitness' SBUs are presented in Table 7.4.

Complete the matrix

- Examine the data in Table 7.4.
- Draw two axes and label them (as explained above).
- For the vertical axis (Market Growth Rate), the midpoint is 10%.
- For the horizontal axis (Relative Market Share), the division between Low and High is 1.5x.
- Calculate the relative market share for each SBU (SBU's sales relative to its next biggest competitor).
- Mark the spot on the matrix where each SBU should be placed, roughly calculating the size of the circle that represents each SBU according to its sales provided in Table 7.4.

   Based on the outcome of your evaluation process, you are now in a position to select the best strategy for your sport organization to help you gain or sustain a competitive advantage.

TABLE 7.4   BCG Matrix data for South East Fitness

South East Fitness SBU:	Number of competitors	Market growth rate (%)	$M sales	$M sales of industry leader	Relative market share
Shenzhen	20	15	1.0	1.4	1/1.4 = 0.71
Mumbai	18	20	4.2	4.2	
Toronto	3	7	4	5	
Paris	4	4	6.6	4.0	
Brisbane	4	4	0.7	3.0	

(Relative market share for Shenzhen has been done for you.)

1 South East Fitness is a pseudonym.

Summary

Strategy evaluation and selection focuses on evaluating high-level strategic options for the overall sport organization and its SBUs, products/services, and activities. After gathering all relevant information through a SWOT analysis and building a list of potential strategic options, the task then is to evaluate each option. It is important to use consistent criteria for all options.

In this chapter, we presented six imperatives that non-profit sport organizations can use to evaluate their program attractiveness (fundability, client base size, volunteer appeal, and support group appeal) and competitive position (equipment costs and affiliation fees) (Thibault et al., 1993).

However, sport organizations can also draw from and adapt a variety of tools created for non-sport organizations: (1) the suitability-feasibility-acceptability-competitive advantage approach, (2) the strategic options grid, and (3) portfolio analysis techniques such as the Boston Consulting Group (BCG) Matrix.

Once you have picked a set of criteria and overall strategy evaluation approach, you can evaluate each strategic option. We suggest taking one option at a time and evaluating it across the set of criteria before moving on to the other options. The outcome of this evaluation will direct you to the best possible strategy option for your sport organization to provide for the best chance of gaining or sustaining competitive advantage.

CLOSING CASE: STRATEGY EVALUATION AND SELECTION IN THE GOLF INDUSTRY – THE CASE OF THE CLUBLINK CORPORATION (By Eric L. Lachance)

The golf industry focuses on offering a service and leisure experience to its members. Within this industry, the traditional strategy has been to offer membership and privileges at only a single golf club. In fact, semi-private and private golf clubs often rely on current members to bring in new members, such as their children, business partners, or friends. The changing landscape of the golf industry in the 1990s called for a different approach given the growing participation rate in which "golf [had] replaced hockey as the number one activity reported in 1998" (Sport Canada, 2000, p. 22).

John Simmonds is the son of a prominent family who runs a business known as A. C. Simmonds and Sons Inc. The business specializes in the acquisition of businesses for expansion and development in international food, waste management, renewable energy, and leisure (Jermyn, 2014). Mr. Simmonds recognized this change in the golf industry, and proceeded to evaluate the industry in terms of its current and new participants as well as their demands. For instance, younger individuals who weren't familiar with the sport beforehand began to participate. These individuals wanted the ability to play a variety of courses but not have the financial strain of paying daily greens fees. In turn, John Simmonds also recognized the inability for private clubs to promote a welcoming and positive environment for businesses, such as meetings, corporate events, and entertaining guests.

Following his evaluation of the golf industry, John Simmonds determined possible options, including purchasing a variety of golf courses, purchasing land and building new golf courses, the location of golf courses and of purchased land (i.e., near major highways), membership structure, and additional privileges.

Ultimately, John Simmonds chose to first purchase a struggling golf club in 1989 in the Greater Toronto Area (GTA) in the province of Ontario, Canada. Within a few years, he proceeded to turn around Cherry Downs Golf Club by improving food and beverage practices and introducing a new computerized billing system (Gillespie, 2000). Following this successful turnaround, Mr. Simmonds wanted to implement two strategies, developed and aimed at meeting the demands of the golf industry: reciprocal play and clustering.

First, reciprocal play enabled golfers to pay membership fees at one golf course but have the ability to play a range of golf courses. This led to the development of what would eventually be known as ClubLink's slogan: one membership, more golf (ClubLink, n.d.a). Next, a clustering strategy was introduced in relation to reciprocal play, as purchased golf courses or land would be located close to one another (e.g., the same geographical region) and major highways (e.g., the 401 series highway) or metropolitan areas (e.g., GTA).

With the introduction of these two strategic concepts, ClubLink was born and John Simmonds proceeded to purchase three golf courses in 1993: King Valley Golf Club, Heron Point Golf Links, and Emerald Hills Golf Club. As such, ClubLink now officially owned and operated four golf courses within the GTA.

Since the corporation's inception in 1993, ClubLink continued to purchase struggling golf courses and various parts of land in the GTA and the nearby Muskoka region, known as cottage country. For instance, ClubLink purchased Glen Abbey Golf Club in 1999, which has hosted ten RBC Canadian Opens since then, and built three new golf courses in the Muskoka region during the late 1990s: the Lake Joseph Club, Rocky Crest Golf Club, and Grandview Golf Club.

During the early 2000s, ClubLink also entered the golf market in the nation's capital, Ottawa, with the purchase of three golf clubs (GreyHawk Golf Club, Kanata Golf and Country Club, and Club de Golf Hautes Plaines), and two golf clubs across the river in the province of Québec (Val des Lacs Golf Club and Golf Le Maître de Mont-Tremblant). Between 2003 and 2010, ClubLink's expansion in Ontario and Québec slowed down as only eight golf clubs were purchased or built.

ClubLink began expanding into the United States in 2010, with the purchase of nine golf clubs in Florida. ClubLink's newest addition occurred in 2014 with the purchase of Hidden Lake Golf Club. Today, ClubLink operates 41 golf courses in Canada and the United States and is known as the largest golf operator in Canada (ClubLink, n.d.b).

However, the golf industry is changing again as stakeholders, such as golfers, golf operators (e.g., board of directors, golf management staff, and superintendents), local communities, and media outlets, have discussed the decline in participation (Sorensen, 2014). This has resulted in golf club closures or golf clubs being sold for redevelopment.

ClubLink is no stranger to these industry changes, as it has been attempting to redevelop Glen Abbey Golf Club in order to build 3,222 residential units, 69,000 square feet of commercial and retail space, and 107,000 square feet of office space (Lea, 2019). Furthermore, ClubLink has recently announced a partnership with Minto Communities and Richcraft Homes to redevelop Kanata Golf and Country Club in the Ottawa region (ClubLink, 2018; Gibbons, 2018).

Although ClubLink and other golf operators have begun to sell golf courses to developers, local communities have shared their outrage in the media and through forums with local government or committees. For instance, individuals from the Oakville community challenged their local government to name Glen Abbey Golf Club as a cultural heritage site, which was eventually granted in 2017 under the Ontario Heritage Act (Lea, 2019). Furthermore, communities surrounding the Kanata Golf and Country Club have been outraged with the decision to redevelop the golf club as they will lose their valuable green spaces, and suffer financial losses because many homeowners have paid higher taxes and premiums to be near the golf club (Gibbons, 2018).

Chapter review questions

1   Pick a sport organization you know and evaluate it using Thibault et al.'s (1993) seven imperatives.
2   Looking specifically at the SFACA approach, if a particular strategic choice is suitable and feasible, how and why could it possibly be unacceptable? Try to use real-world examples in explaining your answer.
3   Using the same sport organization from Question 1, evaluate it using one of the other approaches provided in this chapter.
4   What is the overall aim of portfolio analysis?
5   As you now know, portfolio analysis relies upon the availability and accurate analysis of data relating to market share and industry growth rates. Not all sport organizations have the capacity to generate that sort of data themselves. So, with a partner, identify the types of resources that are available to managers, both for free and paid, to access the type of data they need for accurate portfolio analyses.
6   With a partner, identify a well-known sport conglomerate. Discuss the SBUs that make up that conglomerate. Now, using as much actual evidence relating to market share and growth rates as you can find, try to work how you might categorize these SBUs as Stars, Question Marks, Cash Cows, or Dogs. At the end of your analysis, discuss whether your chosen organization has a good mix of risk and opportunity in its corporate portfolio. What would be your advice to senior executives around strategic choices for the ongoing management of their corporate portfolio?
7   From the closing case, what strategic approach could be applied by ClubLink to evaluate the current golf industry environment and select an appropriate strategy? What would you do if you were John Simmonds?
8   Based on your answers above, and considering the turbulent state of the golf industry, what do you foresee as being the future of this corporation?

Additional resources

- Websites
  - How to evaluate corporate strategy: https://hbr.org/1963/07/how-to-evaluate-corporate-strategy
  - BCG's portfolio x-ray: www.bcg.com/capabilities/strategy/portfolio-xray.aspx
- Videos
  - Strategy evaluation: definition, methods, and tools: https://study.com/academy/lesson/strategy-evaluation-definition-methods-tools.html

o   Evaluating business strategy: suitability, feasibility, and acceptability: https://
     study.com/academy/lesson/evaluating-business-strategy-suitability-feasibility-
     acceptability.html
- Books/articles
  o Barksdale, H. C., & Harris, C. E. (1982). Portfolio analysis and the product
     life cycle. *Long Range Planning*, *15*(6), 74–83. https://doi.org/10.1016/0024-
     6301(82)90010-3
  o Johnson, G., & Scholes, K. (2002). *Exploring Corporate Strategy* (6th ed.). London:
     Prentice Hall.
  o Miles, R. E., & Snow, C. C. (1978). *Organizational strategy, structure, and process*.
     New York: McGraw-Hill.
  o Suarez-Gonzalez, I. (2001). Downsizing strategy: Does it really improve organizational
     performance? *International Journal of Management*, *18*(3), 301–307.

References

Clegg, S. R., Schweitzer, J., Whittle, A. & Pistelis, C. (2017). *Strategy: Theory and practice* (2nd Ed.). Los Angeles: Sage.

ClubLink Corporation. (2018, December 14). *ClubLink initiates planning for the redevelopment of Kanata golf lands* [Press release]. Retrieved from www.newswire.ca/news-releases/clublink-initiates-planning-for-the-redevelopment-of-kanata-golf-lands-702776132.html

ClubLink Corporation. (n.d.a). *About us*. Retrieved from https://clublink.ca/about/

ClubLink Corporation. (n.d.b). *Our story*. Retrieved from https://clublink.ca/about/our-story/

De Bosscher, V., De Knop, P., van Bottenburg, M., & Shibli, S. (2006). A conceptual framework for analysing sports factors leading to international sporting success. *European Sport Management Quarterly*, 6, 185–215.

Evans, N., Campbell, D., & Stonehouse, G. (2003). *Strategic management for travel and tourism*. London: Routledge.

Gibbons, R. (2018, December 17). Is ClubLink's Kanata proposal a bit of good green space spoiled? *Ottawa Sun*. Retrieved from https://ottawasun.com/news/local-news/gibbons-is-clublinks-kanata-proposal-but-good-green-space-spoiled

Gillespie, C. (2000, July 28). Making the green. *The Globe and Mail*. Retrieved from www.theglobeandmail.com/report-on-business/rob-magazine/making-the-green/article25467854/

Grundy, T. (2018). *Dynamic competitive strategy: Turning strategy upside down*. London: Routledge.

Henderson, B. (1970). *The product portfolio*. Retrieved June 3, 2018 from www.bcg.com/publications/1970/strategy-the-product-portfolio.aspx

Hubbard, G., Rice, J., & Galvin, P. (2015). *Strategic management: Thinking, analysis, action* (5th ed.). Melbourne, Australia: Pearson Australia.

Hunger, J. D., & Wheelen, T. L. (2011). *Essentials of strategic management* (5th Ed.). Upper Saddle River, NJ: Pearson.

International Olympic Committee. (n.d.). *Olympic-results*. Retrieved from www.olympic.org/olympic-results

Jermyn, D. (2014, July 18). ClubLink co-founder is obsessed with buying businesses. *The Globe and Mail*. Retrieved from www.theglobeandmail.com/report-on-business/small-business/sb-growth/club-link-founder-success-stories/article19658942/

Lea, D. (2019, January 8). ClubLink takes aim at Oakville's Glen Abbey Golf Course heritage designation. *Toronto Star*. Retrieved from www.thestar.com/news/gta/2019/01/08/clublink-takes-aim-at-oakvilles-glen-abbey-golf-course-heritage-designation.html

LeBlanc, J. (2018, May 16). *From vision to action, Creating your strategic blueprint for success* [webinar]. Ottawa, Canada: Ottawa Sport Council. Retrieved from http://sportottawa.ca/webinars/from-vision-to-action-creating-your-strategic-blueprint-for-success/

Morden, T. (2007). *Principles of strategic management* (3rd ed.). London: Routledge.

Own the Podium. (2017). *Annual report 2016–2017*. Ottawa: Own the Podium.

Robinson, P. (2009). *Jamaican athletics: A model for 2012 and the world*. London: BlackAmber.

Slack, T. & Parent, M. M. (2006). *Understanding sport organizations: The application of organization theory* (2nd Ed.). Champaign, IL: Human Kinetics.

Sorensen, C. (2014, July 4). Why Canadian golf is dying. *MacLean's*. Retrieved from www.macleans.ca/economy/business/the-end-of-golf/

Sport Canada. (2000). *Sport participation in Canada: 1998 report*. Ottawa, ON: Department of Canadian Heritage. Retrieved from http://publications.gc.ca/collections/Collection/CH24-1-2000-1E.pdf

Thibault, L., Slack, T., & Hinings, C. R. (1993). A framework for the analysis of strategy in nonprofit sport organizations. *Journal of Sport Management, 7*, 25–43.

Toomer, R. (2015). Jamaica. *International Journal of Sport Policy and Politics, 7*(3), 457–471.

8 Strategy implementation and organizational change

OPENING CASE: "GET OFF THE BUS": BAD CHANGE
MANAGEMENT PROCESSES IN THE NHL AND
THE FLORIDA PANTHERS
(By Ashley Thompson and Eric L. Lachance)

Professional sport teams are notorious for making changes to their coaching staff during times of poor team performance. Between 2010 and 2018, the National Hockey League (NHL) saw 34 in-season coaching changes (Leahy, 2018; Servalli, 2018). Despite existing research that highlights how coaching changes do not result in an immediate increase in team performance (e.g., Besters, van Ours, & van Tuijl, 2016; Esteve, Di Lorenzo, Inglés, & Puig, 2011; Flint, Plumley, & Wilson, 2014), NHL teams – and professional sport teams in general – continue to replace head coaches in the hope of better team performance. There is no better example of this than the NHL's Florida Panthers.

Between 2012 and 2018, the Panthers struggled to find a winning formula. In the 2012–2013 and 2013–2014 seasons, the team finished at the bottom of the league's overall standings, prompting the hiring of head coach, Gerard Gallant, in the 2014 post-season (Reynolds, 2014). In his first season as the Panthers' head coach, Gallant helped the team move up the standings to a 20th overall finish. In the following 2015–2016 season, under Gallant's leadership, the team had a breakout season, finishing 1st overall in their division (7th in the league), setting the team record for most wins (47), and most points in the regular season (103). As a result of their regular season success, the Panthers clinched their first playoff spot in four years.

Following their breakout year, the Panthers' poor performance returned early in the 2016–2017 season. On November 27, 2016, after the Panthers blew a 2–0 lead against the Carolina Hurricanes, which dropped their record to a mediocre 11–10–1, Gallant was fired (Cotsonika, 2016). The firing was called the worst in NHL history (Boylen, 2016), after pictures of Gallant taking a taxi home with luggage in hand flooded social media (The Associated Press, 2016). Despite the firing, the Panthers continued to underperform in the 2016–2017 and 2017–2018 seasons, finishing sixth in their division and 23rd overall in the league's standings.

In this case, the Panthers' change management seemed questionable in two ways: (1) the way in which Gallant was fired and (2) how the organization failed to realize that the team's performance was perhaps not solely related to the head coach, as Gallant went on to coach the Las Vegas Golden Knights to a Stanley Cup final in the team's first expansion year (The Associated Press, 2017). The latter point highlights a broader change management issue in professional sport, where there exists a belief that poor performance can be resolved through the firing of coaches, despite research disproving these beliefs (e.g., Besters et al., 2016; Esteve et al., 2011; Flint et al., 2014).

Introduction

Although you will have done significant work by now in analyzing your internal and external environments (Chapters 2 and 3), developed potential strategic options and evaluated your selections (Chapters 3 through 7), and even chosen the best strategic option to help your organization gain or sustain a competitive advantage (Chapter 7), this is only half the work.

You now need to implement that strategy. You need to transform your strategic plan into action. This means change is coming to your organization. Implementing a strategy is not easy and may have negative consequences. As a manager, you will need to pay careful attention to the strategy's implementation, not the least of which because people will likely have an automatic resistance to any suggested changes brought to them. This chapter will help you understand change and how you can successfully implement your strategy and help your sport organization gain or sustain a competitive advantage. We review the concept of change, then move to examining entrepreneurship, innovation and types of change, and end with organizational structural and design considerations. First, however, we provide basic tools for turning your chosen strategy into action.

Implementing your chosen strategy

It is all well and good to have a good understanding of which strategy will help you gain or sustain a competitive advantage, but the reality is that the strategy won't magically provide desired outcomes. It needs to be implemented properly.

So far, we've covered why a (new) strategy is needed, such as to gain a competitive advantage, to grow, or to survive, and what the strategy is. But we are missing the how, the who, and the when. This is the core of strategy implementation, a step sometimes forgotten by sport organizations and even governments. National governments, for example, are known to develop policies (or strategies in public administration speak), only to have them sit on the proverbial shelf and never be implemented.

Your overall strategy can be broken down into more specific objectives. Each of these objectives will have one or more tactics associated with it. But in order for the tactic to happen, you will need to identify who is responsible for undertaking that tactic and meeting that objective, with what resources, and by when. Table 8.1 provides a template you can use to help develop strategy implementation.

TABLE 8.1 Strategy implementation template

Overall goal/strategy				
Specific objectives	Tactic	Who is responsible	Timeline	Resources (financial, material, time, human)
Objective 1				
Objective 2				
...				

Once you complete this step, you should create benchmarks or indicators to know if you are on the right track. In Chapter 9, we address strategic control systems. An effective strategic control system provides management with information on past strategy implementations (feedback mechanisms), how current implementations are faring (concurrent mechanisms), and what future issues should be considered (feedforward mechanisms). Complementing strategic control, however, Chappelet (2005) suggests following the SPORTS acronym when developing benchmarks and indicators of implementation success:

- Specific
- Pertinent
- Objective
- Representative
- Transparent
- Simple.

Like the previous step, you should identify who will measure and keep track of the progress. Now that you have the tools to implement your strategy, you need to be aware of the impact its implementation will have on the organization and its members. This is where a well-conceived strategic control system (see Chapter 9) comes in. Based on the information generated through your strategic control system, some level of organizational change will be necessary, as we will see in the remaining sections of this chapter.

Defining change

There is an interesting paradox in organizations. Generally, managers want their organizations to be stable, to keep things the same; this tendency is called inertia and speaks to management's desire for predictability. Yet in order to be competitive, to gain and sustain a competitive advantage, organizations need to innovate and change (Peters, 1990). They need to stand out. Some sport organizations that operate in a fluctuating or unstable environment need to change if only to survive. In sport event organizing committees, for example, change is the only constant.

According to Welty Peachey and Bruening (2011, p. 202), change is a "planned or unplanned response to external or internal pressures and forces which can be developmental (small-scale), transitional (mid-level range) or transformational (large-scale) in nature." Change relates to "a difference in form, quality, or state over time in an organizational entity" (Poole & Van de Ven, 2004, p. xi).

There are four main areas where change occurs in organizations (Slack & Parent, 2006):

- *People*: This type of change relates to employee turnover but also to modifying the way individuals think, act and/or interact. A new leader would be an example of people-related change.
- *Structures and systems*: This type of change involves modifying the organization's division of labor, roles and responsibilities, departments, and reporting, operating, and/or control systems. Moving to a flat structure by removing middle management would be an example of structure-related change, while implementing a strategic plan could be an example of a system-related change.
- *Technology*: This type of change includes not only the introduction of new technologies (e.g., wearable sport performance tracking devices, augmented and

virtual reality applications, cloud computing, digital media) but also modifications to the organization's production processes, the ways it operates, and the materials and equipment it uses. A sport organization moving to a paperless registration system would be an example of technology-related change.

- *Products and services*: This type of change refers to the addition, expansion, reduction, or elimination of an organization's product and/or service portfolio. A sport organization adding a new sportswear line would be an example of a product-related change, while another organization cutting out grassroots sport programs to focus only on elite-level programs would be an example of a service-related change.

Although we generally focus on organizational change in this chapter, it is important to be aware of two related concepts – entrepreneurship and innovation – before we delve deeper into the types and sources of change. Understanding entrepreneurship and innovation is important when undertaking strategic change to gain or sustain a competitive advantage.

Critical thinking Box 8.1

Investigate organizational change that has taken place within an international federation, such as the IOC, the Fédèration Internationale de Natation (FINA), or FIFA. Can you find specific details on the changes that were implemented in the four categories listed above? Were the changes a response to internal or external pressures? Did the changes improve the competitive advantage of the organization?

Entrepreneurship

Rumelt (1987) defined entrepreneurship in terms of the creation of new businesses, businesses that are not exact duplicates of existing businesses (i.e., that have an element of novelty to them). The role of the entrepreneur is to gather, evaluate, and use the information; the entrepreneur is the instrument that directs the competitive process to its fruition (Jacobson, 1992). The entrepreneur "undertakes risk and innovation for the purpose of economic benefit in business transactions" (Byers, Slack, & Parent, 2012, p. 60). Knowledge is critical. "Opportunities in profit are rooted in private information, ambiguity, special instructions, and entrepreneurial insights. . . . [If] a phenomenon is understood well enough to model it, it is too late to make money from it" (Jacobson, 1992, p. 803).

Economic development occurs when firms engage in entrepreneurial activities (Schumpeter, 1950; Jacobson, 1992). The competition that counts is the competition from the

> new commodity, the new technology, the new source of supply, the new type of organization . . . competition which commands a decisive cost or quality advantage and which strikes not at the margins of the profits and the outputs of the existing firms but at their foundations and their very lives.
>
> (Schumpeter, 1950, p. 4112)

Finally, entrepreneurship is facilitated by management's ability to acquire resources and manage (large) projects (Rumelt, 1987).

Innovation

The concepts of change and innovation are often used interchangeably. However, there is a distinction. A change is more about the process: it can be new or not. In contrast, an innovation must be new to the organization (Hoeber & Hoeber, 2012). An organizational innovation refers to the adoption of an "internally generated or purchased device, system, policy, program, process, product, or service that is new to the adopting organization" (Damanpour, 1992, p. 556). Innovation is an important concept in our discussion on strategy implementation, as it is meant to help improve not only the organization's performance, generally speaking, but it is also a source for gaining or sustaining a competitive advantage (Damanpour, 1992; Hoeber & Hoeber, 2012), as we will see below.

Types of change

There are two basic types of changes: strategic and operational. Strategic change is a change that flows from high-level decisions and affects the whole organization, its strategic business units/departments, and their positioning in terms of their products/services and competitors. Operational change is usually seen at lower levels of the organization.

Strategic change is a complex, situation-dependent, continuous process that includes three dimensions to consider:

- *Context*: both internal and external resources, capabilities, culture, and politics;
- *Content*: the assessment and choice of products/markets, objectives and assumptions, targets and evaluation; and,
- *Process*: involving change managers, considering different models of change, formulations and implementation patterns, and considering these patterns over time.
   (Pettigrew, 1973, 1985; Pettigrew & Whipp, 1991)

Thus each strategic change initiative will be unique. There is no place for a "cookie-cutter" approach. However, as you will see in this chapter and the next, there are key tools and competencies that will serve you well when it comes time to implement a strategy and the organizational change it precipitates.

Strategic change can be radical or convergent, evolutionary or revolutionary. *Radical change*, also known as frame bending or divergent change, refers to "busting loose" from an existing orientation leading to deep organizational transformation, whereas *convergent change* refers to an organization fine-tuning its existing orientation (Greenwood & Hinings, 1988, 1996). *Evolutionary change* is a change that occurs slowly, gradually, whereas *revolutionary change* is a change that occurs swiftly and affects most or all parts of the organization simultaneously (Greenwood & Hinings, 1988, 1996).

Radical and revolutionary changes are of particular interest here. Schumpeter (1950) argued that each innovation is destroyed and replaced by another innovation, a process called "creative destruction." Essentially, the equilibrium is disrupted or punctuated to start the process over again. As new information and opportunities arise all the time, the marketplace continually changes. The entrepreneur will stay on top, sometimes by chance, but mainly through having new, more or better information than others in order to discover a given innovation. In our knowledge economy, where increasing technical expertise speeds up the pace of doing business, embracing change is the key to survival and to gaining/sustaining a competitive advantage (Parent, 2001).

Sources of change

Entrepreneurial managers are alert to their environment and use their creativity and knowledge to find appropriate markets (Kirzner, 1973). From an internal perspective, new leadership dominates sources of internal change, as can employee turnover. Just look at what often happens when a team hires a new coach. However, research has shown that changes mainly stem from external sources, more so than internal ones, with new technology being a recently popular source of change (Barley, 1986; Bartunek, 1984). So your SWOT analysis (see Chapters 2 and 3), and especially the external environment's opportunities and threats, become important to identify areas of potential changes.

Typical factors that can lead to organizational change include, for example, geography, a disadvantaged position as compared to competitors, regulatory requirements/legislation, norms/values, and non-local models of change (D'Aunno, Succi, & Alexander, 2000). Regulatory agencies, such as the state, professional boards, associations, and commissions, are particularly important; they can be seen as an external pressure that precipitates change but also as a key player in the change process, as they allow for the formulation, diffusion, reproduction, and legitimization of the innovation in question (Greenwood, Suddaby, & Hinings, 2002). Policy changes, particularly around funding, by state or national sport organizations, for instance, can have a domino effect on lower-level sport organizations as they seek to (re)position and sometimes (re)structure themselves in order to access valuable resources (e.g., provincial and local sport organizations; Legg, Snelgrove, & Wood, 2016).

In a sport context, Welty Peachey and Bruening (2011) found that competitive pressures from conference affiliation, poor economic environment, and external stakeholders (e.g., parents and alumni) were major catalysts for organizational change in athletic departments. In turn, regulatory changes by international sport federations impact not only national sport organizations but also players and managers, as was the case in the International Rugby Football Board's decision to repeal its amateur principles and its impact on the Queensland Rugby Union, as well as its players and managers, who subsequently felt pressure to professionalize (Skinner, Stewart, & Edwards, 2004).

Finally, changes in the legal environment (see Chapter 3) in Canada for all national not-for-profit organizations, including national sport organizations, have significantly affected how these national sport organizations can be governed, resulting in sweeping structural and people-based changes: people-based changes included new hires (new leaders, gender diversity; see Chapter 4) and changing the internal culture (see Chapter 2), while structure-based changes included moving from an operational to a governance board and even a full restructuring of the organization's structure and complexity (see Parent, Naraine, & Hoye, 2018). As we have already discussed people-based aspects, we now review how structural aspects play a part in the process of strategy implementation and organizational change.

◼ Organizational structure and design considerations

There is a long-standing debate on the strategy-structure relationship (cf. Amburgey & Dacin, 1994; Chandler, 1962; Rumelt, 1987) that asks the question, which comes first: strategy or structure? Does structure follow strategy, or does strategy follow structure? Suffice to say, strategy and structure go hand in hand. Your organization's structure affects your strategic options, and your strategy can be a source of change for inside the organization, as we noted earlier. But what do we mean by organizational structure? Three key concepts are important here: complexity, formalization, and centralization (Pugh & Hickson, 1976; Pugh, Hickson, Hinings, & Turner, 1968).

Complexity

The larger the organization, the more differentiated and, therefore, complex it is (Pugh & Hickson, 1976; Pugh et al., 1968). Differentiation, in this sense, can occur in three ways:

- *Horizontal differentiation*: Just like an American football team will have offensive, defensive, and special teams as well as coaching staff, equipment staff, support staff, marketing staff, ticketing staff, and so forth, a sport organization will have different departments such as finance and administration, marketing and communications, research and development, and so on. The more complex the organization, the more individuals will have specialized tasks and the more departments there will be. This is what we call:
  - *Specialization*: Separating people based on task/function (e.g., marketing, finance, and communications) or skills/training (e.g., coaches, kinesiologists, physiotherapists, and nutritionists);
  - *Departmentalization*: Separating groups of individuals by product/service (e.g., athletic shoes, lifestyle clothing, and food); function (e.g., marketing, legal, communications, finance and administration, and research and development); or geography (e.g., North America, Europe, Africa, and Asia).

  As we discussed in Chapter 3, depending on the nature of the environment, there may also be a need to have departments that deal specifically with certain parts of the environment or stakeholders in order to respond appropriately and, hopefully, proactively (Lawrence & Lorsch, 1967).
- *Vertical differentiation*: This is simply the number of hierarchical levels in an organization. For example, a local family-owned sporting goods store may have the owner as the top level and then a select number of employees reporting directly to her, thus meaning only two hierarchical levels – also known as a flat structure (i.e., fewer than three levels). In contrast, an organizing committee for an Olympic Games will have volunteers at the lowest level, then coordinators, managers, directors, vice presidents, executive/senior vice presidents, chief executive officer (CEO), and a board of directors at the top, thus meaning upwards of eight levels – also known as a tall structure.
- *Spatial differentiation*: This differentiation refers to the geographical differentiation of an organization. We traditionally expect a sport organization to be located in one place. However, some organizations may have two or more headquarters or locations where they operate. For example, the Canadian Olympic Committee used to operate only out of Ottawa (Ontario), the nation's capital. However, the organization's president opted to split the headquarters between Toronto (Ontario) and Montreal (Quebec), with a six-hour drive difference between the two locations. This made the organization more spatially differentiated.

Formalization

The second key concept is formalization, which refers to the extent to which procedures, rules, policies, communications, and/or activities are written down (Pugh & Hickson, 1976;

Pugh et al., 1968). Formalization is not to be confused with standardization, which refers to the degree to which there are informally established ways of doing or procedures. For example, an organization's leadership may have a way it likes to approach potential sponsors; if it isn't written down, this approach relates to standardization. If, however, the approach is written down, then the approach is formalized.

As you may have guessed, formalization helps when there is staff turnover. Formalization is also an indication of an organization's professionalization. Increasingly, societal and government expectations regarding good governance, as well as rules and laws, create expectations for sport organizations that they will formalize their procedures and activities, including formalizing their strategic plans (Parent et al., 2018). Risk management and mitigation is another area in sport where formalized policies and procedures are absolutely critical to organizational survival.

However, too much formalization can also be unnecessarily restrictive and may stifle creativity and innovation. For example, Kelly, Fairley, and O'Brien (2019) investigate how formalized regulations of the International Cricket Council (ICC) influenced how two host nations leveraged the ICC Cricket World Cup. Results revealed that while leveraging was still possible, the highly formalized hosting rights actually limited host countries' ability to generate benefits from hosting.

Centralization

The third key concept is centralization. Centralization refers to the "locus of authority to make decisions affecting the organization" (Pugh et al., 1968, p. 76). The higher up in the organization the "last" person or group is that makes such decisions, the more centralized the organization. For instance, decisions perceived to have potentially less significant impact across the organization can be pushed down the hierarchy, such as more operational decisions regarding when to buy more stationery. In contrast, a decision to liquidate assets or to expand into a new territory is likely a more centralized process.

Depending on the structural design of the organization, you will see differences in centralization or decentralization. Larger organizations tend to push decision-making down the hierarchy; however, this can be modified in times of change or increased risk/uncertainty. Let's look at organizational design to see how these concepts can be integrated.

Organizational design

Different authors have developed various ways to combine complexity, formalization, and centralization to create organizational designs. Henry Mintzberg (1979, 1984) examined for-profit organizations and proposed a typology of seven organizational designs:

- *The simple structure or entrepreneurial organization* is focused on the strategic apex (i.e., its owners/leaders) and has a flat structure – think the family-owned local sporting goods store. In such an organization, we expect to see less formalization and more centralization.
- *The machine bureaucracy* is focused on standardizing work through its technostructure (e.g., analysts, IT specialists). This is usually a larger organization that wants to produce standard products/services – think factories and government – which means higher formalization and often decentralization of decision-making.

- *The divisionalized form* is focused on standard outputs and run by the middle line, that is, the heads of divisions. These are usually very large (often multinational) organizations, so each division can be its own legally incorporated organization and have its own design. Complexity is high here. For example, Nike has its world headquarters in the United States (Beaverton, Oregon), but its various divisions (e.g., Nike Canada, Nike Europe, Nike China) have their own corporate headquarters in their respective geographies, and each division is run by its own executives and coordinates with Nike world headquarters. Nike's affiliate brands (i.e., Converse, Hurley, and Jordan) are also run in the same manner (Nike, 2018).
- *The professional bureaucracy* is focused on its operating core composed of professionals. The professionals' training means a standardization of skills but often means less formalization and fewer hierarchical levels – think a sport medicine clinic.
- *The adhocracy or innovative organization*, as the name suggests, is focused on research and development, with the support staff being present for mutual adjustments. This organization fits particularly well in more turbulent environments because it can respond quickly and be proactive, which means formalization is usually low.
- *The missionary or ideology-driven organization* is focused on driving a particular ideology, so it is about standardizing norms. It is the ultimate form of decentralization, as all members are charged with acting for the benefit of the organization. Olympic Solidarity, as the foundation arm of the International Olympic Committee, could be defined as an ideology-driven organization because it promotes Olympism and the Olympic Values around the world on behalf of the International Olympic Committee.
- *The political organization* is an unstable organization given the tensions found within it that pull people apart. No level of centralization or decentralization can help here, as the organization is usually in trouble. You will see this in organizations with bad/negative organizational culture, which will need a strong leader to turn things around. Chapter 9 can help in this regard.

Within sport, Kikulis, Slack, Hinings, and Zimmermann (1989), Kikulis, Slack, and Hinings (1992), and Stevens (2006) presented a taxonomy for (non-profit) national sport organizations:

- *The kitchen table*: this is the sport equivalent to Mintzberg's (1979) simple structure. Many local and state/provincial sport organizations and clubs (and even some national and international sport federations) with very few (if any) paid staff members, low formalization, high centralization, and an operational-type board fit this design.
- *The boardroom*: this intermediate sport organization will have some staff members as well as medium levels of formalization and centralization.
- *The executive office*: this sport organization has professionals leading decision-making, which means higher complexity, high formalization, and low centralization (high decentralization). The larger organizations like the US Olympic Committee fit this description.
- *The amateur sport enterprise*: this revenue-focused, corporate-like organization is highly complex, with a governance-based board and operational-based staff.

It is important to note that these design archetypes are ideal types. This means that an organization may not fit exactly into one type. This is even more the case if the organization is undergoing change. Nevertheless, an organization should tend toward a particular archetype. If it doesn't – if it is all over the map, so to speak – this may be an indication of potential issues within the organization, which need to be addressed if the strategy implementation is to be successful.

Critical thinking Box 8.2

Reflect on the sport organizations in your country, and those you are familiar with. Prepare a table with four headings: Kitchen table, Boardroom, Executive office, and Amateur sport enterprise. Under each heading, categorize sport organizations into the various archetypes – do they fit into one, or perhaps a couple? Can you determine any commonalities between organizations within each archetype, for instance funding, size, board structure, volunteers? What conclusions can you draw when you examine your table?

▮ Summary

In this chapter, we examined the implementation of strategy, which by its very nature involves undergoing strategic change. We started the chapter by examining how, once you've chosen your preferred strategy, you take the next step to implementing that strategy that, hopefully, will help your sport organization gain or sustain a competitive advantage. This included breaking down the strategy into more specific objectives. Tactics are then developed for each objective. Next, the individual(s) responsible for undertaking the tactic and meeting the objective are noted, as are timelines and resources. To monitor progress, we suggested benchmarks and indicators be developed using the SPORTS acronym.

Next, because strategy implementation often entails organizational change, we moved to examining the general concept of change. We defined it and highlighted that it can occur in four areas of the organization: people, structures and systems, technology, and products/services. We highlighted the role of entrepreneurship and innovation in the change process before further delving into the different types of changes (strategic/operational, radical/convergent, and evolutionary/revolutionary). We underscored the fact strategic change is complex, situation-dependent, and continuous, making each strategic initiative unique. We also emphasized that while change can come from internal and external sources, external ones are more likely to lead to radical change, and regulatory agencies are a key external source of change.

In addition, as structure and strategy go hand in hand, we focused on organizational structure and design considerations. We defined the concepts of complexity, formalization, and centralization. This led us to explore design options for for-profit and non-profit sport organizations.

CLOSING CASE: A CASE ON THE CHANGES OCCURRING IN THE IAAF IN RESPONSE TO CORRUPTION AND BAD GOVERNANCE (By Ashley Thompson)

In late 2014, the sport of athletics was placed under a microscope as a result of a worldwide doping scandal. News outlets revealed extensive doping violations in Russian athletes as well as the extortion of Russian athletes who were allegedly paid off by International Association of Athletics Federations (IAAF) officials in exchange for hiding failed drug tests (Ingle, 2016; Shryack, n.d.). As a result of these allegations, the World Anti-Doping Agency (WADA) established an Independent Commission with the purposes of investigating these allegations against Russian athletics and the IAAF (WADA, 2016). The Independent Commission released a two-part report, in which part 1 exposed the existence of a state-sponsored doping program in Russia. These doping violations led the IAAF to suspend the Russian Athletics Federation. The second part of the Independent Commission's report unmasked the corruption existing in the IAAF and the illegitimate governance structure, then led by President Lamine Diack (now ex-president), which operated informally alongside the organization's formal structure. The Independent Commission's report also highlighted the issues with IAAF's existing governance structure as one that was poor in preventing corruption. As a result of this report, several members of the IAAF leadership team resigned and remain under investigation.

As a result of the scandal, in late 2016 the IAAF engaged in widespread organizational change, specifically targeting its governance structure (Phillips, 2016). These changes, outlined in a reform document titled *Time for Change*, included reducing the decision-making power of the president, reducing the president's authority over all day-to-day management of IAAF staff (with the exception of the CEO), introducing vetting requirements for all IAAF officials, and creating a vetting panel composed of people independent of the IAAF (Gibson, 2016).

The IAAF also created a new Independent Athletics Integrity Unit (IAIU) with the responsibility of managing doping and non-doping integrity-related matters (WADA, n.d.). The IAIU was also responsible for investigating and prosecuting doping violations committed by international-level athletes, a responsibility formerly undertaken by the national federations. In order to remain independent from the IAAF and free from potential corruption, it was decided that the IAIU would be housed separately from the IAAF and have its own board of directors to govern the operations of the unit.

■ Chapter review questions

1   Explain the process of strategy implementation.
2   What are the different types of organizational change? Provide a concrete example from sport for each.
3   Do a little research on the strategy and structure relationship. Which one do you think comes first? Provide literature and a concrete example to support your explanation.
4   Think of a sport organization you know and describe it using the concepts of complexity, formalization, and centralization.
5   Using the same organization as in Question 4, state which organizational design archetype it most resembles and explain your rationale.
6   Think about times in your life where you've experienced organizational change. How did the change process make you feel? Explain, using an example(s) from the sport industry, why it is that people seem to have almost innate resistance to change.

Additional resources

- Books/articles
  - Amis, J., Slack, T., & Hinings, C. R. (2004). Strategic change and the role of interests, power, and organizational capacity. *Journal of Sport Management, 18*(2), 158–198.
  - Kim, W. C., & Mauborgne, R. (2009). How strategy shapes structure. *Harvard Business Review, 9*. https://hbr.org/2009/09/how-strategy-shapes-structure
  - O'Brien, D., & Slack, T. (1999). Deinstitutionalizing the amateur ethic: An empirical examination of change in a Rugby Union Football Club. *Sport Management Review, 2*, 24–42.
  - Romney, M. (2004). *Turnaround: Crisis, leadership, and the Olympic Games.* Washington, DC: Regnery Publishing, Inc.
- Websites
  - OnStrategy: https://onstrategyhq.com/resources/strategic-implementation/
  - Strategic management: Formulation and implementation: www.strategy-implementation.24xls.com/en101
  - 5 structural elements of strategy: www.entrepreneur.com/article/196932
  - Aligning structure with strategy: www.strategybydesign.org/aligning-structure-to-strategy/
- Videos
  - Bob Legge (2013). What is strategy implementation? A quick overview: www.youtube.com/watch?v=EBZgXM-dKA
  - Patrick Sanaghan (2014). 10 critical lessons I've learned about implementing a strategic plan: www.academicimpressions.com/blog/10-critical-lessons-ive-learned-about-implementing-a-strategic-plan/Books/articles

References

Amburgey, T. L., & Dacin, T. (1994). As the left foot follows the right? The dynamics of strategic and structural change. *Academy of Management Journal, 37*(6), 1427–1452.

The Associated Press. (2016, November 27). Florida Panthers fire head coach Gerard Gallant – Sportsnet.ca. *Sportsnet.ca.* Retrieved from www.sportsnet.ca/hockey/nhl/florida-panthers-fire-head-coach-gerard-gallant/

The Associated Press. (2017, April 13). NHL notes: Vegas Golden Knights hire Gerard Gallant as first head coach. *NBCSports.ca.* Retrieved from www.nbcsports.com/philadelphia/philadelphia-flyers/nhl-notes-vegas-golden-knights-hire-gerard-gallant-first-head-coach

Barley, S. (1986). Technology as an occasion for structuring: Evidence from observation of CT scanners and the social order of radiology departments. *Administrative Science Quarterly, 31*, 78–109.

Bartunek, J. M. (1984). Changing interpretive schemes and organizational restructuring: The example of a religious order. *Administrative Science Quarterly, 29*, 355–372.

Besters, L. M., van Ours, J. C., & van Tuijl, M. A. (2016). Effectiveness of in-season manager changes in English premier league football. *De Economist, 164*(3), 335–356. https://doi.org/10.1007/s10645-016-9277-0

Boylen, R. (2016, December 3). Coach's Corner: Gallant firing "worst" in NHL history. *Sportsnet.ca*. Retrieved from www.sportsnet.ca/hockey/nhl/coachs-corner-gallant-firing-worst-nhl-history/

Byers, T., Slack, T., & Parent, M. M. (2012). *Key concepts in sport management*. London: Sage.

Centre for Creative Leadership. (2018). *How to be a successful change leader*. Retrieved from www.ccl.org/articles/leading-effectively-articles/successful-change-leader/

Chandler, A. D. (1962). *Strategy and structure*. Cambridge, MA: MIT Press.

Chappelet, J.-L. (2005). The process of strategic management and its practical tools. In J.-L. Chappelet & E. Bayle (Eds.), *Strategic and performance management of Olympic sport organizations* (pp. 7–15). Champaign, IL: Human Kinetics.

Cotsonika, N. J. (2016, November 29). Panthers take blame for Gerard Gallant firing. *NHL.com*. Retrieved from www.nhl.com/news/panthers-players-take-blame-for-firing-of-head-coach-gerard-gallant/c-284184866

Damanpour, F. (1992). Organizational size and innovation. *Organization Studies, 13*, 375–402. https://doi.org/10.1177/017084069201300304

D'Aunno, T., Succi, M., & Alexander, J. A. (2000). The role of institutional and market forces in divergent organizational change. *Administrative Science Quarterly, 45*, 679–703.

Esteve, M., DI Lorenzo, F., Inglés, E., & Puig, N. (2011). Empirical evidence of stakeholder management in sports clubs: The impact of the board of directors. *European Sport Management Quarterly, 11*(4), 423–440. https://doi.org/10.1080/16184742.2011.599210

Flint, S. W., Plumley, D. J., & Wilson, R. J. (2014). You don't know what you're doing! The impact of managerial change on club performance in the English Premier League. *Managing Leisure, 19*(6), 390–399.

Gibson, O. (2016, January 14). Sebastian Coe admits IAAF is a "failed organisation" but is backed to reform it. *The Guardian*. Retrieved from www.theguardian.com/sport/2016/jan/14/sebastian-coe-iaaf-wada-report

Greenwood, R., & Hinings, C. R. (1988). Organizational design types, tracks, and the dynamics of strategic change. *Organization Studies, 9*, 293–316.

Greenwood, R., & Hinings, C. R. (1996). Understanding radical organizational change: Bringing together the old and the new institutionalism. *Academy of Management Review, 21*, 1022–1054.

Greenwood, R., Suddaby, R., & Hinings, C. R. (2002). Theorizing change: The role of professional associations in the transformation of institutionalized fields. *Academy of Management Journal, 45*, 58–80.

Hoeber, L., & Hoeber, O. (2012). Determinants of an innovation process: A case study of technological innovation in a community sport organization. *Journal of Sport Management, 26*, 213–223.

IAAF. (2016). *Time for change*. Retrieved from www.iaaf.org/about-iaaf/documents/iaaf-reform

Ingle, S. (2016, January 7). IAAF in crisis: A complex trail of corruption that led to the very top. *The Guardian*. Retrieved from www.theguardian.com/sport/2016/jan/07/russia-doping-scandal-corruption-blackmail-athletics-iaaf

Jacobson, R. (1992). The "Austrian" school of strategy. *Academy of Management Review, 17*, 782–807.

Kelly, D., Fairley, S., & O'Brien, D. (2019). It was never ours: Formalised event hosting rights and leverage. *Tourism Management, 73*, 123–133.

Kikulis, L. M., Slack, T., & Hinings, C. R. (1992). Institutionally specific design archetypes: A framework for understanding change in national sports organisations. *International Review for the Sociology of Sport, 27*, 343–370.

Kikulis, L. M., Slack, T., Hinings, C. R., & Zimmermann, A. (1989). A structural taxonomy of amateur sport organizations. *Journal of Sport Management, 3*, 129–150.

Kirzner, I. (1973). *Competition and entrepreneurship.* Chicago, IL: University of Chicago Press.

Lawrence, P. R., & Lorsch, J. (1967). *Organization and environment.* Boston, MA: Harvard Graduate School of Business Administration.

Leahy, S. (2018, April 5). *Which NHL teams will make a coaching change after the season?* Retrieved from https://nhl.nbcsports.com/2018/04/05/what-nhl-head-coaches-will-be-shown-the-door-after-the-season/

Legg, J., Snelgrove, R., & Wood, L. (2016). Modifying tradition: Examining organizational change in youth sport. *Journal of Sport Management, 30*, 369–381. https://doi.org/10.1123/jsm.2015-0075

Mintzberg, H. (1979). *The structuring of organizations.* Englewood Cliffs, NJ: Prentice Hall.

Mintzberg, H. (1984). A typology of organizational structure. In D. Miller & P. Friesen (Eds.), *Organizations: A quantum view* (pp. 68–86). Englewood Cliffs, CA: Prentice Hall.

Nike. (2018). *About Nike.* Retrieved December 19, 2018 from https://about.nike.com/

Parent, M. M. (2001, September 26). *Strategy, structure & entrepreneurship.* Unpublished paper prepared for ORG A 703: Seminar in Strategic Management. Edmonton, Canada: University of Alberta.

Parent, M. M., Naraine, M. L., & Hoye, R. (2018). A New Era for governance structures and processes in Canadian National Sport Organizations. *Journal of Sport Management, 32*(6), 555–566. https://doi.org/10.1123/jsm.2018-0037

Peters, T. (1990). Get innovative or get dead. *California Management Review, 33*, 9–26.

Pettigrew, A. (1973). *The politics of organizational decision making.* London: Tavistock.

Pettigrew, A. (1985). *The awakening giant: Continuity and change in ICI.* London: Blackwell.

Pettigrew, A., & Whipp, R. (1991). *Managing change for competitive success.* London: Blackwell.

Phillips, M. (2016, November 30). IAAF plans transparency amid new corruption claims. *Reuters.* Retrieved from www.reuters.com/article/us-athletics-corruption/iaaf-plans-transparency-amid-new-corruption-claims-idUSKBN13P1EB

Poole, M. S., & Van de Ven, A. H. (Eds.). (2004). *Handbook of organizational change and innovation.* Oxford and New York, NY: Oxford University Press.

Premier League. (2018). *Manager profile: Alex Ferguson.* Retrieved from www.premierleague.com/managers/344/Alex-Ferguson/overview

Pugh, D. S., & Hickson, D. J. (1976). *Organisation structure in its context: The Aston Programme I.* Farnborough, Hants: Saxon House.

Pugh, D. S., Hickson, D. J., Hinings, C. R., & Turner, C. (1968). Dimensions of organizational structure. *Administrative Science Quarterly, 13*, 65–105.

Reynolds, T. (2014, June 21). Panthers hire Gerard Gallant as coach. *The Globe and Mail.* Retrieved from www.theglobeandmail.com/sports/hockey/panthers-hire-gerard-gallant-as-coach/article19282391/

Rumelt, R. P. (1987). Theory, strategy, and entrepreneurship. In D. J. Teece (Ed.), *The competitive challenge* (pp. 137–158). Cambridge, MA: Ballinger.

Schumpeter, J. (1950). *Capitalism, socialism, and democracy.* New York, NY: Harper & Row.

Seravalli, F. (2018, March 16). Record year for NHL head coach job security – Article. *TSN.ca.* Retrieved from www.tsn.ca/record-year-for-nhl-head-coach-job-security-1.1029384

Shryack, L. (n.d.). Pound: Corruption was everywhere at IAAF, says Coe right man to fix problem. *Flotrack.* Retrieved from www.flotrack.org/articles/5048899-pound-corruption-was-everywhere-at-iaaf-says-coe-right-man-to-fix-problem

Skinner, J., Stewart, B., & Edwards, A. (2004). Interpreting policy language and managing organisational change: The case of Queensland Rugby Union. *European Sport Management Quarterly, 4,* 77–94.

Slack, T., & Parent, M. M. (2006). *Understanding sport organizations: The application of organization theory* (2nd ed.). Champaign, IL: Human Kinetics.

Stevens, J. A. (2006). The Canadian hockey association merger and the emergence of the amateur sports enterprise. *Journal of Sport Management, 20,* 74–100.

WADA. (2016). *The independent commission report #2.* Retrieved from www.wada-ama.org/sites/default/files/resources/files/wada_independent_commission_report_2_2016_en_rev.pdf

WADA. (n.d.). *Independent Athletics Integrity Unit is operational| News | iaaf.org.* Retrieved July 11, 2018 from www.iaaf.org/news/press-release/independent-athletics-integrity-unit

Welty Peachey, J., & Bruening, J. (2011). An examination of environmental forces driving change and stakeholder responses in a football championship subdivision athletic department. *Sport Management Review, 14*(2), 202–219. https://doi.org/10.1016/j.smr.2010.09.002

9

Strategic control systems and change management

As Donna Spethman flicked on her television on Friday morning November 30, 2018, she felt sick to her stomach. It wasn't her breakfast or anything she ate or drank the night before that unsettled her; it was the lead story on the morning news that focused on a massive data breach in Marriott Hotels' Starwood chain. The report revealed that unauthorized access to guests' private details had compromised the confidentiality of 500 million customers of Marriott's Starwood network since 2014 (ABC News, 2018). As the general manager of education, training and risk at UniSport Australia (UniSport), the peak governing body for Australian university sport, Donna's role obviously had nothing to do with the Marriott data breach. But she considered the implications a similar breach could have for her organization.

UniSport has 43 member universities that jointly represent more than one million students across Australia. Donna wondered what would happen in the event of a similar hacking episode of UniSport's data. What mechanisms were in place to stop or even detect such a breach? If the worst happened and such a breach transpired, how soon would she know they'd been hacked? What actions would need to be taken, when, and by whom? For a large multinational corporation like Marriott, the effects would be devastating enough, but with economies of scale borne through its large size, Marriott would eventually absorb the shock. Conversely, for a comparatively small organization like UniSport, or an even smaller community sport club, the impacts of a similarly scaled data breach could be catastrophic for their survival. It was a horrifying thought.

However, Donna was buoyed by the knowledge that at the start of 2018, UniSport had undertaken a review of its policy framework and response mechanisms to address just such a risk and had, in fact, implemented training and policy to manage a data breach event. The personal information that UniSport collects varies among individuals, depending on the nature of their interaction with UniSport. But the types of information can be incredibly sensitive, ranging from name, address, and contact information, through to passport number, credit card details, and health information. So within UniSport's privacy policy, it was critical to communicate why they actually need stakeholders' personal information and to include clauses around data protection – how they collect and use personal data; security measures around data storage; the length of time data are kept; which third parties UniSport will and will not disclose personal information to; the relevant laws pertaining to privacy; and the course of action individuals should take if they consider their privacy to have been breached by UniSport.

Meanwhile, Donna also led the development of an internal data protection process in the form of a workbook for employees that outlines basic data monitoring procedures, the types of data breaches that are possible, and the sequencing of who does what and when in the event of a worst case scenario: an actual data breach. All of these actions are aimed at averting data breaches in the first place, but also detecting and minimizing the impact if one does actually occur.

▌ Strategic control systems and managing change

As the opening case suggests, the environment that sport organizations operate in is not always a friendly one. Accidents can and do happen, as can more malicious terror or cyber incidents, and of course, good old human error always plays its part in disrupting the best-laid plans. This is one of the reasons we need strategic control systems. Strategic control systems provide managers information on how their strategy is faring before, during, and after implementation – are we achieving what we set out to achieve, and if not, why not? And equally, if we are actually achieving our strategic targets, what are we doing right? What factors are aiding our success? In terms of organizational change, the extent of change required is in many ways a function of the information derived through effective strategic control. This means that a key part of strategic management, and strategic control in particular, is figuring out what strategic success should look like, and what, when, and how to actually measure levels of success and failure. Based on all of the above, we then assess if change is required, and if so, how much, and by whom will it be implemented.

The Asian Games, also known as Asiad, is a quadrennial multi-sport event second in size only to the Olympic Games and is organized by the Olympic Council of Asia under the auspices of the International Olympic Committee (IOC). In September 2018, the Indonesian cities of Jakarta and Palembang hosted the 2018 Asian Games. After the Games, Indonesian President Joko Widodo announced his country's intention to bid for the 2032 Olympic Games, an announcement warmly welcomed by IOC President Thomas Bach (Diamond, 2018). However, without an event evaluation, which is an example of a feedback mechanism in a strategic control system, Indonesia's 2032 bid plans would have no foundation from which to build, and President Widodo's announcement would not have been possible. Feedback mechanisms help those responsible for implementation know where strategic targets were met, exceeded, or missed, and they provide the basis for subsequent actions, such as in this case, an Indonesian bid for the 2032 Olympic Games. A comprehensive strategic control system includes not only feedback mechanisms, but also concurrent and feedforward mechanisms, and helps managers evaluate the extent to which their sport organization is meeting strategic goals and progressing toward achieving their overall strategic direction.

Effective management of a comprehensive strategic control system requires skills in data analytics and at least adequate levels of data literacy among managers. Having (or developing, if necessary) that analytical mindset is key. As Fried (2017) states:

> When examining the past [feedback], analytics examine what happened and why it happened. When examining current conditions [concurrent], analytics can help identify what is happening now and what might be the next best action. Using predictive analytics [feedforward], a manager can try to figure out what will happen in the future.
>
> (p. 232, brackets added)

The control process enables management to monitor organizational activities and strategy implementation so that *actual* performance can be compared with *desired* performance (Hunger & Wheelen, 2011). Such mechanisms provide a "report card" to help management know where deficiencies exist and where and when corrective actions are needed; equally, it is also important to inform management where gains can and actually are being made. Historically, strategic control systems have been thought of mainly in terms of financial

FIGURE 9.1 The strategic control process

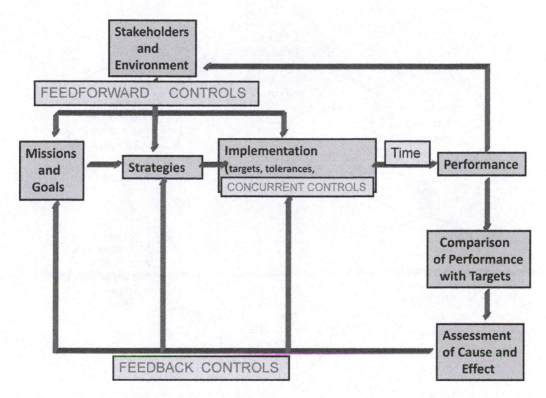

performance measures (Harrison & St. John, 2014). So this meant that goals were expressed purely in financial terms, and success was measured according to whether these financial goals were met or exceeded. This type of approach is obviously far too simplistic; strategic success is also dependent on myriad other types of internal, community, and environmental objectives. A comprehensive strategic control system will also work as an "early warning system" to keep managers apprised of trends that may impact future organizational performance. Three main mechanisms for strategic control will be explored in this chapter, as depicted in Figure 9.1: feedback, concurrent, and feedforward control systems. We will then explore some of the ways that management may respond to the information derived through strategic control. This material builds on Chapter 8's focus on implementation and organizational change.

Feedback control mechanisms

Effective feedback controls provide managers with information about results from organizational activities that have already been implemented and allow managers to know whether the strategies pursued have indeed moved the sport organization in the desired strategic direction. Once goals and objectives are set, examples of feedback control mechanisms include surveys, budgets, reports, audits, and ratio analyses. As shown in Figure 9.2, Harrison and

FIGURE 9.2   Establishing feedback control
Source: Harrison and St. John (2014, p. 167). Reprinted with permission of Jeffrey S. Harrison, all rights reserved.

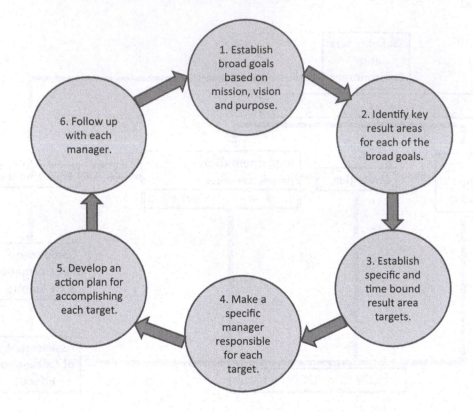

St. John (2014) provide a six-step feedback model by which organizational performance results can be assessed. The model's six steps consist of:

1   *Establishing broad goals based on mission, vision, and purpose*: As discussed in Chapter 4, a sport organization's strategic direction is a function of its vision, mission, and purpose. While a vision expresses where the organization is heading and a mission defines its activities, purpose speaks more directly to the key stakeholders involved. Collectively, these elements of strategic direction provide the foundation for organizational control mechanisms. For example, adventure sport equipment provider Patagonia's mission is to "build the best product, cause no unnecessary harm, use business to inspire and implement solutions to the environmental crisis" (Patagonia, 2018a, ¶1). Clearly, the company's strategic direction seems unequivocal – although it is a for-profit enterprise, profits are only important insofar as their pursuit raises awareness about environmental issues and does not cause undue negative ecological impacts.

2   *Identifying key result areas*: This step is essentially about identifying what to measure and pinpointing measurable processes and result areas that will objectively indicate levels of strategic success. Focus should be directed toward those elements that account for the highest proportion of problems such as completion times, labor, or expense. Earlier, we referred to Patagonia and the company's stringent strategic focus on ecological principles. In order to achieve that strategic direction, management had to work out

key result areas to know whether they were achieving that direction. As fabrics and raw materials used for adventure sport equipment are at the core of Patagonia's mission and strategic direction, they established four key result areas in which to measure progress toward achieving that direction:

> Our search for the best materials starts with our material development team. It is their job to research, develop, and approve materials and suppliers by evaluating performance in four key areas: quality, traceability, environmental health and safety, and social responsibility.
>
> (Patagonia, 2018b, ¶2)

3   *Establishment of specific targets and time frames*: Specific targets and time frames are statements that articulate the standards of performance thought necessary in each key result area such that broad goals will be achieved. These targets, called objectives, are more specific than broad goals in that clear outcomes and timelines for accomplishment are identified. As well as establishing standards for final output, setting standards for intermediate stages of production can also provide a barometer of progress toward strategic objectives.

4   *Assignment of responsibility*: An effective feedback control process is wide-ranging and inclusive because strategic success never depends on merely one or a few factors. There are any number of interrelationships and processes that determine strategic success. At a more micro-level, therefore, this means that responsibility for achieving objectives needs to be assigned. Ideally, if the planning process was inclusive, managers most influential in identifying the original key result areas will hopefully be the same ones assigned responsibility for achieving success in those areas.

5   *Development of an action plan*: This step involves the development of action plans toward achieving the targets set in each key result area. Again, the managers identified as responsible for developing action plans will be the same ones assigned responsibility for identifying and achieving in the key result areas. Specifically assigning responsibility like this provides a high level of accountability and recognition of interdependencies (Harrison & St. John, 2014), but also encourages individual and/or departmental ownership of the targets and their achievement. In their study of management control in six "pulsating" sport event organizations, Carlsson-Wall, Kraus, and Karlsson (2017) found that detailed action planning,

> . . . served as the backbone in the chain of control in each case, connecting the evaluation based on non-financial measures with the budgeting, and with policies and procedures that were applied during the process. . . . Detailed action planning created a shared understanding of the breakdown of activities . . . it also made it possible to clarify the role each individual plays within the system.
>
> (p. 31)

6   *Accountability and review*: This final step in establishing a feedback control system involves confirming feedback mechanisms for regular oversight and review. At a minimum, the review process should establish that all activities and interdependencies are accounted for, as well as identifying: the role of chance in the final result; whether processes were carried out correctly; whether the processes themselves were appropriate; and last, who is best placed to undertake any required corrective actions (Hunger & Wheelen, 2011).

Concurrent control mechanisms

Concurrent controls are usually associated with quality assurance in production and service processes. They are similar to feedback control mechanisms, but rather than looking back after implementation, the time horizon is "real time" during the actual implementation of strategy. Broadly speaking, concurrent controls fit into two categories: process controls and behavioral controls.

Process controls: If you think about it, sport organizations consist of innumerable processes: how new staff are inducted and trained; how major decisions are made; the technology platforms used for marketing and sales; team selections – the list goes on! And when you consider the larger scale of sport leagues and the international scope of some sports, and add in the governance and strategic processes, the picture gets even more complex and the need for process controls grows exponentially. Process controls consist of statistical process controls and real-time inventory controls.

Consider the processes involved in athlete preparation – a task that is absolutely central to the mission of most participative sport organizations from amateur to professional levels. We now have wearable GPS-based technologies and "smart clothing" to optimize athletes' training loads, monitor injury prevention, performance enhancement, and stress factor estimations, to name just a few areas of statistical data collection and goal setting. These data represent an example of a (statistical) process control because athletes, coaches, and medical staff are enabled to respond in real time to the statistical data generated. The Sydney Swans AFL club, for example, utilizes a neural network system to identify injury risk in players. Based on the data generated, medical and conditioning staff modify players' training loads accordingly. Not surprisingly, the club regularly records one of the lowest player injury rates in the league (Fried & Mumcu, 2017).

Equally, the rise of sports wagering means statistical controls are critically important to the mission of professional sport leagues. As in many countries, sports wagering is now pervasive in the United States, and it presents as many challenges as it does opportunities to sport stakeholders. The main challenge has been effectively maintaining sport integrity and detecting suspicious activities, such as fraud and match fixing and being seen by the general public as making efforts to do so. If the general public sees a particular sport as "bent," that is, lacking integrity, they are unlikely to watch, attend, or wager on the results. However, the sheer amount of data is far too large for any individual sport governing body or sports wagering operator to monitor. And, with dozens of American states and sovereign tribal nations set to pursue legal sports betting in the United States in 2019, according to Sara Slane, senior vice president of public affairs for the American Gaming Association, the stakes have never been higher to provide "robust consumer protection, increased transparency and additional tax revenues for state and local governments" (Slane, 2018, in Lemire, 2018, ¶9). In response, two of the biggest US sports wagering operators, MGM Resorts and Caesars Entertainment, along with most major US betting operators, have joined forces to create the non-profit Sports Wagering Integrity Monitoring Association (SWIMA). SWIMA, based in Atlantic City, will partner with regulators, law enforcement, and other stakeholders to identify betting fraud as it actually happens (Lemire, 2018). Explaining the real-time nature of this concurrent control mechanism, David Rebuck, the director of the New Jersey Division of Gaming Enforcement, stated:

> Every operator who has unusual or suspicious activity that they see – whether it be fraud or potential match-fixing – is required to notify every other operator and

required to notify the gaming regulator, who will then notify law enforcement, if need be, and will also notify the leagues, if it impacts them.

(Rebuck, in Lemire, 2018, ¶3)

Meanwhile, real-time inventory controls relate more to monitoring stock and inventory levels in retail environments. Obviously, these types of controls are appropriate for sport equipment and apparel providers. But inventory controls may also be applicable in other sport contexts where, for example, it is important to monitor crowd flows and foot traffic through particular event precincts or parts of stadia. Computerized ticketing and closed-circuit television (CCTV) solutions meet these types of inventory controls for larger events. At smaller events, a low-tech solution (and low-cost if sponsored by a local business or charity!) of colored wristbands can perform a similar function to computerized ticketing where patrons get a wristband on entry and deposit the wristband at a central point on exit. A simple check by event staff as to whether there are wristbands available provides real-time inventory control as to how many seats are left in the venue.

Behavioral controls: This category of concurrent controls addresses the types of behaviors management hopes to see in organizational members. Obviously, managers cannot, and should not, supervise employees 100% of the time. So behavioral controls are about creating a framework for organizational members such that they understand what behaviors, norms, and values are expected of them, especially in times where direct supervision from management is not possible. So, short of inventing a remote control for employees, how can management achieve this? Well, there are three main ways: bureaucratic controls, clan controls, and human resource systems (Harrison & St. John, 2014).

First, *bureaucratic controls* refer to the formalized rules, procedures, and policies that prescribe and proscribe the general behaviors expected of organizational members in particular situations. For example, in the opening case, UniSport, through its privacy policy, has prescribed why, how, and by whom its members' personal information is to be collected, used, stored, and disposed of. Any behavior that deviates from those procedures is proscribed, and consequences and courses of action are recommended. Similarly, each UniSport employee is trained in "what to do in case of a data breach incident," and each employee also has a manual to help prompt the processes that need to occur in order to lower the impact of the breach.

Second, *clan controls* are enacted through socialization processes and are used to impress upon individuals the values, behaviors, and organizational culture of the sport organization. For example, in the off-season before the 2019 NRL season in Australia, the Gold Coast Titans NRL franchise employed current Australian national coach and former national and State of Origin great, Mal Meninga, as the club's inaugural head of performance and culture. By aligning performance and culture in this way, the appointment alone sent a message to stakeholders. But when Meninga informed the club's players shortly after assuming the role that they would be spending part of their off-season in the summer heat volunteering with local businesses doing "heavy physical labor," this too sent a message about the values of hard work and "giving back" to their community. Jarrod Wallace, a senior player in the club stated: "It's good for the young guys who come straight into footy contracts. It can be a bit of a rude shock what a full day of work is like and for the older guys who have played for a long time, I think it's a nice change up" (Titans, 2018, ¶7).

Often, behavioral controls are implicit; that is, they may not be found in a manual or other formalized document. However, a more strategic approach is to explicitly state and model the values and behaviors that are prized by the organization so that stakeholders can see unequivocally what the organization stands for. Sportswear multinational adidas, for example, uses the company's human resource systems to communicate the values and behaviors expected of employees. New employees go through an induction process that includes the "Book of aditudes" – a booklet that lists and describes the company's core values and the related behaviors that employees will hopefully take on. In this way, the sport organization's human resource systems such as screening, selection, induction, training, and rewards processes can act to reinforce and/or change the values, behaviors, and overall culture of the organization.

Critical thinking Box 9.1

Go to www.sportsdigita.com and read about the company called Sports Digita. With a partner, discuss what business this company is in and list some of its clients.

Now go to www.sportsdigita.com/case-studies/yankees and read the New York Yankees case study. In particular, go to the section titled, "The Result." With your partner, discuss the type of control mechanism(s) "The Digideck" provides for clients like the Yankees.

Feedforward control mechanisms

Feedforward control mechanisms are management's "crystal ball" to anticipate future changes in their sport organization's internal and external environments. Such mechanisms are sometimes referred to as surveillance systems or competitive business intelligence systems (Harrison & St. John, 2014). Feedforward controls help managers forecast change based on examination of inputs from stakeholders and the broad environment. Like the general business environment, the sport business environment is replete with turbulent social, economic, technological, and political landscapes that often precipitate change responses within organizations. This is why effective feedforward control systems are essential for strategic planning: they provide context around what the future may look like and how best the sport organization can strategically plan for and respond to different scenarios.

Harrison and St. John (2014) propose that feedforward controls depend upon two main mechanisms: premise control and strategic surveillance/monitoring systems. Premise control refers to whether the information and assumptions used to plan current strategies and their related goals are still valid. For example, in the opening case, the fact that Donna Spethman, as UniSport's manager in charge of risk, undertook a complete review of UniSport's privacy policy reflected the organization's recognition that assumptions around the security of members' personal information had shifted. New and sophisticated cyber threats had emerged, and the organization could not afford to be cavalier with members' personal information if they wished to fulfill their mission and achieve their desired strategic direction. Despite this, many people still adopt an "it will never happen to us" mentality, and this is a common reason why people resist putting controls in place. As Donna Spethman observed:

There are some in our organization that had that thought about a data breach. . . . But then they thought that it would never happen to us. But finally, I was able to convince them that the impact from "what if it did happen?" outweighs the no action and the "it will never happen to us" mentality.

(Donna Spethman, personal communication, January 25, 2019)

Another feedforward control is strategic surveillance, which is about gathering business intelligence to create a clear picture of the sport organization's competitive environment. Zajac and Bazerman (1991) suggested that strategic decision makers often do not sufficiently consider the decisions of competitive rivals, and this deficiency can lead to "blind spots" in their strategic planning. To avoid these "blind spots," some organizations employ competitive intelligence analysts whose sole job is to monitor the actions of competitors and report back to senior management. Thompson, Peteraf, Gamble, and Strickland (2018) sum up the significance of strategic intelligence:

> As in sports, scouting the opposition is an essential part of game plan development. Gathering competitive intelligence about the strategic direction and likely moves of key competitors allows a company to prepare defensive countermoves, to craft its own strategic moves with some confidence about what market maneuvers to expect from rivals in response, and to exploit any openings that arise from competitors' missteps.
>
> (p. 74)

So where should sport managers look for this type of strategic intelligence? Formal and informal networking with colleagues from other organizations in your competitive environment is one way, so liaising regularly with managers from suppliers, distributors, regulatory agencies, and even competitors can lead to exchanges of critical information.

Michael Porter's (1980) *Framework for Competitor Analysis* is pretty old now, but it is still extremely relevant and puts some structure around how you might go about this intelligence gathering. First, Porter suggests that in order to predict competitors' next moves, we need to have a good understanding of their *current strategy* in terms of market positioning, basis for competitive advantage, and even the types of investments they are making as an indicator of their growth trajectory. Second, we should analyze competitors' *objectives*, both financial and strategic. If a key competitor is currently meeting financial objectives, it is highly likely they will continue on their current strategic trajectory; whereas, if they are not, we should expect new strategic moves from them. Third, analyzing competitors' *resources and capabilities* will tell us where they might be enabled and constrained in attempting future strategic actions.

Fourth, we discussed earlier the utility of premise control – regularly assessing and reassessing the validity of the basic assumptions that underpin our own strategic direction. Porter suggests it is also important to consider competitors' basic *assumptions* about themselves and their industry/sector. For example, if executives in your professional football club see themselves as competing in the sport industry while your key rival's executives consider their industry to be entertainment, this will profoundly influence the respective strategic actions and broader directions each are likely to pursue.

◾ OK, we have our strategic control system in place . . . what now?

So far in this chapter, we've explored the characteristics of comprehensive strategic control systems. For a strategic control system to be considered "comprehensive," it needs three broad sets of data that relate to (1) past events (feedback controls), (2) present implementations (concurrent controls), and (3) potential future scenarios (feedforward controls). It would be a stretch to assume that all sport organizations have comprehensive strategic control systems in place. The mechanisms described here can be costly to establish in terms of time and resources and, let's face it, most sport organizations simply don't have access to those kinds of resources, and besides, not everyone likes dealing with numbers and datasets. Nevertheless, with the increasing prevalence and sophistication of data and data collection opportunities across the sport industry, being data literate and having an analytical mindset have never been more important for sport managers. Fried and Mumcu (2017) summed this up nicely when they said, "That is why being data literate is so important. Without knowing what data to look for, a person can spend years searching through data and not finding the right material" (p. 1).

This means that there can sometimes be a delay in moving from strategy formulation to implementation, then from implementation to control, and finally from control to formulation again. Depending on the interpretation of strategic control mechanisms, this last step may involve implementing organizational change (e.g., changing organizational structures and systems, as discussed in Chapter 8). The delays in the system regarding change typically come from a combination of three main sources: (1) managers fail to perceive organizational problems correctly, (2) they don't have or fail to develop the required skill sets to handle them, or (3) there is a resistance to change within the organization (Chandler, 1962). We dealt briefly with the first two sources above when we discussed the need for managers to have or to develop an analytical mindset and the skills to go along with that. But the third area – resistance to change – is often a problem. So let's explore resistance to change and ways we can manage that resistance so that, based on how we interpret our strategic control data, we can successfully implement our chosen strategy.

Resistance to change

There are various sources of resistance to proposed changes you could face when trying to implement your chosen strategy (Clarke, 2010; Slack & Parent, 2006):

- *Personal self-interest*: An important source of resistance is an individual's own fears, self-interest, and emotions. You will hear statements like: What's in it for me? I don't want to try something new. I'm afraid of what it means for me/my job. I don't see myself in this new direction. I'm going to lose the influence I currently have.
- *History/experience*: For most organizations, change should not be a new phenomenon. Yet, and often due to poor change management and a lack of communication about the process, previous efforts fell flat, leaving a sour taste in organizational members' mouths and increasing feelings of resistance to new changes. If this is the case, you will hear statements like: It hasn't worked before. We've always done it this way.
- *Lack of understanding of the context or change implications*: Lower-level organizational members may not have the same entrepreneurial spirit as the leader and may not understand the opportunities and threats emerging in the external environment. They may also not understand the full potential of an innovation or a suggested change. In this case, you will hear statements like: It's the same everywhere else, so why should we change? We don't do that. It's not in our mission.
- *Lack of trust in the change implementers*: If there is a history of failed changes, a new leadership implementing change, or a lack of communication, uncertainty will reign and rumors will start, misinformation will be disseminated, and organizational members will become defensive. If mistrust exists, you will hear statements like: They don't know what they're doing. They don't understand us. They're not telling us anything.
- *Time, effort, and/or financial costs of the change*: Sometimes resistance comes from the perception that it will be too much work on the part of organizational members and/

or the perception the organization lacks the capacity to undertake the change, despite the change being potentially good for the organization. You will hear statements like: We don't have the budget for it. I don't have time to learn something new. The change is too big or complex.

- *Differing opinions and assessments regarding the change outcomes/consequences*: Just as organizational members may not perceive the external environment the same way as the organization's leader, so too can they perceive the potential benefits (and costs) of the change differently. If this is the case, you can hear statements like: It won't work. It's not worth it.

These sources are not mutually exclusive and can manifest at different times in the change process. You may also see individuals support the change, only to shift their own beliefs/perceptions at one point during the change process (Stagl, 2015). Being aware of these potential sources of resistance allows you to preempt them and manage your strategic change process, which we now discuss in the next section.

Critical thinking Box 9.2

With a partner or on your own, and using a sport organization you are familiar with, think of a time when you have heard organizational members utter one of the statements listed above in the "Resistance to Change" section. What was the nature of the change process involved in this case? What was the change in response to? Can you identify a control mechanism or process that the change would have been prompted by? Explain the manner by which the change process was/was not managed effectively.

All the concepts noted above (e.g., strategy, change, entrepreneurship, innovation, resistance, and environment) are, of course, interrelated within the strategic management process. Figure 9.3 provides an overview of how these concepts can be linked.

FIGURE 9.3   Relationship between strategy, structure, environment, entrepreneurship, and innovation
Source: Adapted from Parent (2001).

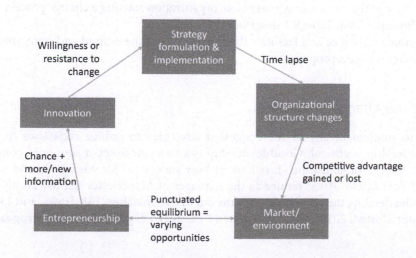

Managing change

A key step to successfully managing the strategic change process is to deal with (and better yet, overcome) resistance, and it starts with you. As Stagl (2015) points out, whatever people say, whatever their reactions, as managers, we can't take it personally. Next, to mitigate some of the above noted sources of resistance, it can be helpful to (cf. Slack & Parent, 2006):

- *Educate* organizational members about why the change is needed (need, potential benefits, etc.), how it will happen, and when;
- *Communicate* regularly on progress and next steps. Often, noting a short-term win or positive aspect can help increase motivation and positive perceptions about the change, and avoid perceptions that changing is negative because "it's taking too long";
- *Involve* organizational members so they take ownership of the change process;
- *Create* a change team to oversee the change process, train, counsel, motivate, and communicate the need for the change; and
- *Designate* idea champions, individuals who wholeheartedly believe in the change, are committed to it, can decrease opposition through charisma and/or power, and can act as transformational leaders.

The idea champions and change team should not only facilitate the change process but also provide support for organizational members and create a favorable culture for the change to occur. Other ways to address resistance and implement the desired change, though sometimes less effective, and sometimes even unethical, include negotiating with or providing incentives to powerful groups so they endorse the change process; manipulate information or potential resisters; co-opting resisters or influencers; and outright coercion through threats of demotion, dismissal, and so forth (Slack & Parent, 2006).

The change process

Besides the ability to reduce or eliminate resistance to change, it is important to understand strategic and radical change will not necessarily occur in a clear, linear manner. There are four main change tracks we can witness in an organization starting a change process (Greenwood & Hinings, 1988). Table 9.1 describes these changes.

To reduce resistance and facilitate the change toward the desired end state, you need to lead the change process properly.

Leading the change process

In order to implement any of the suggested strategies to reduce resistance to change, proper leadership is critical. Good leadership is a strategic asset, a source of competitive advantage for the organization. Just look at how successful Sir Alex Ferguson was during his 27-year (1986–2013) tenure as the manager of Manchester United Football Club. Under his leadership, the team had 528 wins out of 810 matches, 168 draws, and 114 losses (Manchester United, 2018). The team won 13 Premier League titles, two European Cups,

TABLE 9.1   Organizational change track options

Track		Description
Inertia		A non-starter – the organization never changes its structural design, it stays the same
Aborted execution		The organization starts to change, morphing into an embryonic state, where the structure is relatively coherent with a few discordant aspects, only to revert back to the original design
Reorientation	Linear progression	The most linear path, where the organization moves into an embryonic state, then into a schizoid state (half original and half desired outcome), then to an embryonic state of the desired outcome, and finally into the full-fledged, coherent, final desired structural design
	Oscillation	The organization's design fluctuates back and forth between original embryonic and desired embryonic states, to eventually end in the full-fledged, coherent, final desired design
	Delay	The organization's design remains in its original state, resisting the change, and finally, rapidly changes into the full-fledged, coherent, final desired design
Unresolved excursions		The organization starts to change, moving into various embryonic and schizoid states, but then never reaches its final desired design, remaining in a schizoid state

five FA Cups, four League Cups, and 11 Community Shields (Manchester Evening News, 2018; Premier League, 2018). Sir Alex was also named the Premier League Manager of the Season 11 times, the LMA Manager of the Year, and the LMA Manager of the Decade (Premier League, 2018). After Sir Alex's retirement, the club has been under the leadership of four different managers in five years, with none winning the Premier League title, though one manager led the team to an FA Cup title in 2015–2016. In the 2016–2017 season, Jose Mourinho took over leadership and led the club to first place in the League Cup, Community Shield, and Europa League in his first season, but was dismissed in December 2018, midway through his third season at the club after a run of losses despite big-budget spending on a string of high-profile players (Wright, 2018).

As you can see, quality of leadership is critical for the long-term survival and success of the sport organization; it provides stability and strategic direction (Morden, 2007). In its analysis of effective change leaders, the Centre for Creative Leadership (2018) found three common themes, labeled the three Cs, that can describe effective change leaders: communicate, collaborate, and commit. Figure 9.4 details what these three Cs constitute. Effective change leaders also go through three steps, which parallel the strategic planning process: they initiate, strategize, and execute (Centre for Creative Leadership, 2018). Figure 9.5 illustrates this process.

As you may have guessed from the above and from previous chapters, the leader does not do the change by herself. It is not a hero-type leader required here (Pugh & Hickson, 2007). Two critical elements for successful strategy implementation and change are successfully managing your human resources and creating the right culture,

FIGURE 9.4   The three Cs of effective change leadership
Source: Based on data from Centre for Creative Leadership (2018).

Communicate

Effective leaders **focus on the why** to increase buy-in and urgency in the change. They:

- Explain the purpose and benefits

- Link the change to organizational values

Collaborate

Effective leaders create a team to plan and implement the change by **involving employees early** in the decision making. They:

- Break down existing silos

- Work across boundaries

- Don't accept competition

Commit

Effective leaders model the desired behaviors: persistence, resilience, positivity, and patience. They:

- Step out of their comfort zone

- Devote personal time to the change effort

- Adapt to challenges

- Focus on the larger picture

FIGURE 9.5   Leading the change
Source: Based on data from Centre for Creative Leadership (2018).

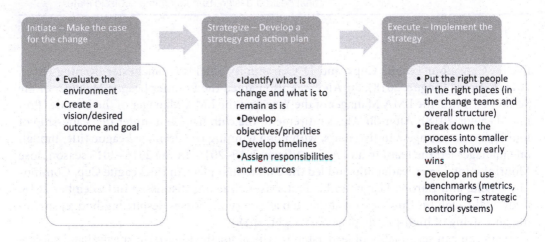

Initiate – Make the case for the change

- Evaluate the environment
- Create a vision/desired outcome and goal

Strategize – Develop a strategy and action plan

- Identify what is to change and what is to remain as is
- Develop objectives/priorities
- Develop timelines
- Assign responsibilities and resources

Execute – Implement the strategy

- Put the right people in the right places (in the change teams and overall structure)
- Break down the process into smaller tasks to show early wins
- Develop and use benchmarks (metrics, monitoring – strategic control systems)

a learning culture. Effective change leaders will do the following (Centre for Creative Leadership, 2018):

- *Support* their employees by addressing their sources of resistance (e.g., egos, fear, and perceived costs, such as a lack of time or resources). Effective leaders spend much of their efforts on the process of change.
- *Sway* key individuals and stakeholders, both internal and external, to convince them of the necessity and benefit of the change. It is a team effort.
- *Learn* through informal and formal feedback and adjust the course whenever necessary. Effective leaders do not assume they know everything.

The three Cs, the three change process steps, and the three behaviors constitute what the Centre for Creative Leadership (2018) calls the nine competencies of effective change leaders. This learning aspect also links to the ideal culture for successful strategy implementation, a learning culture. We already briefly addressed the learning culture in Chapter 2, indicating it can be a source of competitive advantage and it must be seen at all levels of the sport organization (Zong, Duserick, & Rummel, 2009).

To become a learning organization, various approaches can be used. Senge (1992) argues leaders can (1) instill personal mastery in themselves and organizational members so they can comprehend who they are and know what they hope to achieve personally; (2) continually review and challenge the organizational members' mental models, biases, and assumptions; (3) build a shared vision of what the leader *and* the organizational members can strive toward, together; (4) commit to team learning through open dialogue, cooperation, and collaboration; and (5) unite organizational members into a systems way of thinking instead of an individual/personal way. One way leaders can foster and facilitate learning, innovation, and master – in themselves and in organizational members – is through the concept of communities of practice. For more information on communities of practice, see Wenger (1998) and Wenger-Trayner and Wenger-Trayner (2015).

Finally, change leaders should be aware of five main problems when implementing strategic change (Pettigrew & Whipp, 1991; Pugh & Hickson, 2007):

1   *Assessing the environment*: this task, which we detail in Chapters 2 and 3, should not be viewed as simply a technical step in the process, but as a continual learning activity that involves all top managers.
2   *Leading change*: this aspect, which we describe in this chapter, should be seen as a complex and situation-specific task, one that includes building a learning culture, trust, and of a team of change leaders from all levels of the organization.
3   *Linking strategic and operational change*: this aspect refers to ensuring that operational aspects don't challenge the overall strategy, that the operational changes don't become the de facto tactics after the fact. Targets and benchmarks need to be developed, supported by the proper resources, communicated throughout the organization, and monitored.
4   *Treating human resources as assets and as liabilities*: this aspect refers to recognizing not only the importance of your human resources in implementing the change, but also in the need to educate them/have them learn new skills and unlearn "old" skills, which in itself can be a cost or liability and therefore accounted for in the change plan.
5   *Developing a coherent approach*: this problem is also a complex one, in that leaders need to foster unity while the sport organization is being dismantled and put back together. As such, leaders need to ensure that all aspects (goals, capabilities, skills, resources, etc.) are consistent; the chosen strategy is consonant with the environmental analysis; strategy should lead to a competitive advantage; and the strategy is feasible. Hopefully, by having followed this book, you will see that this problem is readily addressed.

Summary

In this chapter, we discussed strategic control systems and explored how management's interpretation of the data generated through strategic control determines the nature of organizational change required. A comprehensive strategic control system includes feedback, concurrent, and feedforward mechanisms and is a critical component in management's quest to achieve the sport organization's desired strategic direction. Underpinning the establishment and maintenance of effective strategic control is the central role of data literacy and the need for managers to nurture the relevant skill sets both in themselves and their organization. In addition, we explored six sources of resistance to change before detailing how to mitigate these. We also presented the change process and how to lead change effectively with nine key competencies. Finally, we noted five key problems associated with strategic change, all of which you should be able to mitigate with the various tools, processes, templates, and additional resources we provided in this book.

CLOSING CASE: ARE EXCLUSIVITY DEALS STILL THE WAY TO GO IN SPORT BROADCASTING?

For many years now, the general institutional wisdom in sport has been that broadcasters will pay exorbitant fees for exclusive broadcast rights to a focal sport property – be that a particular sport event or professional sport league. It's now common place for broadcast deals to be quoted in the billions of dollars, but the caveat has always been that the deal must be exclusive; that is, only the party paying for the rights can broadcast the actual event. This basic premise has underpinned the revenue generation strategies of many a sport league and event. Added to this, the advent of live streaming and "Over the Top" (OTT) technologies has fundamentally shifted the sport broadcasting landscape to the point where it is now unheard of for sport events and leagues to have traditional free-to-air television as their *only* broadcast platform. However, despite all this change, the practice of "exclusivity" in rights deals seems to have survived where online broadcasters, mainly large telecommunications companies (telcos), pay huge sums for exclusive online broadcast rights. The basic premise here is that by being exclusive broadcasters of the particular sport/event, the telcos can retain their existing customers and attract additional customers. But maybe that basic premise is about to change.

Peter Adderton is the founder of multinational telecommunications company, *Boost Mobile*, known for its youth-based marketing and strong sponsorship alignment with sports like basketball, surfing, NASCAR, and other extreme sports. It has a particularly strong presence in Australia and the United States, with nine million subscribers in the United States alone.

Adderton described the strategy of his major competitors to lock down exclusive sport broadcast deals as "flawed" and "alienating" for consumers. He also said:

> I don't know whether that was necessarily a good strategy. . . . Specifically itemising one code of sport or one code of content and thinking that's going to be enough to drive your business is narrow-minded. . . . Exclusivity deals are dead. I think putting value in Netflix and Stan and all these other value-added cloud services as part of your package is really going to be the thing that drives the businesses forward. If your strategy is that you're going to spend a bunch of money – hundreds of millions of dollars buying sporting codes because 30% of your customers care about it, how is that doing the majority any favours? It's not a strategy that's going to survive for the next three to five years because the market is moving way past exclusivity.
>
> (McDonnell, 2018, ¶¶7–10)

So as a media executive, Adderton is making his call on the pitfalls of the strategies employed by his telco competitors, arguing that exclusivity deals are actually bad for business and bad for sport. He believes that when a sport (event) is only available to subscribers of a particular telco, those fans who are not subscribers are likely to be in the majority and are unlikely to switch providers. And worse, Adderton argues that these fans, denied access to their preferred sport broadcast, are left with feelings of resentment to the telco that has the rights as well as the sport property itself. If Adderton's prediction of the death of exclusivity deals within three to five years is borne out, this will have wide-reaching ramifications for major professional sport leagues and events around the world.

Chapter review questions

1   On an individual level, describe the strategic control processes that indicate to you your level of success as a student.
2   Using a sport organization you are familiar with, explain the types of strategic control that were employed. Would you describe what the organization had as a "comprehensive" strategic control system? Justify your answer and explain what changes you would make.
3   Explain the closing case and Peter Adderton's observations on the future of sport broadcast deals from the perspective of strategic control processes.
4   Imagine you are employed by a professional sport organization that relies heavily on revenue from sport broadcasting. How would you interpret the observations of Peter Adderton and what strategic control mechanisms would you employ in response?
5   Explain how strategic control processes relate to the nature of organizational change required in a sport organization.
6   Why is heroic leadership not appropriate for leading change?
7   Describe the five key problems associated with strategic change and explain how you would mitigate each problem.
8   Think of a strategic change you have lived through. Explain what happened. Then, note what went well and what could have been improved. Finally, explain how you would have improved the process/what you would have done differently if you had been in charge of the change.

Additional resources

- Books/articles
  - Dinwoodie, D., Pasmore, W., Quinn, L., & Rabin, R. (2015). *Navigating change: A leader's role*. Greensboro, NC: Centre for Creative Leadership. Available at: www.ccl.org/wp-content/uploads/2015/02/navigating-change-white-paper.pdf
  - Malmi, T., & Brown, D. A. (2008). Management control systems as a package – Opportunities, challenges and research directions. *Management Accounting Research*, 19, 287–300.
- Websites
  - Centre for Creative Leadership: www.ccl.org/
  - LawInSport. *Sports media rights in 2018 – consumption trends and the growing influence of OTT digital players*: www.lawinsport.com/topics/sports/item/sports-media-rights-in-2018-consumption-trends-and-the-growing-influence-of-ott-digital-players
  - Managing organizational change for managers: www.linkedin.com/learning/managing-organizational-change-for-managers

- Videos
    - ○ Harvard Business Review. Strategies for learning from failure: https://hbr. org/2011/04/strategies-for-learning-from-failure
    - ○ Rosabeth Moss Kanter (2013). Six keys to leading positive change: www.youtube. com/watch?v=owU5aTNPJbs
    - ○ Sillitoe, A. (2016). How to create a high performance culture. *TEDx Talks*: www. youtube.com/watch?v=BAdeFHlhKi4

References

ABC News. (2018). Marriott's Starwood hotels hacked, compromising 500 million guests. *ABC News*. Retrieved December 10, 2018 from www.abc.net.au/news/2018-12-01/ massive-data-breach-at-marriott-starwood-hotels/10573562

Carlsson-Wall, M., Kraus, K., & Karlsson, L. (2017). Management control in pulsating organisations – A multiple case study of popular culture events. *Management Accounting Research, 35*, 20–34.

Centre for Creative Leadership. (2018). *How to be a successful change leader*. Retrieved from www.ccl.org/articles/leading-effectively-articles/successful-change-leader/

Chandler, A. D. (1962). *Strategy and structure*. Cambridge, MA: MIT Press.

Clarke, J. (2010, December 22). Embracing change. *TEDx Talks*. Retrieved from www. youtube.com/watch?v=vPhM8lxibSU

Diamond, J. (2018). Indonesia's President meets Bach and announces bid intention for 2032 Olympics. *Inside the Games*. Retrieved November 27, 2018 from www.insidethegames. biz/articles/1069452/indonesias-president-meets-bach-and-announces-bid-intention-for-2032-olympics

Fried, G. (2017). Putting it all together. In G. Fried & C. Mumcu (Eds.), *Sport analytics: A data-driven approach to sport business and management* (pp. 232–246). London: Routledge.

Fried, G., & Mumcu, C. (2017). *Sport analytics: A data-driven approach to sport business and management*. London: Routledge.

Greenwood, R., & Hinings, C. R. (1988). Organizational design types, tracks, and the dynamics of strategic change. *Organization Studies, 9*, 293–316.

Harrison, J. S., & St. John, C. H. (2014). *Foundations in strategic management* (6th ed.). Mason, OH: Thomson South-Western.

Hunger, J. D., & Wheelen, T. L. (2011). *Essentials of strategic management* (5th ed.). Upper Saddle River, NJ: Prentice Hall.

Lemire, J. (2018). MGM, Caesars lead formation of Sports Wagering Integrity Monitoring Association. *Sport Techie*. Retrieved December 10, 2018 from www.sporttechie. com/mgm-caesars-form-sports-wagering-integrity-monitoring-association/?utm_ source=SportTechie+Updates&utm_campaign=2d36bb1b0f-SportTechie_Weekly_ News_12_2_2018&utm_medium=email&utm_term=0_5d2e0c085b-2d36bb1b0f-294458269

Manchester Evening News. (2018, June 10). *Sir Alex Ferguson*. Retrieved from www. manchestereveningnews.co.uk/all-about/sir-alex-ferguson

Manchester United. (2018). *Manchester United: The story so far*. Retrieved from www. manutd.com/en/history/history-by-decade

McDonnell, J. (2018). Boost Mobile boss shuns "flawed" broadcast deals. *AdNews*. Retrieved December 17, 2018 from www.adnews.com.au/news/boost-mobile-boss-shuns-flawed-broadcast-deals#LM9oYK6RVLtvyhJ2.99

Morden, T. (2007). *Principles of strategic management* (3rd ed.). London: Routledge.

Parent, M. M. (2001, September 26). *Strategy, structure & entrepreneurship.* Unpublished paper prepared for ORG A 703: Seminar in Strategic Management. Edmonton, Canada: University of Alberta.

Patagonia. (2018a). *Patagonia's mission statement.* Retrieved December 3, 2018 from www.patagonia.com/company-info.html

Patagonia. (2018b). *Corporate social responsibility.* Retrieved December 3, 2018 from www.patagonia.com/working-with-mills.html

Pettigrew, A., & Whipp, R. (1991). *Managing change for competitive success.* London: Blackwell.

Porter, M. E. (1980). *Competitive strategy.* New York, NY: Free Press.

Premier League. (2018). *Manager profile: Alex Ferguson.* Retrieved from www.premierleague.com/managers/344/Alex-Ferguson/overview

Pugh, D. S., & Hickson, D. J. (2007). *Writers on organizations* (6th ed.). Thousand Oaks, CA: Sage.

Senge, P. N. (1992). *The fifth discipline: The art and practice of learning organizations.* Boston, MA: Harvard Business School Press.

Slack, T., & Parent, M. M. (2006). *Understanding sport organizations: The application of organization theory* (2nd ed.). Champaign, IL: Human Kinetics.

Stagl, H. (2015, June 30). How to deal with resistance to change. *TEDx Talks.* Retrieved from www.youtube.com/watch?v=79LI2fkNZ2k

Thompson, A., Peteraf, M., Gamble, J., & Strickland, A. (2018). *Crafting and executing strategy: The quest for competitive advantage, concepts and cases* (21st ed.). New York, NY: McGraw-Hill Education.

Titans (2018). Wallace: It's good to be on the tools. *Club News.* Retrieved December 11, 2018 from www.titans.com.au/news/2018/11/27/wallace-its-good-to-be-on-the-tools/

Wenger-Trayner, E. (1998). *Communities of practice: Learning, meaning and identity.* Cambridge: Cambridge University Press.

Wenger-Trayner, E., & Wenger-Trayner, B. (2015). Learning in a landscape of practice: A framework. In E. Wenger-Trayner, M. Fenton-O'Creevy, S. Hutchinson, C. Kubiak, & B. Wenger-Trayner, (Eds.), *Learning in landscapes of practice: Boundaries, identity, and knowledgeability in practice-based learning* (pp. 13–29). Oxon: Routledge.

Wright, D. (2018, December 19). Manchester United decided to cut ties with Jose Mourinho. *The Sun.* Retrieved February 3, 2019 from www.news.com.au/sport/football/manchester-united-decided-to-cut-ties-with-jose-mourinho/news-story/5f9b47f0d56d2b392d92dd1090ebb425

Zajac, E. J., & Bazerman, M. H. (1991). Blind spots in industry and competitor analysis: Implications of interfirm (mis)perceptions for strategic decisions. *Academy of Management Review, 16*(1), 37–56.

Zong, D., Duserick, F., & Rummel, A. B. (2009). Creating a learning culture for competitive advantage. *Competition Forum, 7*(1), 17–24.

10 Strategic planning

Mintzberg, Henry, 'Strategy-making in three modes', 2nd ed. London: Routledge, 1973, pp. 44–53 (September 2012, Strategy at: http://e-entrepreneurnu.). See also the paper for D.A. (1982). Safeguard in subject Management Education. New School: university.

Anderson, O. (2013). Safeguard management. London: Routledge.

Shapiro of our Autumn-Obsession.

Gibson, J.L., et al. (eds), Leadership approaches. Routledge December 2015 Industry perspective. Oxford: our unitary.

Biddy, Lee A., & McAdam, R. (2011). Managing Sport in an essential nation. London: Bloomsbury, 2016, vol. 4, 2. (2016). Management culture. New York: New free press.

OPENING CASE: THE CREATION AND ORGANIC UTILITY OF UNISPORT AUSTRALIA'S "STRATEGY 2020"
(By Don Knapp, CEO, UniSport)

Many of you will have seen examples of strategic plans, but fewer of you will be familiar with the process behind how strategic plans actually come into being. This case study explores one such process and the CEO who led the process walks you through how the current strategic plan of UniSport Australia came into being. As you saw in Chapter 9, UniSport Australia is the national governing body of university sport in Australia – analogous to the National Collegiate Athletic Association (NCAA) in the United States.

UniSport Australia undertook the process of developing its new strategic plan in early January 2016, with its 2013 to 2016 Healthy Body – Healthy Mind plan due to expire at year's end. The CEO, with the support of the board of directors, set about creating a planning framework to develop the new plan. The planning process was referred to as "Strategy 2020."

The planning framework

Every year in January, the UniSport Australia Board commits to a full day of planning at its annual review and planning workshop. The purpose of this two-day workshop is to review the previous year's organizational performance against annual performance goals and to establish or refresh the performance goals for the new year. The format of the 2016 meeting was altered to allow a more singular focus on the importance of developing a new plan for the next quadrennial planning cycle.

The board began by setting a few planning precedents, including:

1 Developing an in-depth understanding of the rapidly evolving changes in both the higher education and national sporting landscapes in Australia; understanding of both environments and how they reciprocally affect one another was critical before planning commenced;
2 It was agreed to "start with the *why* question" in a number of key planning areas (Sinek, 2009);
3 The board agreed its role was to establish the planning framework, steps, and strategic direction; and
4 The board resolved to gather extensive members' feedback to ensure the new plan was relevant, unifying, and purposeful sector-wide.

Tilling the soil

To achieve precedents 1–4 (above), planning tactics adopted by the board were:

1 A PESTLE analysis (see Chapter 3), which was applied to the higher education student services area; and a Boston Consulting Group report on Australian sport was also considered. A SWOT analysis (see Chapter 2) was conducted for both the higher education and national sport areas.
2 The building blocks of key planning considerations were shaped within the framework of Sinek's "start with the *why* question" theory; this applied to developing the plan's foundations, including mission/purpose, vision, values, and key result areas, success indicators, and drivers.
3 It was agreed the board's version of the Strategy 2020 framework would remain an internal document. This decision was made to ensure members had the opportunity to contribute without the influence of previous work completed by the board, and to allow for comparisons to be made between board and member perspectives.
4 Strategy 2020 planning forums were organized in all regions and staged in Queensland, Sydney, Victoria, Adelaide, and Perth. These were full-day planning sessions, and facilitation tactics similar to those used for the board were also used for members' sessions.

Planning workshops were also facilitated for UniSport staff – these workshops were similar to board and members' workshops. Input into the plan was also sought from students and external stakeholders such as NSOs.

Strategy 2020 – Drafts 1 and 2

Early in the process, the board decided that a small reference group would be appointed and tasked with the job of converting all workshop inputs into the Strategy 2020 written plan. The reference group included the board chair, one director, and the CEO. An abundance of data was collected from member forums. Useful input was collated by the CEO and compared with the board's initial work. The CEO was charged with the responsibility for creating the first draft of Strategy 2020. Once Draft 1 was completed, it was circulated to the board, a members' focus group (12 in total who had volunteered), staff, and a ten-member student focus group. Based upon feedback from these groups, Draft 2 was completed by the CEO.

Strategy 2020 – final draft

As planned, the final draft of Strategy 2020 was completed and signed off by three authors, including the president of the UniSport Board, a board director, and the CEO. The focus of work for the final draft was on concise, consistent wording and meaning, as well as clear strategic alignment of the mission, vision, values, and key result areas of the plan, and all of this aligning with measures of success.

The board then ratified the final draft and Strategy 2020 was launched and implemented in October 20, 2016. The planning process was highly consultative, engaging the board, members, staff, students, and external stakeholders. This collaborative process generated rich input into Strategy 2020, enhancing its relevance to all stakeholders: "this plan speaks to UniSport members in a common language" (Liz Brett – CEO Activate University of Technology, Sydney).

(*The full "UniSport Australia Strategy 2020" can be found at www.unisport.com.au/strategy-2020*).

Introduction

You have made it to the final chapter of this textbook and you are now ready to write your strategic plan. The benefits of strategic planning are considerable, but the process needs to be undertaken with care. This chapter will look at putting into practice everything you have read in the preceding chapters and provide a detailed step-by-step guide to assist you in completing your strategic plan. The opening case illustrates an example of the detailed process undertaken by the CEO of UniSport Australia, Don Knapp, in order to develop his organization's strategic plan. The closing case demonstrates how UniSport goes about ensuring its strategic plan is implemented and utilized effectively.

Why plan?

The importance of strategic planning has been outlined throughout this book, and by now you should realize how important it is to plan strategy if you want to manage a successful sport organization. The aim of strategic planning for sport organizations is to articulate the issues that are important in determining the future of the organization, where the organization hopes to go in the future, and the means by which it intends to get there (Viljoen & Dann, 2000). This is ideally done in the form of a document: the strategic plan. Strategic planning enables a sport organization to:

- Be proactive rather than reactive – to clarify club purposes and direction;
- Initiate and influence outcomes in favor of the sport organization;
- Exert more control over its own destiny – deciding and articulating where it wants to be in the future;
- Adopt a more systematic approach to change that helps to reduce resistance to change;
- Improve financial performance and encourage effective resource acquisition and use;
- Increase awareness of its operating environment (for example, competitors, government policy, threats);
- Improve organizational control and coordination of activities; and,
- Develop teamwork off the field.

(Sport Australia, 2018)

What is a strategic plan?

A strategic plan is the culmination of the strategic management process undertaken by your organization, as explained in the previous chapters of this book. It is the physical document that maps where you are, where you want to go, and how you are going to get there. Strategy is about the future! Research suggests there is a positive relationship between formal strategic planning processes and the financial success of an organization (Delmar & Shane, 2003). As a sport manager, you need to develop an overall strategic intention and direction for your organization. The strategic plan articulates your organization's mission, vision, and values. However, the strategy you create is never complete. Ideally, the strategic plan is an evolving, living document that is revisited at regular intervals so there is an inbuilt propensity to accommodate change as your internal and external environments change. Successful strategy is about reacting to events and adopting a fluid approach to the planning process (McKeown, 2012). So let's begin by understanding what the strategic planning process involves.

■ The strategic planning process

The strategic planning process

> is a systematic process through which an organization agrees on – and builds commitment among key stakeholders to – priorities that are essential to its mission and are responsive to the environment. Strategic planning guides the acquisition and allocation of resources to achieve these priorities.
>
> (Allison & Kaye, 2005, p. 1)

To develop a strategic plan requires input and consultation from as many key stakeholders as possible at multiple levels inside and outside of your sport organization. Obviously, it's simply not feasible to include *all* stakeholders in the process, but the opening case gives you a good idea as to how you can be as inclusive as possible in your strategic planning. The strategic planning process is cyclical, and can be very time- and resource-hungry (Chappelet, 2005).

However, done well, strategic planning itself can be a source of competitive advantage, so it is worth the effort to do it properly (Kukalis, 1989; Powell, 1992). Indeed, a formal strategic planning process has been shown to positively impact organizational performance (Brews & Hunt, 1999). The reason strategic planning sometimes fails is due largely to an ineffective planning process – problems with who, what, and even when the process is implemented (Kachaner, King, & Stewart, 2016). The strategic planning process can be done formally or informally, often depending on the size of the organization. Some small, not-for-profit sport organizations outsource the writing of their strategic plan to external consultants; in such cases, it's hard to imagine the plan truly engaging the hearts and minds of those closest to the organization. Can an external consultant really understand your organization and its key stakeholders' interests? As a result, we see some sport organizations' strategic plans gathering dust and not really offering real strategic direction for the organization. A strategic plan is a living document, and successful sport organizations will revisit and review the plan regularly to ensure they are meeting targets and achieving organizational goals.

Sport organizations that conduct formal strategic planning gain insight into their organization that predisposes them to making effective decisions about the direction of their organization and the acquisition and allocation of resources (Dibrell, Craig, & Neubaum, 2014). However, organizations need to adopt some flexibility into the planning process so they can react to environmental opportunities or threats as they emerge (Barringer & Bluedorn, 1999). Dibrell et al. (2014) suggest that organizations should be flexible in their formal strategic planning processes, as flexibility often enables innovation to occur.

Kachaner et al. (2016) propose that successful organizations that benefit most from strategic planning activities have four things in common:

1   They explore strategy at distinct time horizons (e.g., long, medium, and short term);
2   They constantly reinvent and stimulate strategic dialogue (e.g., don't ask the same questions year after year);

3   They engage the broad organization in their strategy development efforts (e.g., both internal and external stakeholders); and

4   They invest in execution and monitoring (e.g., implementing comprehensive strategic control systems).

Many of the strategic planning processes proposed by government agencies and described in textbooks are very similar, but it is important to note that their implementation will always vary depending on the organization. Different organizations will, therefore, adopt different approaches to developing strategy, depending on the size of the organization and the type/volatility/stability of environment the organization operates in. When planning for high-performance sport success, for example, Sport Australia (2016) suggests consideration of the following questions:

- Where does the organization/program want to be? There should be a clear goal for the plan, with a specified time frame detailed.
- Where is the organization/program now? An analysis of the current situation should be performed, identifying gaps and barriers and reflecting on drivers or successes.
- How will the organization/program reach its goal? This should cover strategies, time frames, and priorities.
- What resources are needed? Resources should include financial, people, and where capabilities should be developed.
- How will the organization/program know if they are successful? Strategic control mechanisms that feature ongoing monitoring and key performance indicators should accompany the plan, which also accommodates for evaluation at the end of a cycle.

So, based on the discussion so far, most sport organizations can ask the following five questions when preparing a strategic plan (see Chapter 5):

- Why do we exist?
- Where are we now?
- Where are we heading?
- How do we get there?
- How do we know when we have arrived?

Let's examine how to address these questions using the tools and skills you have learned from the previous chapters. We will incorporate a six-step process in order to address these key questions. The first step is to ensure your organization is ready for the planning process.

Step 1: preparing to plan

Provide an understanding to the board, staff, members, and stakeholders of what strategic planning is and how it is done

An important step is "preparing to plan," and there is much evidence to indicate the benefits of multiple contributions into the strategic design process (Shilbury & Ferkins, 2015). The size of your organization will impact the process and steps undertaken for strategic planning. Assuming you have a medium to large sport organization, one approach is to encourage a cooperative effort between the board and paid staff, with dedicated staff taking responsibility for driving the planning process. However, the strategic team must agree on the best process to develop the strategic plan, and this can be done at a meeting or perhaps a strategic planning retreat, which is quite common for larger organizations. During this time, participants will come to understand what strategic planning is and how it is done, determine the value of a strategic plan to the organization's objectives, highlight the costs associated with developing a strategic plan, consider the plan's long- and short-term perspectives, finalize how to proceed, establish responsibilities for the various steps of the planning process, and finalize timelines for completion. Except for very small sport organizations, it is best to establish a strategic planning committee.

The strategic planning committee

The strategic planning committee should be of a manageable size and may include board, staff, members, community, stakeholders, or volunteers. Ensure the planning committee can devote significant time to the task at hand and allocate committee roles and responsibilities. In federated governance structures, membership of such committees is typically based solely on parochial representation of members' interests. However, on more strategic boards and, in this case, committees, members are selected based on the skill sets (legal, financial, sponsorship, etc.) they bring to the process (Ferkins & Shilbury, 2010, 2012). The organization may want to include an outside facilitator to assist in the preparation process. It is important to note here that the outside facilitator is exactly that – a facilitator – so she/he is not there to do the actual planning but to stimulate the discussion and constructive debate that is required for effective planning.

Step 2: why do we exist?

Define and refine organizational mission, vision, activities, and values

This stage will allow your planning committee to assess the current strategic plan, including the mission, vision, strategic goals, and current activities. It is also a time to reflect on organizational performance – did your organization achieve its previous goals? If not, why? Can you identify what prevented your organization from achieving its goals? If enough reliable data and information is not available, then a resolution to improve strategic control mechanisms will be warranted. Overall, this analysis of the past will provide valuable input into the creation of your new goals and strategies.

The start of your strategic plan includes a brief statement about your sport organization for the benefit of new members, stakeholders, sponsors, parents, and so forth. The statement may include when the organization was formed, where it is located, its governance structure (including management or board members), special achievements, and finally, your mission statement, vision statement, and organizational values.

Next, you must identify the overriding aims of your organization, especially understanding its core purpose. A core purpose includes the values of the organization and addresses the question, why are we here? The core purpose, along with your organization's mission and vision, provides the foundation on which to build your strategic plan (Parent,

O'Brien, & Slack, 2012). Refer to Chapter 5, where you learned the key elements of strategic direction and what questions to address when considering why your organization exists.

Chapter 5 also discussed the importance of your organization's mission, vision, and values. Are the mission, vision, and values of your sport organization still current? It is important to have a good mission statement, as it is a statement of your organization's strategic direction. It communicates ideals, a sense of direction and purpose to all of your organization's stakeholders. The mission statement represents what the organization is all about – why it exists (Harrison & St John, 2014). A vision statement, on the other hand, is a look into the future of what the organization wants to become. Examples of a mission and vision statement from FINA (Fédèration Internationale de Natation, n.d.):

Mission statement from FINA

To increase participation in all aquatic sports.

Vision statement FINA

To enable everyone in the world to swim

(FINA, n.d.)

Critical thinking Box 10.1

Write a mission and vision statement for your club, or for a sport club you may be involved with. Make sure each statement accurately encapsulates what the organization does and what it wants to achieve. Refer to Chapter 5 for more detailed information on preparing mission and vision statements.

Step 3: where are we now?

Conduct an environment analysis (strategic control mechanisms)

While internal and external analysis was explained thoroughly in Chapters 2 and 3, the discussion around strategic control systems in Chapter 9 is also relevant here. Our feedback control mechanisms provide us data on past strategic performance; concurrent control mechanisms may point to problems we're currently experiencing, or alternatively, areas in which we're excelling; and feedforward control mechanisms act as our early warning system for future environmental opportunities and threats.

According to Kachaner et al. (2016), too many strategic planning processes "wrongly focus on analyzing the current market and competitors rather than searching for or anticipating disruptive new entrants or business models" (p. 31). In other words, you need to be competitive in your market, but meanwhile, keep an eye on what the future may look like. Can you predict what future trends may look like? Can you predict what future participants/ clients/members want from your sport organization? For instance, let's examine the changes from the International Olympic Committee (IOC) in relation to the Olympic sport program. The IOC's use of feedforward control mechanisms have led to a belief that the youth of future generations may be less interested in more traditional sports. As a result, they are adding new and more individual sports to the Olympic program. New sports such as surfing, climbing, and skateboarding have been added to the Tokyo 2020 Olympic Games program. As IOC President Thomas Bach explained, "We want to take sport to the youth. With the many options that young people have, we cannot expect any more that they will come automatically to us. We have to go to them" (Corrigan, 2016, ¶2).

Ultimately, strategists are interested in the big picture. So for you as a strategic planner, try to look forward to determine future trends and identify opportunities that you can take advantage of. However, you must also look back, or as described in Chapter 9, implement feedback control mechanisms such as surveys, audits, reports, and budgets to reflect on past performance. What has happened in the past contributes to the bigger picture of your future. Are there lessons to be learned? How can you shape strategy moving forward to make sure you don't make the same mistakes of the past? Refer to Chapters 2 and 3 for further information on undertaking an environmental analysis and how to conduct a SWOT analysis, and Chapter 9 for more information on strategic control systems.

Critical thinking Box 10.2

Consider the preceding example regarding the sport program for the Olympic Games. Do you believe the IOC will be successful in attracting future audiences to the Olympic Games by incorporating more modern, individual sports such as surfing, rock climbing, and skateboarding? Explain your thoughts on whether this strategy is enough to provide a competitive advantage.

Step 4: where are we heading?

Develop strategic directions (priorities)

Now is the time to evaluate all of the data collected in the previous steps. You now know where your sport organization has been; you know where it is today; so now it's time to articulate where you want it to go. Chapter 6 provided an overview of how to write your strategic directions and emphasized the formulation of both business- and corporate-level strategy. Remember that a business-level strategy deals with how a single-business sport organization positions itself relative to its perceived competitors, while corporate-level strategies are more about guiding multi-business sport organizations (conglomerates).

An organization's strategic direction should focus on its future goals. For example, if a long-term objective is to build female participation in the sport, then the strategic direction is one of growth, and to help achieve this, market development (attracting more women consumers) and product development in the form of a new women's league may be appropriate. When writing strategies, you should describe what you are aiming to accomplish by using "doing" verbs at the start of the strategy. Words such as *foster, develop, produce, provide, promote, deliver, adopt, build, prepare*, and so forth are effective in describing the course of action your strategy will take.

◼ Step 5: how do we get there?

Identify strategic issues

Identifying and clearly articulating strategic issues is an important step to ensure your sport organization understands its environment and is prepared and resourced for the future implementation of your new strategic plan. This is done by evaluating the new strategies you have developed to ensure they are the right fit for your organization. The Australian Sports Commission (2004) (now known as Sport Australia) developed a strategic planning guide that suggests the following questions for reviewing your organization's strategies, prior to implementation:

- Do the strategies address internal strengths/weaknesses while averting external opportunities/threats?
- Are the strategies actionable?
- Are they building on the successes of the previous plan?
- Do they enable the organization to achieve its long-term objectives and performance indicators?
- Does the organization have the capacity (resources) to achieve them?
- Will key stakeholders support them (buy in)?
- Will they provide a competitive advantage for the organization?

Important decisions are never easy, and to make the appropriate choice, it is helpful to develop a range of options and then to systematically evaluate each option accordingly. In Chapter 7, we identified three different approaches for evaluating strategic options. They were:

- Approach 1 – Suitability, feasibility, acceptability, competitive advantage
- Approach 2 – The strategic options grid
- Approach 3 – The Boston Consulting Group (BCG) Matrix.

The criteria used for evaluating strategic options are in Table 7.2. This is a practical guide to assist you in your strategy evaluation.

◼ Step 6: how do we know when we have arrived?

Implementing the new strategic plan

The final part of the strategic planning process is the implementation and evaluation of the strategy you have developed. Chapter 8 detailed how to successfully implement your new strategies and manage transitional change. Implementing a new strategy is often difficult and requires various degrees of organizational change, during which you may encounter some resistance.

Engaging internal and external stakeholders in the strategic planning process can act as a catalyst and motivator for the organizational change that strategy implementation often involves. Openly addressing the concerns of organizational stakeholders in a transparent manner can help to overcome any latent or actual resistance you may face. Quite often, the concerns are extremely valid, and incorporating solutions into the evolving strategic plan can save time, resources, and angst for the organization and its stakeholders. Working to ensure that members and stakeholders are aware of the organizational vision and providing opportunities to see the big picture can aid stakeholders' understanding of the direction and changes being proposed. Political support for new strategic initiatives should be gained from the more powerful and influential organizational members and stakeholders. This group is influential and provides legitimacy to the initiatives undertaken by the organization. Once change commences, sport managers must ensure there are sufficient resources to maintain the strategic direction and keep the momentum of new strategic initiatives moving. As stakeholders accept new initiatives, rewarding those embracing the new strategic initiatives can reinforce new behaviors and maintain the momentum of change (Parent et al., 2012).

Evaluating the new strategic initiatives

The overall evaluation of the strategic plan is the final important step of our strategic planning process. Evaluating the strategic plan and organizational activities will provide information and feedback to determine future strategic actions (Daft, 1995). Senior management may ask, have the strategic initiatives achieved the desired goals? Have stakeholders embraced the (new) strategic direction of the organization? (How) do we need to adjust our strategies moving forward? The evaluation process involves assessing the final outputs of the strategic initiatives and comparing them to the outcomes articulated in the original strategic plan (Parent et al., 2012).

According to Hubbard, Rice, and Beamish (2008), many strategic plans fail due to the inability of the organization to determine a clear strategy or to distinguish the purpose of the organization. Plans also fail when there is insufficient focus on their implementation. Completing and distributing the finished strategic plan is one thing, but there must be clear guidelines on the implementation of the strategies included in the plan. Set dates, accountabilities, and processes for evaluating the implementation of new strategies (see Chapter 9).

Implementation relies on the functional and operational groups within your organization, and if the plan has not been fully understood and accepted by these groups, it may be unworkable. This is why it is absolutely imperative to create ample opportunities for these groups to provide input and for them to see clear evidence of that input in the final version. Finally, because successful implementation of the plan is in many ways a function of it being understood by stakeholders, it must be written in a way that facilitates this understanding, thus eschewing unnecessary jargon and overly complicated language.

Summary

Strategic planning is one of the key elements in the governance and management of sport organizations. Therefore, if you do not plan effectively, your organization may suffer from operational inefficiencies and an inability to cope with change. The process of strategic planning is critical and should involve as many stakeholders as is feasible, both internal and external. The planning process in this chapter has provided you with some ideas and methods for strategic planning. You can amend and create your own planning process depending on the needs of your organization. But don't miss any of the steps, as they are all vital to the successful development and implementation of your new strategic initiatives.

CLOSING CASE: THE ORGANIC UTILITY OF UNISPORT AUSTRALIA'S STRATEGY 2020

It is a challenge for many sport organizations to actually use a strategic plan to maximum benefit; most sports managers could cite examples where the strategic plan sat on the proverbial shelf collecting dust and/or was of little use or relevance to the operations or annual key performance goals of the organization. UniSport Australia has adopted a number of tactics that have the effect of embedding Strategy 2020 into essential operational and functional areas, particularly where accountability, decision-making, and policy creation are concerned. Many of these tactical examples are discussed below.

Giving Strategy 2020 life

A common failing of strategy occurs at the execution stage, or when organizations try to put strategy into operation. A number of tactics must be adopted and followed with discipline to ensure the strategic plan has living, functional use and purpose. In the case of Strategy 2020, these tactics include the following.

Strategy 2020 annual rolling planning cycle

The last page of Strategy 2020 clearly defines how the plan will be used in respect to annual organizational performance in a four-step process, including:

- April/May: The board must report to members at the Annual General Meeting (AGM) on organizational performance in respect to the previous year. The CEO delivers this report to members, and also reviews the organization's strategic goals for the current year; these goals, set at the board's two-day strategic review workshops held earlier in the year (January – Step 4 below) must be endorsed by members at the AGM.
- June/July: The CEO and board review the progress to date against annual performance goals and reset planning as required.
- October/November: Management staff review the organization's performance against goals for the year and compile a comprehensive performance report for the board.
- December/January: The board and CEO conduct the end-of-year performance review and set the performance goals for the year at hand. This is perhaps the most important step of the process and relies heavily on the quality and veracity of the performance report (strategic control systems) produced by the CEO and management staff at Step 3 of the cycle.

Aligning organizational objectives and annual performance goals

Strategy 2020 is a four-year plan, and the organization's performance objectives are structured into five key result areas (KRAs), including:

- Sport participation;
- High-performance sport;
- Advocacy and members' services;
- Business development and management; and
- Governance and leadership.

Strategy and execution – who is responsible?

A performance pitfall of many organizations is the failure to execute strategy, with strategy relegated to intent only, and the plan sitting on the shelf. It is vital that the responsibility for strategic execution is clearly in the hands of key staff, and operational systems reinforce this. Key tactics include:

- Assigning the executive staff with the front line responsibility for strategic execution. UniSport executive staff includes the CEO, chief operating officer, and company secretary;
- Executive staff also attend, participate in and report at board meetings; this helps bridge the gap between strategic development and execution; and
- Executive staff, responsible for the performance of management staff, ensure alignment of annual performance goals with departmental management staff.

Annual performance goals – a contract between the executive and the board

It is critical that the executive and board reach agreement on what the annual performance goals are each year. This can require some negotiation, but it certainly brings those responsible for strategy and execution into alignment with common purpose. UniSport generally sets only three or four major annual goals for each of the five KRAs; limiting the number of goals for each KRA increases focus and allows for better prioritization.

Aligning organizational performance with staff performance

- The CEO's annual performance is reviewed directly against how well the organization achieved its annual performance goals;
- The major focus of the CEO's board report at each meeting assesses progress against annual goals;
- Executive and KRA management staff provide written input for the CEO board report to inform and update about KRA progress against annual goals; and
- Executive staff line-manage managers from each KRA. Managers' annual performance plan and appraisal specifically measures progress against their respective performance goals.

Walking the talk

It is important that system documentation supports and reinforces the strategic alignment of all of the above. Strategy 2020 objectives must align with annual performance goals; CEO board reporting must align with annual performance goals; executive and management staff reporting must align with CEO board reporting; and board reporting to members at the AGM must align with all of this. Staff annual performance plans and appraisals must align with the organization's annual performance goals, and the documentation for these functions must reflect this.

An organic strategic plan should also be used as a frame of reference for policy, planning, problem-solving, and decision-making. Revisiting the values and vision of the organization is a powerful tool when confronted with making a tough decision. Finally, a total organizational focus of achieving annual performance goals empowers UniSport to operate a flexible workplace. Rather than sweating the small stuff, we can prioritize achievement against performance goals as what really matters to the board, members, the executive, management, staff,– and external stakeholders.

■ Chapter review questions

1   What do you believe are the greatest challenges a sport organization may face when commencing the strategic planning process?
2   How can you encourage stakeholders and staff to "buy in" to the new strategic plan, and why is this important?
3   Describe the strategic control systems you would implement in your organization. Be sure to include feedback, concurrent, and feedforward mechanisms.
4   What are the challenges associated with predicting future trends in the sport industry, specifically related to your sport and organization?
5   What key points did you take away from the opening and closing cases regarding the strategic planning process of UniSport Australia?

■ Additional resources

- Websites
  o   www.azswimming.org/wp-content/uploads/2017/04/1-Mission-Vision-Statement-4-9-2017.pdf
  o   https://clubspark.lta.org.uk/CityofPeterboroughTennisClub/AboutUs/Vision
  o   www.dsr.wa.gov.au/docs/default-source/file-support-and-advice/file-how-dsr-helps/high-performance-planning-guide-2011.pdf?sfvrsn=4
  o   www.clearinghouseforsport.gov.au/knowledge_base/organised_sport
  o   www.sportaus.gov.au/club_development/governance
  o   https://sport.nsw.gov.au/clubs/ryc/governance/planing
  o   www.sportengland.org/about-us/governance/things-to-think-about/ttta-strategic-planning/
- Strategic plan examples
  Cricket Australia
  o   www.cricketaustralia.com.au/strategy-aus
  New Zealand Rugby
  o   www.nzrugby.co.nz/about-us/governance/strategy-new-zealand-rugby-2020
  Ontario Soccer
  o   https://sirc.ca/news/ontario-soccer-releases-2019-2021-strategic-plan
  Surf Life Saving NSW
  o   www.surflifesaving.com.au/sites/site.test/files/Surf%20Life%20Saving%20NSW%202018%20-%202021%20Strategic%20Plan.pdf
  Tennis Victoria
  o   www.tennis.com.au/vic/files/2016/09/2016-2020_TennisVictoria_StrategicPlan_FINAL_Spreads.pdf
  WA Football Club
  o   www.wafootball.com.au/wafc/strategic-plan

■ References

Allison, M., & Kaye, J. (2005). *Strategic planning for nonprofit organizations: A practical guide and workbook*. Hoboken, NJ: Wiley.

Australian Sports Commission. (2004). *Planning in sport: A good practice guide for sporting organizations*. Australian Sports Commission.

Barringer, B. R., & Bluedorn, A. C. (1999). The relationship between corporate entrepreneurship and strategic management. *Strategic Management Journal, 20*, 421–444.

Brews, P. J., & Hunt, M. R. (1999). Learning to plan and planning to learn: Resolving the planning school/learning school debate. *Strategic Management Journal, 20*, 889–913.

Chappelet, J. L. (2005). The process of strategic management and its practical tools. In J. L. Chappelet & E. Bayle (Eds.), *Strategic and performance management of Olympic sport organizations*. Champaign, IL: Human Kinetics.

Corrigan, K. (2016). Climbing officially approved for 2020 Olympics. *Climbing*. Retrieved November 3, 2018 from https://www.climbing.com/news/climbing-officially-approved-for-2020-olympics/

Daft, R. L. (1995). *Organizational theory and design* (5th ed.). St Paul, MN: West Publishing Company.

Delmar, F., & Shane, S. (2003). Does business planning facilitate the development of new ventures? *Strategic Management Journal, 24*, 1165–1185.

Dibrell, C., Craig, J. B., & Neubaum, D. O. (2014). Linking the formal strategic process, planning flexibility and innovativeness to form performance. *Journal of Business Research, 67*, 2000–2007.

Ferkins, L., & Shilbury, D. (2010). Developing board strategic capability in sport organisations: The national-regional governing relationship. *Sport Management Review, 13*, 235–254.

Ferkins, L., & Shilbury, D. (2012). Good boards are strategic: What does that mean for sport governance? *Journal of Sport Management, 26*, 67–80.

FINA. (n.d.). *FINA Strategic Plan 2018–2021*. Retrieved November 2, 2018 from www.fina.org/sites/default/files/fina_strategic_plan_2018-2021.pdf

Harrison, J. S., & St. John, C. H. (2014). *Foundations in strategic management* (6th ed.). Mason, OH: Thomson South-Western.

Hubbard, G., Rice, J., & Beamish, P. (2008). *Strategic management: thinking, analysis, action* (3rd Ed.). Frenches Forest, Australia: Pearson Education.

Kachaner, N., King, K., & Stewart, S. (2016). Four best practices for strategic planning. *Strategy and Leadership, 44*(4), 26–31.

Kukalis, S. (1989). The relationship among firm characteristics and design of strategic planning systems in large organizations. *Journal of Management, 15*, 565–579.

McKeown, M. (2012). *The strategy book*. Harlow: Pearson Education.

Parent, M., O'Brien, D., & Slack, T. (2012). Strategy and planning in the context of sport. In L. Trenberth & D. Hassan (Eds.), *Managing sport business*. Oxon: Routledge.

Powell, T. C. (1992). Strategic planning as competitive advantage. *Strategic Management Journal, 13*, 551–558.

Shilbury, D., & Ferkins, L. (2015). Exploring the utility of collaborative governance in National Sport Organizations. *Journal of Sport Management, 29*(4), 380–397.

Sinek, S. (2009). *Start with why: How great leaders inspire everyone to take action*. London: Penguin Group.

Sport Australia. (2016). *High performance sport planning*. Retrieved March 22, 2018 from www.clearinghouseforsport.gov.au/knowledge_base/high_performance_sport/Strategy_Planning_and_Practice/high_performance_sport_planning

Sport Australia. (2018). *Club development and planning*. Retrieved December 10, 2018 from www.sportaus.gov.au/club_development/governance#planning

Viljoen, J., & Dann, S. (2000). *Strategic management: Planning and implementing successful corporate strategies* (3rd ed.). Frenchs Forest: Pearson Education Australia.

Index

Note: Page numbers in italics indicate figures and in bold indicate tables on the corresponding pages.